Religion and Society in Industrial England

Themes in British Social History

Edited by Dr J. Stevenson

Religion and Society
in Industrial England

Church, Chapel and Social Change, 1740–1914

Alan D. Gilbert

Longman
London and New York

Longman Group Limited London

*Associated companies, branches and representatives
throughout the world*

*Published in the United States of America
by Longman Inc., New York*

© Longman Group Limited 1976

First published 1976

ISBN 0 582 48322 0 cased
ISBN 0 582 48323 9 paper

Set in IBM Baskerville 9 on 10pt
and printed in Great Britain by
Lowe & Brydone (Printers) Ltd, Thetford, Norfolk

Contents

Preface

This book examines the social history of English religion between 1740 and 1914. Concerned with religion specifically as a social phenomenon, the interpretation it offers emphasises landmarks in the relationship between organised religion and its wider social context rather than purely ecclesiastical landmarks associated either with the careers of outstanding religious leaders, the fortunes of particular church parties or denominational interests, or the development of English theology. The primary object is to explore links between religious and social changes during the crucial metamorphosis from pre-industrial English society to the modern industrial nation of the twentieth century. What were the functions of religion in England during the crisis of early industrialisation? What connexions existed between the emerging religious pluralism of the late eighteenth and early nineteenth centuries and the social and political tensions of the period after 1790? In what ways did the evolution of a mature industrial society alter the character of English religion, and diminish its role within the life of the nation? These basic questions determine the shape of the study.

Traditions of religious dissent in English society go back to the Reformation and beyond, but it was only in the century after 1740—and in the context of the societal upheaval of the Industrial Revolution—that popular extra-Establishment religious movements arose which were capable of challenging and ultimately subverting the traditional monopolistic role of the Church of England. This emergence of religious pluralism during a period when the coherence of the pre-industrial social order was breaking down under demographic, economic, and political pressures was of major importance both for the history of English religion and for the nature of the English adjustment to industrialisation and political transformation in the century and a quarter before the First World War. If the book can be said to have a central thesis, it is that the social history of English religion and the relationship between religion and social change between 1740 and 1914 were dominated by the creation and subsequent gradual resolution of a conflict situation involving the Established Church on the one hand, and on the other a popular extra-Establishment Protestantism embracing both the Methodist movement (despite its Anglican origins) and those sections of the old Dissent which were caught up in the Evangelical Revival during the second half of the eighteenth century.

Examining the origins, historical development, and social

significance of this Church—Chapel confrontation occupies the entire study, and other aspects of English religion are implicated virtually as sub-themes within the overall interpretation. This approach is adopted because it seems to be in harmony with the actual importance of the Church—Chapel confrontation in determining the role of religion in the society during the period under review. There can be no claim to novelty, of course, in emphasising the centrality of the confrontation, but the elaboration of the thesis is novel at least to the extent that on several major points it draws on quantitative evidence previously unpublished. Data on the social composition of Nonconformist communities in early industrial society, and series of annual figures analysing membership turnover, for example, provide a fairly precise basis for explicating links between religious phenomena and developments within the wider society.

In the long run industrialisation abetted the secularisation of English society, but because of the immense, if in many respects transitory, functionality of Evangelical Nonconformity in the early industrial age, and because the Church—Chapel confrontation became implicated deeply in the mainstream of Victorian politics, organised religion continued to enjoy considerable social prominence until the eve of the First World War. By the second half of the nineteenth century English religion was a paradox of manifest vitality and latent secularisation. Processes which in the period after 1914 would produce serious institutional decline were already at work, but their effects were being masked by the persistence of important alignments between religious factors and wider social changes. In seeking to illuminate this paradox, and in its whole approach to religion in industrial England, the study draws freely from sociological insights into the nature of religion as a social phenomenon. Indeed, it is apparent that in this, as in other fields, the line between sociology and social history is very blurred, and sometimes non-existent.

Such an observation leads naturally to the acknowledgement of debts. For while the quality of an historical study depends primarily upon the ability and diligence of its author, the approach owes much to those who have influenced the author's understanding of his discipline. For much encouragement and guidance over a number of years, and for stimulating interest in most of the major questions underlying the present study, I owe a very great deal to Ken Inglis. Robert Currie, my supervisor at Oxford, helped immensely with advice about sources and methods, and by kindly devoting many hours to the stringent and constructive criticism of preliminary drafts of most of these chapters. The book would have been impossible without his help, though doubtless it would be better if more of his criticisms and suggestions had been heeded. Others who contributed a great deal in terms of criticism, encouragement, and advice include Bryan Wilson, John Walsh, R. M. Hartwell, Marc Borg, and Stewart Firth. And to John Stevenson, the editor of this series, I am indebted already for the opportunity to contribute and for the tolerance and understanding with which he has responded to the rather slow emergence of the manuscript. Doubtless the debt will have mounted considerably by the time the book appears.

The work of Ingrid Gilbert in typing, retyping, and proof reading many hundreds of pages of manuscript has been immense.

Finally, I would like to thank the British Council, the directors of the Commonwealth Scholarship and Fellowship Award scheme, and Nuffield College, Oxford, for material assistance which made study in England possible.

Alan D. Gilbert

School of History
University of New South Wales
Sydney

Acknowledgements

We are grateful to the following for permission to reproduce copyright material:

Cambridge University Press for extracts from 'The Tithe Question in England in the early 19th Century' by W. R. Ward, from *Journal of Ecclesiastical History*, xvi, 1 April 1955;

William Collins, Sons & Company Ltd for an extract from 'In Memoriam' Section liv from *The Poetical Works of Lord Tennyson*;

A. & C. Black Ltd for extracts from *The Victorian Church*, vol. i, third edition by O. Chadwick;

the author for extracts from 'Non-Conformity in Country Parishes' by A. Everitt, from *Agricultural History Review*, 18 February 1970;

the author and American Historical Association for extracts from 'The Ethical Revolt against Christian Orthodoxy in Early Victorian England' by H. R. Murphy, from *American Historical Review*, lx, 1955;

the author for an extract from a University of Keele, MA thesis, 1968, 'Methodism and the Working Class, 1760–1821: A Study in Social and Political Conflict' by E. P. Stigant, and the Wesley Historical Society for extracts from 'A Micro-Theory of Methodist Growth' by R. Currie, from *Wesley Historical Society Proceedings*, xxxvi, October 1967.

The cover photographs appear by permission of the Radio Times Hulton Picture Library and the Greater London Council Photographic Library.

Part one

The religious background

The religious background

On 17 February 1739, risking the opprobrium of more punc-
tilious churchmen, George Whitefield preached in the open air to a crowd
of colliers at Kingswood, near Bristol, and by so doing precipitated a major
crisis in his career as an evangelist. Whitefield had no parochial responsibilities in the Kingswood area, and his outdoor preaching was in any case
highly irregular. Yet he had no doubts about the propriety of his conduct.
'Blessed be God that I have now broken the ice', he wrote in his journal on
the evening of the sermon, expressing a determination to persist with the
irregular, extra-parochial ministry even in the face of severe censure[1].
Whitefield was one of a number of young Churchmen whose growing
ecclesiastical radicalism in the 1730s was preparing the way for profound
religious-cultural changes in the century ahead. Like the irregular field-
preaching which Daniel Rowland, Howell Harris, and Howell Davies had
begun a few years earlier in Wales, and like the famous itinerant ministry
on which John Wesley would embark less than two months later, his
unconventional behaviour at Kingswood was a carefully considered
response to an obvious failure of the Established Church to meet the
religious needs of the whole society.

The Church of England's failure to achieve the monopolistic
ideal upon which it had been established was not recent. Partly because in
some areas the services which it offered had broken down almost immediately after the Reformation, and partly because alternative religious traditions had always retained minority support, Anglicanism had never in
practice achieved universality in England. But in the half-century
preceding Whitefield's and Wesley's launching of the Methodist movement
there had been a definite widening of the gap between Establishment
theory and English religious practice. A lowering of the constitutional
status of the Church had followed the Act of Toleration of 1689, and it
had been accompanied by a decline in the social authority of the clergy.
At the same time internal tensions, ecclesiastical, political, and doctrinal,
had compounded the problems of Anglicanism. But while these recent
developments had created the immediate context in which the Methodist
revival began, they had not represented any dramatic reversal in the
evolution of English religion. For to understand the weaknesses of the
Anglican Establishment in 1740 is to recognise social and cultural
processes which had been operating in England since the sixteenth
century.

Weakness is a relative concept. The Church of England, unable fully to realise its universalist goals, inefficient and wasteful in many of its organisational functions, remained nevertheless an immensely powerful social and religious institution in early Hanoverian England. Indeed, its vulnerability lay not so much in the actual flaws of organisation or influence evident around 1740, as in its unpreparedness for the revolutionary social changes of the later eighteenth and nineteenth centuries. But if, as in the present study, the significance of 1740 is that of a starting point rather than a culmination, then the Church's unpreparedness for future developments in English society emerges as the primary reality of the religious situation at the time. The same perspective must be adopted towards the other components of English Christianity around 1740: Dissent, Recusancy, and Methodism. The purpose of this opening chapter is to indicate fairly briefly how their historical inheritance, and their responses to major social and political trends in early eighteenth-century society, had prepared each of these religious cultures for the opportunities and problems which they would face during the century and three-quarters which lay ahead.

The legacy of the sixteenth and seventeenth centuries

An Anglican monopoly of religious practice could be neither instituted nor sustained in England without the determined and continuing support of the Crown, of Parliament, and of those who wielded social and political influence in local communities. The Reformation had been more than an assertion of national independence from the hegemony of Rome; it had also been an assertion of secular authority over ecclesiastical. But the Church had not only become dependent on the State to an unprecedented degree, it had suffered in the sixteenth and seventeenth centuries because of the ambivalence of State policy towards it. Elizabeth I and her successors had legislated to make Anglican worship compulsory, but they had not dealt as peremptorily with religious deviance as had many of their Absolutist counterparts in Europe. Like her father, Elizabeth I had manipulated ecclesiastical structures in pursuit of secular objectives, and she had both participated in and connived at the large-scale depredation of clerical livings which he had begun. The Tudors, in short, had weakened the Church economically while defending it politically.

The Stuarts had left a different legacy, but one equally destructive. Wittingly (by indulging their sympathies for Catholicism), and unwittingly (by precipitating civil war and revolution), they had contributed to an undermining of the political basis of the Establishment. Their demise, moreover, had created a situation in which the legal toleration of religious Dissent had become a matter of political expediency, and in which political power had passed to Whig politicians suspicious about the significant, albeit residual political influence which the Church had still retained at the end of the seventeenth century. By 1740 more than two centuries of conflict and change had left the Church dependent on the State, the parson subordinate to the squire, and once-powerful ecclesiastical courts bankrupt of independent coercive power. The fate of

Anglicanism rested as much on the policies of its secular patrons as on the endeavours of its clergy.

The economic concomitants of Reformation, summarised aptly in Christopher Hill's phrase, 'the plunder of the Church'[2], had affected seriously the religious life of many English parishes. The dissolution of the monasteries between 1536 and 1540 had not only deprived the Church of considerable wealth and influence at a single stroke, but had also altered radically the basis on which much ecclesiastical patronage would be exercised in the future. For with the loss of monastic property, rights of patronage over about 40 per cent of all clerical benefices had fallen into the hands of laymen. Abuses of patronage had long existed in the English Church, but the more or less systematic economic exploitation of clerical livings which had begun with the Henrician Reformation had been something new. The most common and damaging form of exploitation had involved impropriation, an arrangement under which the tithes connected with a living (traditionally the property of the clerical incumbent), had been transferred to non-incumbent rectors, usually laymen, who had then proceeded to pay the incumbent a stipend. By 1603 almost 4,000 of the 9,284 livings in the Church of England had been impropriated[3].

Impropriations had done serious damage to the religious Establishment at its grass roots. In economic terms non-incumbent rectors had been middlemen who had retained for themselves money which previously had gone to support the cure of souls. In many cases they had not been satisfied with a small percentage. A benefice worth £800 had provided the incumbent in Hornchurch, Essex, with only £55 per annum; and from an impropriation valued at £90 the vicar of Hogsthorpe in Lincolnshire had received a stipend of only £10[4]. Such cases had not been atypical. In impropriated parishes, as an early seventeenth-century vicar remarked, the clergy had got 'leavings, not livings'. The dictum that the labourer is worthy of his hire had proved, in the case of the Anglican parochial system, to have an ominous corollary: where the hire had become a pittance, worthy labourers had become fewer and farther between.

The post-Reformation clergy had faced other economic problems besides impropriations. Their incomes had been affected adversely by enclosure and depopulation in certain areas, and by the increasing difficulty of enforcing tithe payments as the ecclesiastical courts which traditionally had settled tithe disputes had relinquished jurisdiction in favour of common law courts. But impropriations had created the most serious and intractable flaws in the parochial system. They had been responsible primarily and directly for a sharp increase of pluralism, absenteeism, and clerical ignorance which had followed the Reformation; and responsible indirectly for much of the serious and widespread physical damage to church property which also had occurred. Clergy demoralised or non-resident had meant churches unused, unrepaired, and unprotected. In many areas lead roofing on deserted churches and manses had become a general target for pilfering in the sixteenth century, other churches had become derelict through simple neglect, and elsewhere the sight of ecclesiastical buildings being used by farmers to house livestock had epitomised the link between the economic problems of the post-Reformation Church and a decline of popular religion. These phenomena had not been general, of course. But while many parishes had remained unaffected and many clergymen unim-poverished, and while the Church as a whole had remained extremely wealthy, the effect of the Reformation on ecclesiastical property, patronage, and parochial endowments had been to produce serious degeneration, localised but widespread, in the services which the Church of England had offered its national constituency.

This damage to the parochial system resulting from changes in the basis of ecclesiastical patronage and clerical emoluments had tended to become permanent. The 'plunder of the Church' had created powerful vested interests in the very economic arrangements which had proved most destructive. There had been sporadic efforts to augment poor livings after the Restoration, the most notable being the inauguration of Queen Anne's Bounty as late as 1704. But these had provided minimal compensation for earlier impropriations. The economic and structural problems which had produced non-resident, unqualified, and otherwise unsatisfactory clergy in the sixteenth and seventeenth centuries persisted in 1740. Churches and vicarages which had become dilapidated or been destroyed had seldom been repaired properly, and in impropriated parishes it had been the non-incumbent rectors, not the parochial clergy, who had been the main beneficiaries of an improvement of tithe values during the almost con-tinuous agricultural prosperity of the period after about 1660. In Oxford Diocese there would remain even at the close of the eighteenth century a clear correlation between benefices inadequate to support an incumbent and livings which had suffered an alienation of tithes at the Reformation; and during the agitation for Church reform in the early nineteenth century, expropriations of sources of ecclesiastical revenue carried out under the Tudors and early Stuarts would be identified as antecedents of the clerical abuses urgently requiring redress in early industrial society[5].

In normal circumstances habits of religion or irreligion in a community are part of the 'world-taken-for-granted' inherited by one generation from another. Continuity is vital, therefore, for the preserva-tion of popular religious beliefs and practices. For while the maintenance of routine religious services usually serves to sustain an existing religious tradition, restoring such a tradition after serious and prolonged disruption involves the much more serious task of altering the norms of social and religious behaviour in a community. Thus in areas where the impoverish-ment of a parochial benefice in the sixteenth or early seventeenth century had left a parish without adequate clerical oversight for any considerable period, the stage had been set, not only for the plunder or decay of church property, but also for the development of a religious apathy which would tend to become increasingly refractory with the passage of time. The extent of the problem cannot be quantified with any precision, but what evidence there is suggests that as early as the end of the Tudor period there had begun a significant deterioration of past standards of Anglican practice. Ecclesiastical courts had been losing ground in their efforts to curb non-attendance at divine worship[6]. A survey conducted in the Diocese of Lincoln in 1603 had shown that even in Easter Week only 75 per cent of those eligible to receive the sacrament had actually done so[7], and this level of participation presumably had been high in comparison with normal services[8]. An observer in 1618 had estimated that one Englishman in four was totally irreligious[9]. High by modern standards, religious practice had nevertheless been far from universal in pre-Revolutionary society.

The Civil War and the Interregnum had involved further serious disruptions of popular religious behaviour. The breakdown of sacramental worship between 1640 and 1660 had in some communities been so complete, an Anglican Bishop had recalled in 1696, 'that in some ages of the Church it would have been interpreted as a downright Apostasie from Christ, and a renunciation of the Christian faith'[10]. As restored after 1660, moreover, the Church had been considerably weaker than in its pre-Revolutionary past. Its independent authority and influence in the society had been further usurped by secular institutions, and not only had the old economic and structural weaknesses produced by the 'plunder of the Church' survived, but to the problems of absenteeism and clerical neglect which they had created the Restoration had added fresh difficulties. The reintroduction of Episcopacy had been accompanied by the resignation or ejection from their livings of many hundreds of clergy-men, and by the alienation of thousands of parishioners who supported these dissidents. Adequate replacements had not everywhere been available, and the legacy of disaffection had in any case proved highly intractable in many parishes. While during the final thirty years of the Stuart era secular support for religious prescription had tended to obscure the full extent of the deterioration, the exigencies of social and religious life between 1640 and 1660 had reduced significantly the degree to which religious conformity was part of the 'world-taken-for-granted' by Englishmen.

By 1740 habits of indifference stretching back several generations had become embedded in the structures of many local communities. When in 1789 Hannah More noted that there were whole village populations in England no less estranged from the services of the Church than heathens were, she was simply recognising for the first time a fact which men like Whitefield and Wesley had been proclaiming for decades[11]. While there is no way of knowing precisely how many communities had become estranged in this way, the number certainly was considerable. The organisational and human resources of Anglicanism changed scarcely at all between 1740 and 1812, when a parliamentary inquiry discovered that there were 4,813 incumbents who were non-resident and not performing the duties of their living[12], but only 3,694 curates serving non-resident incumbents[13]. Over 1,000 parishes, in short, were simply unattended by ministers of the Established Church. Not all neglected parishes contained populations wholly neglected, of course. Extra-Establishment religious services, or the facilities of a neighbouring parish, were sometimes available. Equally, however, in many parishes which did have resident clergy, especially large or scattered parishes, many individuals and even entire communities were without the cure of souls. The monopolistic pretensions of the early Hanoverian Establishment were being frustrated by serious flaws which had developed gradually in the post-Reformation parochial system.

Toleration, voluntarism, and irreligion

The actions of the early Methodists brought into sharp focus for the first time an Anglican dilemma which was to retain primary significance in English social and religious history until the eve of the First World War. The Church of England was confronted with a society beginning to evolve voluntaristic attitudes towards religious behaviour; and while the resulting tensions remained sufficiently small in 1740 to be ignored by a majority of Churchmen, for a religious system which had grown up in a prescriptive society the problem potentially was immense. Anglicanism would have either to resist the social tendencies towards voluntarism and pluralism, or to undergo radical structural and religious-cultural changes. The dilemma inherent in this choice arose precisely because the Church's functions as a monopolistic Establishment were essentially incompatible with the functions required of a religious organisation in a pluralist society. For whereas traditional Establishment theory presupposed religious prescription and conformity, in a *pluralist* situation, in which a plurality of cultural systems and social groupings would coexist within a single society without any emphatic dominance or submission of any one to any of the others, many areas of individual and group behaviour (including religion) would necessarily become private and voluntary concerns.

Thus the concept of religious practice as an associational commitment to be induced voluntarily, not legally or socially prescribed, was not just novel in the ecclesiastical thought of 1740. It was potentially subversive. In retrospect it may be evident that dictating religious mores wherever traditional authority structures survived was to invite the alienation of those sections of the society emancipated already from old prescriptive norms. But to contemporary churchmen the obverse seemed more pertinent: to introduce voluntarism in some areas was to threaten prescriptive authority in others. This was the dilemma posed by the spirit of Methodism. If the primary concern of the Church in 1740 had been to secure the voluntary adherence of constituents whose loyalty it could no longer dictate, or whose religious conformity was prescribed no longer by secular authority, Anglicanism might have jettisoned certain of its traditional functions in the society. But compared with what they would be in the future the social pressures against the religious Establishment were of minor significance in the early Hanoverian era. Traditional Establishment theory was in no immediate danger. The inherited prescriptive structures were too strong, the residual monopolistic advantages too extensive. Yet in rejecting the principle of voluntarism the Church unwittingly committed itself to a long rearguard action against the ultimately irresistible tendencies towards pluralism and individual freedom in English society. Rejection set the stage for the bitter confrontation between Church and Chapel (between Establishment and extra-Establishment religiosity), which was to pervade the social history of the nineteenth century.

Tolerance of religious deviance and religious apathy had increased considerably in English society in the half-century after the Act of Toleration of 1689. Its progress had been related to two social trends which had combined to weaken the Established Church's monopoly of

English religious practice. There had been in the first place a progressive decline of the *independent* social and political influence of the clergy. Where clerical influence remained (and it remained very considerable in 1740), it was exercised in conjunction with secular institutions and interest groups, notably the magistracy and the squirarchy. During the previous 200 years the exclusion of abbots from the House of Lords, which had reduced the clerical vote from an absolute majority to a minority, had been merely the most obvious single example of a systematic secularisation of the institutions of social authority and social control which had followed the Reformation. But while this surrender of effective clerical authority to the civil magistrate and the secularised State had taken place gradually during the sixteenth and seventeenth centuries, its consequences for popular religious practice had not become fully apparent before 1689. For the second of the tendencies towards toleration—the diminution of secular sanctions against Dissent, Recusancy, and irreligion—had not been much in evidence before the Glorious Revolution. Until the Hanoverian era (except during the period of Civil War, Commonwealth, and Protectorate), successive rulers had considered it expedient to make Anglican practice mandatory.

A monopolistic religious Establishment had been a logical instrument of social control in a society in which political protest frequently had taken religious forms. Religious uniformity had been regarded as a partial guarantee of social cohesion and political tranquillity. From the first year of Elizabeth I to the abdication of James II the State had sought to secure such uniformity by prescribing regular parochial worship for all its citizens, and by making non-attendance a penal offence. A fine of twelve pence could be levied for each failure to attend Anglican services on Sundays or Holy Days, and a fine of £20 for persons over sixteen years of age absent for a period of one month[14]. Such legislation had acted not only as a check against religious deviance (its primary purpose), but had also secured the participation in church services of persons whose ideological and devotional commitment had been negligible: persons who under a voluntary system would have been apathetic. Rates of religious practice before 1689 had thus been inflated because in the eyes of the law irreligion had been equated with Recusancy and Dissent.

The effects of the Uniformity Laws on the religious behaviour of the society had been particularly evident during the occasional periods in which these laws had been relaxed. When Charles II had granted a Declaration of Indulgence in March 1672, for example, an official inquiry had discovered that 'many left the church ... who did before frequent it'[15]. The report had not implied that the absentees had gone instead to a Dissenting chapel, but simply that they had ceased to participate in religious services. And just as the Declaration, by suspending penal legislation against Dissent, had had the unlooked-for effect of increasing irreligion, so the hardening of public and parliamentary opinion against Catholics and Dissenters which had forced the King to withdraw the Indulgence in 1673 had effected a revival of the rate of Anglican practice[16]. The late seventeenth-century Church, in short, had been dependent to a significant degree upon the prescriptive powers of the

State; and the authority to impose religious conformity had issued ultimately from lay elements within the society, *not* from the clerical leaders
of dioceses or parishes.

The Church of England consequently had been ill-prepared for
the more tolerant ecclesiastical climate of the Hanoverian age. Except for a
few years under Queen Anne at the beginning of the eighteenth century,
the period between 1689 and 1740 had seen the State controlled by Whig
statesmen whose evident lack of concern about religious apathy in English
society had matched their antipathy towards a religious Establishment
predominantly Tory and partially Jacobite in sympathy. The result had
been a definite decline of popular religious practices. Because of the
relaxation of State sanctions against irreligion, in other words, the generation which produced Whitefield, Wesley, and other early Methodist leaders
had seen the long-standing social and cultural weaknesses of the Church
reflected more fully than ever before in the religious habits of the nation.

In a strictly legal sense the change had not been immense.
Technically the Act of Toleration had conceded very little. It had permitted certain categories of Dissenters to worship outside the Establishment, but it had not relieved them of the civil disabilities inherent in their
nonconformity. Nor had it sanctioned irreligion. For the remainder of the
population the old strictures against non-attendance had persisted—at least
on the Statute Books. But the effect of the Act (as distinct from the inten-
tions of its authors) had been to introduce an important element of voluntarism into matters of religious commitment. An alignment between Whigs
and Latitudinarian churchmen, and an association (real and imagined)
between High Churchmanship and Jacobitism, had combined to create a
situation in which the State and its episcopal appointees had connived at
the misrepresentation of the Act by many laymen.

The right of some to absent themselves from a parish church in
favour of a dissenting chapel had been seen by others as a right to practise
no religion at all. From the very early years of the Toleration legislation
churchmen had noticed that those using it as a shelter for conscientious
Dissent were being outnumbered by those making it a pretext for neglect-
ing 'all manner of worship'[17]. In exasperation the Dean of Norwich had
written:

> Say what the judges can at the assizes, or the justices of the
> peace at their sessions, or we at our visitations, no
> churchwarden or constable will present any for not going to
> church, though they go nowhere else but to the alehouse, for
> this liberty they will have[18].

During the first half of the eighteenth century (before the lax
interpretation of 'toleration' was legitimated by the passage of time),
complaints of this kind often were voiced by the parochial clergy, frequently with the added suggestion that efforts to uphold the law within
their parishes were not receiving support in the ecclesiastical courts. Thus
during Bishop Thomas Secker's Primary Visitation of the Diocese of
Oxford in 1738, from parish after parish came reports of habitual non-
attendance among 'the lowest ranks', 'the poorer sort', and 'the common

people', coupled with appeals for a re-imposition of the legal strictures which previously had dictated conformist religious behaviour[19]. One of the most striking aspects of these reports was the implication that Anglican religious practice had fallen off alarmingly within the lifetime of incumbents still active in the 1730s.

In blaming bishops and church courts for this decline of religious conformity parochial clergy showed a basic misunderstanding of the problem. The abnegation of authority which had occurred had been essentially political and social rather than ecclesiastical. Abandoning the traditional policy of endorsing clerical authority in the interests of social cohesion, the early Hanoverian State under the Whigs had come into conflict with precisely those sections of Anglicanism which would have been likely, under different circumstances, to have shared a strong alliance with the State. Nonjurors and High Churchmen, and indeed that majority of clergymen whose sympathies made them Tories, could expect no favours from the Whigs. For the dominant political party, tacit acceptance of religious apathy had become part of a policy of increasing the subordination of the religious Establishment to the secular.

Thus what the parochial clergy were saying to the bishops about the rise of irreligion under the aegis of 'toleration', the bishops in Convocation had said already, unavailingly, to the State. In 1711, for example, a statement issued by the Upper House of Convocation in the Province of Canterbury had drawn attention to what it had called 'the late excessive Growth of Infidelity, Heresy, and Profaneness'. Many Englishmen, Convocation had alleged, had

> taken occasion from the relaxation of those laws which made absence from the established church penal, to withdraw themselves entirely from all religious assemblies, although the very act of exemption, which gave liberty in one respect, equally restrained it in the other[20].

The law, in short, had been popularly misconstrued, and wherever secular authorities had remained aloof the Church had been powerless to reverse the consequent decline of conformist practice. When Convocation was prorogued in May 1717 following a confrontation with the State over the question of ecclesiastical authority[21], its fate had symbolised the growing inability of the Church to *impose* its services upon English society.

What was beginning to emerge by 1740 was a situation of *de facto* voluntarism. It was not a general phenomenon, for the norms of religious behaviour in English society were heavily dependent upon local influences. But a new tolerance of irreligion, adding to the older problems of pastoral neglect dating back to the sixteenth and seventeenth centuries, was creating a context for the operation of voluntary religious agencies, notably Methodism. There is good statistical evidence to support a claim by the rector of Bladon, in Oxfordshire, that in 1738 more people went nowhere than went to a dissenting chapel[22]. In the entire Oxford diocese there was an average of little over one communicant for every three households, and only a small proportion of communicants actually received communion at any given time[23]. While attendance figures, where given, showed that many people attended church services without receiving the sacrament, they indicated also that non-attendance was widespread. The same was true of the diocese of York in 1743 when the newly appointed Archbishop Herring made his inaugural Visitation[24].

Precisely how much religious practice had diminished during the previous half-century is unclear, partly because there is no firm evidence about the number of people who had succeeded in evading or ignoring the provisions of the Uniformity Laws in the period before 1689. In some areas, certainly, pressures to conform had disappeared well before the Act of Toleration, notably in parishes without a resident clergyman to provide services for the people to attend. Nevertheless, the impact of the Act had been considerable. In Clayworth, Nottinghamshire, the average number of parishioners participating in Easter communion had fallen by almost 40 per cent within a decade or so of 1689[25], and judging from observations which parochial clergy recorded in Visitation returns, comparable lapses had occurred in many other parishes[26]. By 1740, in other words, the Church of England was beginning to experience, on a significant scale, the problem of being a religious Establishment in a society no longer constrained to accept its leadership.

Squire, parson, and the Establishment ideal

But to picture the Church of England as an institution weakened by serious organisational and economic problems, ignored by some of the clients whose adherence it claimed, and unable everywhere to supply adequate religious services to its national constituency, is not to tell the whole truth about the religious situation in England in 1740. For while the Church was far from being the universally patronised monopoly envisaged in traditional Establishment theory, its wealth, influence, and authority remained immense. In much of England Anglicanism and society remained virtually coterminus. Indeed, the fact that the Church of England was in a precarious position in 1740 is evident only in retrospect. For contemporary churchmen, who could not know that England stood on the brink of profound industrial, demographic, and social changes which would threaten the Establishment with redundancy, the great residual strengths of the Anglican system generally obscured the underlying weaknesses.

It was greatly to the advantage of the Church that political authority and social control were highly localised in eighteenth-century England. The Anglican clergy, who since the Reformation and particularly since 1689 had witnessed the gradual erosion of their traditional independent authority over the moral and religious behaviour of their parishioners, very often remained in a position to dictate religious norms by virtue of an alliance with local ruling elites. When a resident clergyman in a manageable parish enjoyed the wholehearted support of the local landowners and the magistracy, he could guarantee high rates of religious practice and make religious Dissent virtually untenable. The cementing of

a strong squire—parson alliance thus mitigated the unwelcome consequences of Whig policies and limited the spread of voluntarist attitudes
towards religious behaviour.

Social control and authority in local society stemmed less
from formal institutions than from informal 'influence' based upon
hereditary status and landed wealth. This is not to imply that the formal
power was lacking. By the eighteenth century county justices had accumulated, albeit without statutory warrant, immense executive, judicial, and
even legislative authority which they exercised through the Quarter
Sessions and the Assizes[27]. But their influence transcended these
definite administrative and legal functions. Together with their fellow
squires who were not magistrates, they were arbiters of local culture and
social behaviour. Their social subordinates, economically dependent on
them as landowners, directly or indirectly, were also socialised to respect
them on grounds of status. Paternalism on one side, deference and social
dependence on the other, were the motive forces of much of the society of
pre-industrial England.

The role of the Anglican parson within this 'dependency
system'[28] had been changing significantly during the period immediately
before 1740. Previously competition had been as characteristic as cooperation in the relationship of squire and parson. As late as 1700 there had
remained considerable clerical resentment about the subordination of the
clergy to wealthy laymen, as well as residual lay suspicion about the
political threat posed by churchmen, particularly in Convocation[29]. But
the further erosion of their independent influence and authority had
predisposed the clergy to rely increasingly on the patronage of the lay
ruling classes; and no longer threatened by clerical competition, the landed
gentry had shown increasing readiness to welcome the local parson as an
ally. The result, as G. F. A. Best has pointed out, had been the emergence
of 'a new version of establishment theory, emphasising the social affinities
of clergy and laity, tending to glorify their interconnexions and mutual
dependence'[30]. Where this alliance between squire and parson worked
well—and it was ideally suited to the conditions prevalent in a majority of
rural parishes, especially in southern England[31]—the Anglican parochial
system remained impervious to the forces of religious toleration and
voluntarism. The Church of England could remain more or less complacent
in 1740 because the most serious problems it faced arose in social contexts
which could be regarded as anomalous in a pre-industrial society.

But while the Establishment ideal of an Anglican monopoly of
English religion was able, in many parts of the country, to survive the
operation of the Toleration Act, the alliance between parochial clergy and
landed gentry which preserved it was a mixed blessing. A more independent clergy might have been able to react differently to the social and
political pressures of the century after 1740. As it was the history of the
previous 200 years had left the parochial system of the Hanoverian Church
almost totally dependent on the patronage of a class whose position, based
on landed wealth and inherited political influence, was to come under
mounting pressure from alternative economic and political forces. For the
'dependency system' itself was to become one of the casualties of the
industrial revolution era. From the late eighteenth century onwards the

squire, like the Anglican parson, would be thrown increasingly on the defensive by the forces of social change; and while in the case of the landed interest the defences would remain formidable, even in the second half of the nineteenth century, the fact remains that the squire—parson alliance had brought together two parties with vested interests in preserving as much as possible of the pre-industrial *status quo*. Ironically, while the Church remained too strong in 1740, too secure, to welcome the drastic remedies advocated by Whitefield and Wesley, its strengths were located in precisely those social structures and cultural values which would inhibit easy adjustment to the religious needs of an emerging industrial society.

Religion outside the Establishment

Although the Church of England was confronted with mounting public apathy and irreligion in 1740, its problems seemed minor compared with those of Recusancy and Dissent. As recently as the 1680s James II had been harbouring the notion of returning England to the Catholic fold; and while the scheme had been essentially impractical, Catholics clearly had remained a significant and influential minority in English society. Possibly as much as 10 per cent of the population had been Catholic, including numerous members of the landed gentry and a fair sprinkling of knights, baronets, and peers[32]. Protestant Dissent, likewise, had been a vigorous and determined minority religious movement in the generation following the Restoration. Together these two streams of extra-Establishment religiosity had drawn significantly on the national catchment over which the Church of England had claimed a monopoly. Yet by 1740—only half a century later—each stream appeared to be in serious danger of drying up.

Being a Catholic in early eighteenth-century England involved severe social and legal disabilities, some of which arose directly from anti-Catholic penal legislation. Catholics were disenfranchised, barred from the military and legal professions, forced to pay double land tax, and subject to a law (never actually executed) making them ineligible to inherit or purchase real property. Their rights of religious practice were restricted and subject to official surveillance. Much of this discriminatory legislation was enforced only occasionally, and at a local rather than a national level; some of it probably was unenforceable. But quite apart from the latent threat of systematic legal persecution, it symbolised for Catholics the social reality of inferior status. The English Catholic faced general antipathy and suspicion in a society deeply imbued with anti-Catholic prejudices dating back to the Reformation. He had to live with more or less constant insinuations of disloyalty, and during phases of Jacobite activity or periods of international tension involving England and Catholic Europe he suffered particular opprobrium. Yet what in the long run was even more depressing than discrimination or persecution—with which, after all, he had lived for 200 years—was the gradual evaporation after 1688 of prospects of a Catholic restoration in England.

From a sociological perspective the problems of Catholicism and Dissent had much in common. Like Catholicism, Puritanism and later Separatism had been capable of attracting the socially and economically privileged in considerable numbers in the uncertain religious climate of the sixteenth and seventeenth centuries. Many families of wealth and status had been on the side of Dissent in 1662. But the social significance of religious deviance had changed fundamentally as the ascendancy of Anglicanism had become increasingly secure and unmistakably permanent. From being important opposition parties in a fluid religious situation, both Catholicism and Dissent, well before 1740, were tending to become fairly marginal minority groups without any great significance in the ordering of the wider society. One result of the change had been serious numerical decline.

The social and political problems of extra-Establishment religion in the early Hanoverian age can be analysed in some detail in the case of Dissent. Men had become Dissenters at the Restoration who earlier had failed only narrowly to secure political and social pre-eminence. Independence had dominated the Commonwealth, and in the 1640s the religious Establishment had for a time been annexed by Presbyterianism. A feature of the social and religious conflicts underlying these upheavals had been the significance of vertical as well as horizontal divisions within the society. The groups in confrontation had represented divergent interests *within* the ruling classes. They had also represented divergent religious positions, for another feature of English social history in the sixteenth and seventeenth centuries had been the close alignment of socio-economic, political, and religious values. In Puritanism, as R. H. Tawney has argued in *Religion and the Rise of Capitalism*, the various 'rivulets of discontent' had been drawn together, and had been swept forward with 'the dignity and momentum of a religious and social philosophy'[33]. It was a confluence of religion and politics which had much to do with the social character of early Dissent.

The Restoration had represented a defeat, not only for this Puritan ideology, but also for the social and economic interest groups with which Puritanism had been associated. Like the Reformation and the Civil War before it, it had been a culmination of vertical conflicts within English society[34]. Consequently in early Dissent, the ideological home of Protestants opposed to the Settlement of 1662, the wealthy, the gentry, and even the nobility had been well represented[35]. Dissent, in short, had been more than a movement of articulate artisans and small tradesmen: it had harboured a disappointed elite, and had functioned for them as a political and religious alternative to the Restoration Establishment.

But the function had been a precarious one. For as the restored Establishment had received the legitimation of time, and as the social and political alignments of 1662 had disintegrated gradually, the original *raison d'être* of Dissent as a social movement had become increasingly anachronistic. The social and cultural commitment inherent in Dissent had become less viable and less relevant, particularly for members drawn from the upper echelons of the social order. The result, E. R. Bebb has shown in a thorough examination of the social composition of early dissenting communities, had been a 'decline in the support of Dissent among the aristocracy', evident by 1715, 'which was before long to be reflected in the growing secession of the gentry'. Reviewing the period before about 1740 Bebb has explained that 'first the socially distinguished, then the economically powerful sections of early Nonconformity almost disappeared, having been for the most part re-absorbed into the Anglican Communion'[36].

This contraction of the social catchment area of Dissent during the half-century before 1740 had been accompanied by rapid numerical decline. Contrary to suggestions by enemies as well as friends, Dissent never had been quantitatively powerful. Unlike later Nonconformity it never had functioned as a viable alternative to the Church of England for the great majority of Englishmen. Yet at its peak around 1700 there had been about 300,000 people, 5 per cent of the national population, associated with its communities. By 1740 this number had been halved, and the fully committed members of Dissenting congregations (as distinct from the penumbra of hearers and sympathisers), scarcely had exceeded 50,000[37]. Dissent, as Isaac Watts put it at the time, seemed to be moving rapidly 'in the course to be found nowhere but in books'[38].

Underlying this decline had been the fact that loss of support at the upper limits of its social spectrum had been accompanied in Dissent by a failure to appeal effectively to the one section of the wider society from which it might have replenished, or even expanded, its numbers of members and adherents. Philip Doddridge, the best-known Dissenter of the day, had argued in 1730 that Dissent generally was failing to cater for 'the plain people of low education and vulgar taste', who were 'strangers to the refinements of learning and politeness'. Echoing, but with regret, the forecasts of many sanguine Anglicans, he had predicted a future in which, as he put it,

> we ... shall have the great pleasure of being entertained with the echo of our own voices, and the delicacy of our discourses, in empty places, or amidst a little circle of friends, till perhaps (like some of our brethren) we are starved into a good opinion of conformity[39].

The picture was of an increasingly demoralised, introverted movement, which, having lost much of its original social and cultural impetus, was being prevented by its elitest self-conceptions from fashioning for itself a new social base among the lower classes.

There was evident truth in this understanding of Dissent's decline. As Doddridge looked about him he saw on one hand his Presbyterian brethren moving towards a theological liberalism which, even when it stopped short of Socinianism or Deism, produced a rational and intellectual faith unconducive to conversionist activity, particularly among the lower classes. On the other hand, in his own Independent denomination and among the Particular Baptists he saw a majority turning to a hyper-Calvinist theology equally effective in stultifying conversionist zeal. But theological and cultural trends alone did not account for the problems of extra-Establishment religion in 1740. As Catholic and dissenting leaders alike had learned by unhappy experience, winning or retaining the allegiance of subordinate classes in pre-industrial society often was primarily a matter of social influence. The diminishing political and social significance of Dissent and Recusancy in the early eighteenth century had therefore eroded the strength of these movements at all social levels.

The erosion process can be illustrated by returning to the problems facing English Catholicism in 1740. Like their dissenting counterparts, growing numbers of wealthy Catholic families were finding intolerable the prospect of more or less permanent marginality within the society. Losses of any kind were serious, but disenchantment within the rich and influential sections of the Catholic community threatened Recusancy as a whole. The survival of Catholicism among subordinate social groups was heavily dependent upon the patronage of this elite, and a single defection could mean the disappearance of an entire Catholic congregation. The readiness of Viscount Montague of Cowdray to maintain a Catholic chapel for his tenants after conforming to the Church of England in 1742 was unusual. 'When a family of distinction fails', Joseph Berington, a priest, wrote later in the century, 'the neighbouring Catholics soon fall away: and when a priest is still maintained, the example of the lord is wanting to encourage the lower class to the practice of their religion.' In a typical example of this kind of decline, Berington cited a district in which thirteen Catholic congregations had been reduced to five in the space of sixty years[40]. Even in 1740 the Catholic population in England was only about half what it had been half a century earlier, and for the remnant the future would become more depressing with the defeat of the final Jacobite uprising of 1745. Until the century's final decade, which would open with an influx of Catholic emigrés from revolutionary France and close with the constitutional union of England with a largely Catholic Ireland, the very existence of Catholicism in England would be in jeopardy.

Methodism and the Church of England

'I went upon a mount', wrote Whitefield, describing the setting in which he preached the famous open-air sermon of 17 February 1739. And when John Wesley took the same radical step two months later it was 'from a little eminence' that he spoke[41]. Whether or not the obvious analogy of the Sermon on the Mount was intended by either man, both reports conveyed a sense of the historic importance of these occasions. Neither Wesley nor Whitefield was acting in ignorance of the contemporary religious situation. They had embarked on a course which, if successful, would change the nature of the religious Establishment in the interests of the cure of souls. Their actions were subversive, if not of the Establishment *per se*, then certainly of the religious *status quo* of 1740.

The era of toleration inaugurated by the Act of 1689 was a crucial phase in the progress of English religion towards genuine religious pluralism. If the ecclesiastical leaders of 1740 had been able to look into the future they would have seen the Established Church facing increasing competition from rival religious and non-religious institutions for the associational allegiance of the society. Neither the squire—parson alliance nor the various residual advantages still inherent in the historical State—Church compact, however successful they might be in the short term in shoring up the prescriptive authority of the clergy, could postpone indefinitely the day when Englishmen would be able to choose freely which church to attend or neglect. The forces of pluralism and voluntarism were in league with the future.

Religious pluralism would mean the end of the Church of England as a monopolistic institution. 'The key characteristic of all pluralistic situations', Peter L. Berger has explained,

> is that the religious ex-monopolies can no longer take for granted the allegiance of their client populations. Allegiance is voluntary and thus, by definition, less than certain. As a result, the religious tradition, which previously could be authoritatively imposed, now has to be *marketed*. It must be 'sold' to a clientele that is no longer constrained to 'buy'. The pluralistic situation is, above all, a *market situation* [42].

Such situations develop gradually, however, and in England in 1740 the implications of advancing religious toleration were but dimly perceived even by the more progressive members of the Established Church. Without the gift of prescience no one could know certainly that the forces making for religious voluntarism would in the long run prove irresistible. Yet it was the fate of the early Hanoverian Church to make an initial, crucial decision about the role of Anglicanism in the emerging 'market situation'. Was Anglicanism, as Whitefield and Wesley wished, to be 'marketed'; or should the Church of England resist voluntarism by continuing to behave as a monopolistic institution?

For perhaps seventy years after the Glorious Revolution efforts to transform Anglicanism into a popular (as opposed to prescribed) form of religiosity appeared to hold out genuine prospects of success. From the 1690s onwards the Church was the home of numerous voluntary agencies dedicated to augmenting the regular operation of the parochial system. 'Religious societies' (voluntary associations of clerics and laymen meeting regularly in search of spiritual fellowship unavailable in the ordinary services of the Church) had existed since 1678, but from the 1690s their numbers grew rapidly [43]. Under the functioning of the Toleration Act other more formal voluntary agencies had also been established, the best known being the Society for the Promotion of Christian Knowledge (1698) and the Society for the Propagation of the Gospel in Foreign Parts (1701). It was under the auspices of the latter that John Wesley travelled to Georgia late in 1735.

This upsurge of voluntarism had received a mixed reception within the religious Establishment. 'I myself have always been averse to such sort of confederacies or combinations, whether of clergy or others, as are now on foot everywhere', John Sharp, the High Church Archbishop of York, had written in 1699. He had feared vaguely that 'some time or other we may feel ill consequences from them' [44]. Disagreeing, supporters of the religious societies had emphasised their pastoral utility in subordination to the parochial clergy. While a lone clergyman might tend to lose touch with his more independent parishioners under the lax regimen of toleration, the existence of a religious society within his parish would not only provide him with dedicated lay assistants, but, precisely because it was a voluntary institution, might appeal effectively to those sections of the community whose religious behaviour could no longer be prescribed. Samuel Wesley, a man whose sons would make him famous, had remarked at the end of the seventeenth century that instead of 'injuring the church', the expanding voluntary societies would provide Anglicanism with 'new bulwarks against its enemies'[45].

John and Charles Wesley shared their father's conception of the role of voluntary agencies within the parochial system, as did the pioneers of Calvinistic Methodism, Whitefield, Rowland, Harris, and Davies. Methodism, in fact, arose directly out of the religious societies of the 1730s[46]. John Wesley was converted at a society which met in Aldersgate Street, London; the rudiments of Wesleyan organisation were borrowed from the rules of typical religious societies[47]; and from the memberships of such societies most of the initial Methodist converts were drawn. In certain cases there was direct continuity between the older voluntary associations and the earliest specifically Wesleyan communities.

Yet by its very success, and by carrying the principle of voluntarism to a logical conclusion, Methodism was destined to come into conflict with the traditional institutions and structures of the Established Church. There was an obvious ambiguity in the claim of voluntary agencies to be subordinate to the authority of the parochial clergy. Their very existence reflected both the partial breakdown of the organisational machinery of the Church and the increasing erosion of the prescriptive powers of its ministers, and they performed religious-cultural and social functions which the majority of the parochial clergy were capable of performing only inadequately, if at all. In joining them their members expressed an implicit dissatisfaction with traditional ecclesiastical institutions. As Archbishop Sharp had feared, the voluntary principle would end up producing an alternative to the parochial system, not an auxiliary. But to elaborate the significance of the new Methodist movement in the religious situation of 1740 it is necessary to anticipate the development of Anglican—Methodist relations during the quarter-century which followed.

From the very early years of his ministry John Wesley was aware that Methodism was confronting the Church of England with an option which it could accept only by adopting extensive structural and religious-cultural changes. In the long term, he told the inaugural Conference in 1744, Methodists would either 'leaven the whole Church' or be 'thrust out' of it[48]. While committed to Anglicanism all his life, Wesley became committed even more deeply to the irregular forms which he believed were essential to the growth of his voluntary 'United Societies'. He made a firm distinction between 'regular' and 'irregular' clergymen, and was convinced that the former, even when preaching 'the genuine gospel', tended to have 'no effect at all'. The parochial clergy of the Church of England, he believed, would remain ineffective until they 'formed irregular Societies and took in laymen to assist them'[49].

In his optimism that Methodism could 'leaven the whole Church' Wesley was underestimating the strength of the forces within the

Establishment resistant to change. Of these forces simple inertia was the most powerful. Institutions as embedded as the Anglican parochial system accept radical change only under immense pressure, and the Hanoverian Church of England was not marked by any great sense of insecurity, despite the legacy of the previous 200 years. If religious apathy was on the increase, Dissent and Recusancy, the old enemies, apparently were in decay. Like the secular State under Sir Robert Walpole, the Church from which Methodism emerged eschewed extremism. People advocating voluntary auxiliaries to the parochial system were liable to be dismissed as 'enthusiasts', and bluntly opposed whenever their innovations threatened to disrupt the 'regular' functioning of the Establishment.

The Church was not easily mobilised by the advocates of voluntarism because in many areas, and particularly in the wealthiest and most influential parishes, the strength of the squire—parson alliance obviated the need for seeking to induce voluntary commitment. In 1740, in other words, Anglicanism was not yet weak enough to adopt desperate or unpalatable remedies. The challenge to its traditional monopoly of popular religion was neither sufficiently pervasive nor sufficiently serious to induce the average Churchman to begin thinking in terms of the harsh alternative of a market situation in English religion. Conservatism was reinforced, moreover, by the ultimate incompatibility of the methods and institutions appropriate to a situation of religious pluralism and voluntarism, on the one hand, and to a situation of monopoly and prescription on the other. A Church seeking to *induce* voluntary religious conformity in some areas would find it increasingly difficult to *impose* conformity in others.

Thus Methodism had profound implications for the future of the Church of England. Even at the most obvious organisational level several facets of the new movement could be construed, with some justification, as subverting the traditional role of the clergy. Itinerancy ignored parish boundaries, and in many cases was carried out by unordained preachers; laymen also assumed pastoral responsibilities in local communities as preachers and class leaders; and Methodism, with its tight-knit connexional organisation and its own meeting houses, appeared from very early in its history to be evolving ecclesiastical structures independent of the parochial system. These facts did not deter some clergymen from embracing the new movement, and adopting its methods. But from a purely professional viewpoint those clergy who did not welcome Wesley or his colleagues were justified in regarding them as dangerous competitors. As Wesley himself remarked rather blandly in 1744, Methodism posed no threat to the parochial clergy as a body: it threatened to weaken the positions only of those who opposed it[50].

Methodism, in short, would either revolutionise the Church or be ejected from it. Granted this choice, it was inevitable that eighteenth-century Anglicanism would adopt a conservative and ultimately reactionary attitude towards the use of voluntary agencies of the Methodist variety. At the local level rejection was often emphatic and almost immediate, and it was not unprovoked. The Wesleyan society founded in Wednesbury, Staffordshire, for example, quickly alienated the local vicar. On his first visit to the town in 1742 Charles Wesley arrived at the vicarage with assurances that Methodism would create no disaffection among parishioners, nor cause them to withdraw from the regular services of the Parish Church. Yet within two years both things were happening. The society of 200 members was being ministered to, not by the ordained (albeit irregular) Wesleys, but by 'a Bricklayer, and then a Plumber and Glazier', and by another itinerant who attacked the Anglican clergy, 'calling them dumb Dogs, that would not bark'[51]. Not surprisingly, incumbents in parishes like Wednesbury regarded Methodism as a major threat to the parochial system almost as soon as a society was established in their vicinity.

As a practical policy Wesley's maxim, 'go always, not only to those that want you, but to those that want you most'[52], meant that Methodist societies sprang up primarily in parishes where the traditional parochial machinery was least effective. In such circumstances there was an understandable tendency for rank-and-file Methodists to regard their local society, not as an adjunct to their parish church but as their primary associational commitment, and to regard the Wesleyan Connexion, not as ancillary to the parochial system but as an institutional alternative. Whether the fact was articulated contemptuously (as in Wednesbury) or concealed behind conformist behaviour (as when Wesley had his way), diminished respect for the Established Church and diminished loyalty towards it stemmed from these attitudes. So, too, did mounting pressures within Methodism impelling it towards overt nonconformity.

The frequency with which Wesley had to insist on the subordinate role of the Methodist movement was itself evidence of the persistence of separatist tendencies. As early as 1755 the question, 'Whether we ought to separate from the Church?' dominated the Annual Conference for three days[53], and while the adamant views of Wesley made a negative conclusion inevitable, the time allotted to the problem was an index of the strength of counter-Establishment forces within the movement. During the following thirty-six years Wesley never abandoned the conception of Methodism as *ecclesiola in ecclesia*, but his reasons for retaining it (certainly insofar as he explicated them) do appear to have revolved increasingly around the practical danger that separatism might lead to the fragmentation of the Connexion. 'Over and above all the reasons that were formerly given for this [remaining within the Church], we add another now from long experience', he told the Conference of 1769. To leave the Church, he said, could be tantamount to leaving Methodism: 'The clergy cannot separate us from our brethren, the Dissenting ministers can and do: therefore carefully avoid whatever has a tendency to separate men from the Church'[54].

Thus, paradoxically, Wesley's advocacy of religious conformity ended up serving his primary interest in protecting and strengthening the Methodist Connexion as a cohesive, independent ecclesiastical entity. As early as the 1760s he appears finally to have despaired of the possibility of 'leavening' the parochial system sufficiently, or rapidly enough, to transform Anglicanism into a popular evangelical church. His disillusionment arose not because, as he put it later, 'the far greater part' of the clergy were 'not devoted to God'[55], but because most of the minority which was genuinely devout (the evangelical clergy) were too embedded in the old prescriptive system fully to support the work of voluntary agencies. Evangelical theology and conversionist zeal were insufficient in themselves, Wesley believed: they were effective only when mediated through irregular societies gathered on the principle of voluntary commitment. 'The grand breach', he wrote in 1761, 'is now between the regular and irregular clergy'[56].

In April 1764, after long deliberation, Wesley sent to about fifty clergymen in England copies of a letter in which he appealed for unity of purpose among those who shared the fundamental principles of evangelicalism[57]. Receiving only three replies, he lost whatever doubts he may have retained about the need for his 'United Societies' to provide the organisational structure for a new popular evangelicalism in England. 'So I gave this up', he said, reporting to the 1769 Conference about his efforts to mobilise the 'regular' evangelical clergy. 'I can do no more. They are a rope of sand, and such they will continue'[58].

In contrast, Wesley explained, Methodism could cope with the social context in which the parochial system was labouring badly. The time had come, therefore, to plan for the growth and continuity of the Connexion as an autonomous institution; and in this planning the lure of 'preferment in the Church' was to be regarded as a danger against which Methodist itinerants were to be warned and protected[59]. Thus the Methodist movement, heir to the voluntary societies of the late seventeenth century, had ended up in competition with the parochial polity the limitations of which had prompted its emergence in the first place. But granted the strength of traditional elements within the religious Establishment, this conflict had been inevitable as soon as Wesley had begun to operate outside the parochial system just before 1740.

The religious situation in England in 1740 is important historically because it represents English Christianity on the eve of its gravest crisis. Recusancy and Dissent were weak; the Church of England, still powerful, was inflexible and ill-prepared for change; Methodism, in its infancy, was already showing signs of dynamism. In retrospect, however, the true strengths and weaknesses of these divergent religious cultures were not reflected in their relative positions in English society in 1740. What would prove more significant in the long run would be the capacity of each to cope with the revolutionary social changes which were imminent. A century later there would be more than three people in England for every one alive in 1740, and these people would be clustered in settlement patterns unlike those with which the Churches had coped reasonably well up to the eighteenth century. Industrialisation, political changes, and a complex of accompanying developments in the social structures, the values, and the beliefs of the society would be well on the way to creating the modern industrial nation of twentieth-century England. The aim of the chapters which follow will be to examine the ways in which the various religious organisations responded to this crisis.

Patterns of religious practice,
           1740-1914

Much of the social history of English religion has been written
by scholars interested in particular aspects of the relationship between
religion and society. Faulkner's pioneering study, *Chartism and the
Churches*, Inglis's *Churches and the Working Classes in Victorian England*,
Harrison's work on the Temperance Question, and the work of Hobsbawn
and Thompson on links between Methodism and the rise of working-class
consciousness, to cite a few obvious examples, are studies of religion as a
social phenomenon in which the perception of an important question or
cluster of questions has preceded the analysis, and indeed inspired it[1].
But the present more general survey has no comparable thematic basis for
problem identification. Criteria must be adduced for locating basic themes
in the relationship between religion and society between 1740 and 1914,
for identifying the major trends in the development of organised religion
during this period, and for isolating the central problems requiring
resolution.

Among the most obvious and useful criteria for this purpose
are those relating to popular religious practices. The social significance of
religion in England in the eighteenth and nineteenth centuries was
reflected fairly accurately in patterns of religious activity and apathy
within the society. A wide variety of such patterns must be considered, for
religious adherence and religious behaviour varied significantly with
geographical, cultural, class, and occupational factors, as well as with the
passage of time. But it is patterns tracing changes over time in rates of
religious practice which provide the best overall perspective of religious
developments in industrial England. Changes in the religious-cultural or
structural character of a Church or denomination, or in its orientation to
the wider society, tended very quickly to be reflected in its pattern of
growth. The analysis begins therefore by focusing on English Church
growth throughout the period from the birth of Methodism to the First
World War.

The measurement of Church growth

Religion is a complex phenomenon embracing a variety of
religious sub-activities which are only partially interdependent. In a
famous analysis of the nature of religious commitment two American

sociologists, Charles Glock and Rodney Stark, have distinguished five 'dimensions' of religious sub-activity: religious experience, religious belief, religious practice, religious knowledge, and such secular activities, values, or norms as are shaped by one or more of these specifically religious elements[2]. They have concluded that while it is implausible to suggest that the various sub-activities are entirely unrelated, 'being religious on one dimension does not necessarily imply being religious on another'[3]. This dimensional approach to the study of religious phenomena has obvious implications for the historian of religion. In particular, it raises the problem of choosing between alternative indices of progress and decline in the development of a religious movement.

The present study focuses primarily on what Glock and Stark have called the 'associational' dimension of religiosity. The concepts 'growth' and 'decline' relate to observed social behaviour: to the participation of individuals in religious practices, acts, and rituals. For the social historian this is an obvious approach, despite the fact that some students of religion have tended to question its usefulness and even its validity. The possible objections to it are worth noting nevertheless. One such objection is that evidence about religious practice does not necessarily measure genuine religiosity. Thus Roland Robertson has argued that 'commitment to participate in the affairs of organizations and collectivities that proclaim themselves to be religious' cannot always be regarded as 'religious' commitment[4]. 'It is possible that church membership *per se* is a particularly poor measure of religiosity', Demerath has suggested, elaborating a similar theoretical position. 'Membership', he has written,

> need not connote a commitment to religion. It may take a
> status claim or serve as a vehicle for mobility. . . . It may be a
> prerequisite for something as basic as credit or a job. . . . Or it
> may simply represent a penchant for formal associations. In
> fact, it can be argued that the churches have sought to
> capitalize upon all of these motives[5].

This implied distinction between genuine and surrogate religious practice is illuminating in certain contexts. Few would deny that the ranks of churchgoers include a proportion of hypocrites, unbelievers, and charlatans, or that some non-churchgoers adhere privately and genuinely to the beliefs and values of some religious system. Thus religious practice represents a category in one sense too broad, and in another too narrow, to provide a precise index of 'genuine' religiosity in a society. But the problem of what is genuine and what is not lies outside the province of the social historian, whose task is to account for observed social behaviour, however motivated, and to evaluate its importance within a wider societal context. The social act of participation in a religious organisation or a religious ritual has an intrinsic significance, irrespective of whether any specifically religious-cultural commitment has inspired it.

The significance of religious practice does of course vary from one cultural context to another. Participation means one thing in a culture prescribing religious observances, quite another in a secular culture; it does not have the same meaning in a national Church as it has in a religious sect.

Its significance varies with the theological, ecclesiastical, and liturgical character of the religious bodies concerned, as well as with more mundane cultural and organisational factors. It is worth stressing, moreover, that to regard associational commitments as intrinsically significant, whether or not they mirror other dimensions of religiosity, is not to minimise the effects of spiritual beliefs and values or the influence of religious norms upon social behaviour. It is to recognise, rather, that the social reality of religion reflects an interaction between such specifically religious influences and the many secular, this-worldly factors which play an important and often dominant role in shaping religious trends at the level of organisational structures and aggregate patterns of religious practice. Hence, while patterns of associational religiosity determine the overall framework of the investigation in the pages which follow, other dimensions of English religion retain a central place in the analysis. They are considered in relation to trends of associational commitment, but without them such trends are essentially meaningless.

Quite apart from the theoretical problems encountered in ascribing major importance to the associational aspects of religion, patterns of religious practice are useful only within the practical limits imposed by the reliability and completeness of the evidence on which they are based. This is the second possible objection to the approach here adopted. Scholarly scepticism about religious statistics has until very recently virtually precluded a systematic quantitative approach to the study of English religion. The British State has only rarely sought statistical evidence about the religious habits of its English subjects[6], and religious statistics consequently lack the ostensible guarantees of reliability normally attributed to social statistics of an official nature. Their quality is dependent largely on the care with which local churches, parishes, or circuits have compiled and maintained their records, and the diligence with which this local material has been collected and collated at a national level.

Statistics so collected inevitably contain errors, some tending to exaggerate and others to understate the incidence of religious practice at a given time. Moreover, for some religious organisations series of comparable statistical data are non-existent or very incomplete for periods before 1900; and in the case of other bodies which did preserve early statistical records, the data relate to somewhat unilluminating aspects of organisational development, such as the number of hearers churches could have accommodated *if* they had been filled. Nevertheless, there are good reasons for regarding the official statistics of at least some of the major religious bodies as fairly sensitive indices of their growth. Even if absolute figures have magnified somewhat the strength of the organisation, in the case of national data the degree of distortion produced by the imprecision of local records can be expected to have remained relatively constant from year to year. Thus while in absolute terms the quantitative strength of associational religion may be somewhat lower or higher than the returns for a given year suggest, a time series traces fairly accurately the direction and rate of change.

The problems of using this kind of evidence have been confronted often by scholars in other fields of historical research. Statistical series dealing with social phenomena such as unemployment and trade union membership present the social historian with the same kinds of problems as statistics of religious practice, but such material has been used to good effect by scholars willing to recognise, and work within, its limitations[7]. Indeed, it would be difficult to demonstrate that denominational statistics are not as intrinsically well-based as much of the quantitative evidence already being used by economic historians to add precision to the study of economic growth. In the collection and collation of statistical data religious organisations behave very much like other rational bureaucracies. Error and even deliberate falsification may occur at various levels of the collection process, but both sources of distortion tend to be minimised by the bureaucratic preoccupation with accuracy. As an analysis of denominational policy-making shows, annual statistical returns, when available, have been used to rationalise such bureaucratic tasks as the deployment of the professional ministry, the formation of clergy-training policies, and the development of church and school building programmes. This functional incentive for statistical accuracy was already powerful in the Methodist movement well before the end of the eighteenth century, and throughout the nineteenth century it contributed to a steady improvement in the data of most other religious bodies[8].

Intrinsic evidence of their accuracy does not provide the only grounds for confidence in the reliability of statistics of religious practice, however. In particular, tests of the kind used in regression analysis point almost conclusively to the general accuracy of membership and other associational indices of Church growth and decline. The various religious bodies have not all followed the same pattern of growth, but their growth patterns have exhibited common characteristics, and where they have diverged they have done so in apparently systematic ways. The kinds of arbitrary variations which would tend to arise as a result of errors or fabrications in particular series are very largely absent. Most available series, in short, are correlated sufficiently highly, positively or negatively, with other series, to indicate the operation of general factors common to many forms of organised religion.

A good example of high positive correlation between series collected, collated, and published quite independently is afforded by Evangelical Nonconformity[9]. Patterns of growth and decline of membership in Evangelical Nonconformist bodies, as they become discernible from the early decades of the nineteenth century onwards, reveal correlations which are not confined to the broad contours of changing absolute membership, nor even to the short-term trends evident in series on annual turnover of membership, but which are characteristic also of the sensitive indices which disaggregate membership turnover into various components of gain and loss[10]. It is implausible that fabrications or errors with virtually identical consequences would have been repeated from denomination to denomination consistently over many decades. A vastly preferable conclusion is that the data reflect common growth processes throughout Nonconformity: that whatever the deficiencies of collection and collation, they are not sufficiently significant to vitiate the usefulness of these religious statistics as fairly precise quantitative evidence about the development of the denominations concerned.

Problems of reliability and methodological questions about the meaning of data measuring associational religiosity will not be pursued further within the scope of the present study. But the study itself, as a reappraisal of the religious history of industrial England based on the kind of quantitative analysis rarely exploited by ecclesiastical historians, will provide a practical test both of the data and of the methodological orientation which it adopts. It is time, therefore, to turn to actual patterns of English Church growth as they can be measured by statistics of religious practice, and to the questions which they raise about the development of organised religion in England in the eighteenth and nineteenth centuries. In the interests of clarity, there are good reasons for distinguishing from the outset of the discussion between Anglican, Methodist, Dissenting, nineteenth-century sectarian, and Catholic growth patterns.

The Church of England

There were two distinct phases of Anglican growth between 1740 and 1914. The period 1740—1830 was an era of disaster, for whereas the Church of England had controlled something approaching a monopoly of English religious practice only ninety years earlier, in 1830 it was on the point of becoming a minority religious Establishment. There may even have been an *absolute* decline of conformist practice during this period, despite the rapid expansion of English society. The evidence is inconclusive. Figures dealing with Anglican church-building and Anglican clergy in the early nineteenth century, presented in Table 2.1, indicate rates of increase so minimal as to suggest little or no pressure on the physical and manpower resources of the Church at the time. The decline of Anglican practice noticeable in the half-century before 1740 may, in short, have continued throughout the eighteenth century. A sample of thirty Oxfordshire parishes, drawn from periodic episcopal and archdiocesan visitation returns, does show a progressive decline in the number of communicants. There were 911 communicants in these parishes in 1738, 896 in 1759, 868 in 1771, and 682 in 1802: a decline of 25 per cent. The number rose to 755 by 1810, but this was still substantially below than the 1738 level[11]. How typical these south Midland parishes were of the country as a whole remains conjectural, of course. It is possible that they actually fared better than many other areas.

But even in areas where the incidence of religious practice did not decline absolutely in the eighteenth and early nineteenth centuries, Anglicanism did experience massive decline both in relation to the size of the wider society, and in relation to the strength of rapidly growing extra-Establishment religious movements. There may have been more practising Anglicans in England in 1830 than there had been in 1740—Table 2.1 records evidence of a gradual increase in the quarter-century immediately preceding 1830—but there were vastly more non-Anglicans. This was the crux of the Anglican failure in early industrial society. Little was done between the reign of Queen Anne and the second quarter of the nineteenth century to enlarge the Church of England as a religious service

Table 2.1 The Church of England
Churches, clergy, and Easter Day communicants, 1801—1914

Year	Churches and chapels	Clergy	Easter Day communicants ('000s)	Easter Day communicant density
1801	11,379	—	535	9.9
1811	11,444	14,531	550	8.9
1821	11,558	—	570	7.9
1831	11,883	14,933	605	7.2
1841	12,668	15,730	755	7.9
1851	14,077	16,194	875	8.1
1861	14,731	17,966	995	8.3
1871	15,522	19,411	1,110	8.2
1881	16,300	20,341	1,225	7.9
1891	16,956	22,753	1,490	8.4
1901	17,368	23,670	1,945	9.4
1911	—	23,193	2,293	9.8
1914	—	—	2,226	9.2

Notes (Sources for Tables are given in the reference section, p. 214)
1 In 1966 Anglican 'churches', 'clergy', and 'Easter Day communicants' numbered 17,761, 20,008, and 1,899,000 respectively. The 1966 Easter Day Communicant density index was 5.4.
2 The density index expresses Easter Day communicant figures as a percentage of the population aged fifteen and over.
3 The figures on 'clergy' for 1811—41 include a few hundred Welsh clergy. Welsh clergy have been excluded from the subsequent figures. The increase of clergy in the 1840s consequently was greater than the series indicates.

organisation. Historians have argued about its pastoral and administrative effectiveness, but by virtual consensus they have recognised the eighteenth-century Church as a static institution, characterised by inertia if not always by complacency[12]. The facilities at its disposal, measured in terms of personnel or in terms of accommodation for religious worship, increased only marginally, if at all, while the English population rose from about 5,500,000 in 1740 to over 13,200,000 in 1831[13].

The concept of *density* (the perception that the relative strength of a religious organisation within a society can be at least as important as its absolute strength) has an obvious relevance for an analysis of Anglican growth in the period 1740 to 1830. A density index relates the incidence of participation in a religious organisation to the size of the constituency within which the organisation operates. Expressed as a percentage, the density index of a village church attracting the active support of half its village community would be 50 per cent; and in density terms a congregation of fifty in a village of 100 people would rank above a congregation of 500 in a vast urban constituency. Clearly, in a society expanding as rapidly as that of early industrial England, density must be the primary measurement of growth. And assuming that the absolute volume of participation in Anglican worship remained stationary between 1740 and 1830 (an assumption sufficiently accurate for the purpose of the present broad comparison), the Church in density terms was well over 50 per cent weaker in 1830 than it had been less than a century earlier. For the religious Establishment this had been a phase of prolonged, rapid, and disastrous decline.

But the Church of England growth pattern changed significantly in the 1830s and 1840s. As Table 2.1 shows, Anglican expansion, negligible before about 1830, began to gather pace in the 1830s, and the period between this revival and the First World War saw a phase of continuous increase of Anglican churches, of Anglican clergy, and of participation by laymen in the institutions of the Church. The population continued to grow, from over thirteen million in 1830 to well over thirty-four million in 1914, but the expansion of the Church was even more rapid. Anglican density indices show progressive improvement throughout this period, especially between 1880 and 1914, although even in 1914 much of the ground lost before 1830 had not been regained.

The evidence of these figures suggests a need for reappraisal in the continuing debate between the 'optimistic' and 'gloomy' schools of Victorian church history[14]. 'Assessment of the "success" or "failure" of the Victorian Church of England', an Anglican historian has written recently,

> depends largely on the criteria employed and on the relative
> weight given to quantitative and qualitative evidence.
> Generally speaking, those writers who emphasise quality of
> pastoral care as a guide to success or failure can remain
> cheerful about the performance of the Victorian Church
> despite gloomy statistics and evidence of intellectual weakness
> and political decline[15].

In point of fact, however, quantitative evidence comes to the defence of the Victorian Church. Statistical indications of Anglican failure in particular urban contexts and among working-class sections of English society[16] must be placed in the perspective of rising density indices within the society *as a whole*. Quantitatively the Victorian Church failed only in the sense that most of the ground lost between 1740 and 1830 was not regained, and it is a measure of the gravity of this Anglican failure in early industrial society that the substantial recovery of the Victorian era was too little and too late to reverse the tendency towards institutional decline in Anglicanism. But however it is to be explained, and however much it is overshadowed by the seriousness of the decline which preceded it, the phase of Anglican growth spanning the Victorian and Edwardian years represents the one prolonged period after the Restoration in which the Church of England succeeded in improving its quantitative position within English society.

Methodism

Table 2.2 traces the growth of all major Methodist bodies in England between 1767 and 1914, and also includes a composite series based on the aggregated membership of all those connexions which, either independently or as parts of Methodist organisations which had been created by earlier unions, merged in 1932 to form the present Methodist Church. The composite series serves to simplify the organisational complexity of the Methodist movement. While it does not trace the development of a single institution, except during the thirty years before the Methodist New Connexion schism of 1797, such a series, by minimising distortions due to Methodist divisions and reunions, provides a fairly accurate picture of the overall growth of Methodism[17].

These Methodist figures are particularly reliable. Wesleyanism and its offshoots produced some of the earliest and most painstaking collectors of social statistics in Britain. Wesley himself not only took seriously numerical evidence of progress and decline, but inculcated the habit of quantitative accuracy into those responsible for maintaining local records. His successors were careful enumerators. Not only was tightly knit connexional organisation a guarantee of virtual completeness: Methodist polity also ensured a minimum of distortion due to merely nominal membership. Membership was subject to quarterly review, and at least until there was a significant relaxation of Methodist discipline late in the nineteenth century, 'members' meant regular participants in the affairs of a connexion. Annual series unbroken since 1766 allow over 200 years of Methodist growth to be plotted with a fairly high degree of precision. The quinquennial series presented in Table 2.2 thus provide a clear picture of the general trends within this growth process.

As far as absolute membership is concerned the period 1740 to 1914 includes three broad phases of Methodist growth: a period of sustained rapid expansion from the birth of the movement to about 1840[18]; a period of considerable, although much slower and decelerating expansion until 1906; and the early stages of a still continuing period of decline between 1906 and the outbreak of the war in 1914. Even more revealing, perhaps, is the density series abstracted from the composite membership data. Relating the growth of Methodist membership to the growth of the English population aged fifteen years and over, it shows, initially, that up to the end of the 1830s Methodist membership had expanded much more rapidly than the total adult population[19], and that in 1840 the relative strength of Methodism within English society was greater than at any period before or since.

As in the case of the Church of England, so with Methodism the second quarter of the nineteenth century saw a major change of growth pattern. Between 1840 and 1885 the ratio of membership to adult population remained more or less constant, and the slight decline in the density index which is apparent almost certainly would have been avoided but for a period of serious internal dissension and schism in Wesleyanism between 1849 and 1857. But this stabilisation of Methodist strength was in marked contrast to the rapid rate at which the movement had outstripped population growth in the period before 1840. And after 1885—

Table 2.2   Methodist membership in England, 1767–1914

A. *Wesleyan membership, 1767–1796*

1767	22,410	1776	30,875	1791	56,605
1771	26,119	1781	37,131	1796	77,402
		1786	46,559		

B. *Wesleyan, New Connexion, and total Methodist membership, 1801–1819*

	W	NC	Total		W	NC	Total
1801	87,010	4,815	91,825	1816	181,631	8,146	189,777
1806	103,549	5,586	109,135	1819	184,998	9,672	194,670
1811	135,863	7,448	143,311				

C. *Wesleyan, New Connexion, Primitive Methodist, Bible Christian, United Methodist Free Churches, and total Methodist membership, 1821–1906*

	W	NC	PM	BC	UMFC	Total
1821	188,668	10,404	16,394			215,466
1826	217,486	10,233	–	6,433		267,652
1831	232,883	11,433	37,216	6,650		288,182
1836	273,588	18,248	62,306	10,499		364,641
1841	305,682	20,506	75,967	11,353		435,591
1846	319,770	15,610	85,500	12,181		452,238
1851	285,000	16,962	106,074	13,324		490,000
1856	242,296	18,380	104,178	13,894		443,493
1861	291,288	22,732	127,772	16,866	52,970	513,628
1866	303,500	24,064	140,905	18,758	60,386	547,613
1871	319,495	22,870	148,597	18,050	61,924	570,936
1876	342,612	23,055	160,737	19,665	64,777	610,846
1881	349,695	25,797	168,807	21,209	65,067	630,575
1886	378,518	27,720	179,726	23,614	66,964	676,542
1891	387,779	28,756	180,518	25,769	67,200	690,022
1896	395,588	29,932	181,079	26,306	69,506	702,411
1901	412,194	32,324	187,260	28,315	72,568	732,668
1906	447,474	37,017	203,103	32,317	80,323	800,234

D. *Wesleyan Methodist Association and Wesleyan Reformers membership, 1837–1856*

	WMA		WMA		WMA	WR
1837	21,262	1846	19,177	1856	18,136	46,609
1841	22,074	1851	20,557			

E. *Wesleyan, Primitive Methodist, United Methodist, and total Methodist membership, 1911–1914*

	W	PM	UM	Total
1911	436,356	202,479	144,888	783,723
1914	432,370	202,420	143,096	777,886

Continued on p. 32

Table 2.2 – *continued*

F. *Total Methodist membership as a percentage of the adult English population,*
1801—1914

1801	1.6	1841	4.5	1881	4.0
1806	1.9	1846	4.3	1886	4.0
1811	2.3	1851	4.4	1891	3.8
1816	2.8	1856	3.8	1896	3.6
1821	2.9	1861	4.1	1901	3.5
1826	3.3	1866	4.2	1906	3.6
1831	3.4	1871	4.1	1911	3.3
1836	4.0	1876	4.1	1914	3.2

Notes
1 The *Total Methodist Membership* Series is based on an aggregation of the following connexional memberships: 1801—19, Wesleyan and New Connexion; 1821, Wesleyan, New Connexion, and Primitive Methodist; 1826—36, Wesleyan, New Connexion, Primitive Methodist, and Bible Christian; 1836—56, Wesleyan, New Connexion, Primitive Methodist, Bible Christian, Wesleyan Methodist Association, and (1851 and 1856) the Wesleyan Reformers; 1861—1906, Wesleyan, New Connexion, Primitive Methodist, Bible Christian, and United Methodist Free Churches; 1911—14, Wesleyan, Primitive Methodist, and United Methodist Church.
2 For the purpose of computing the density series of Section F (above), 'Adult population' has been defined as the population aged fifteen years and over.
3 Wesleyan density in 1767 was around 0.5.
4 In 1968 membership of the Methodist Church in England was 603,100 and Methodist density was 1.7. Following the Union of 1932 these figures represent a continuation of the *Total Methodist Membership* series.

although absolute membership continued slowly to increase for over twenty years—in relation to the adult population Methodism began to lose ground. The Methodist movement, spectacularly successful throughout the pre-Victorian century, was facing serious institutional difficulties well before the Victorian era had run its course.

Protestant Dissent

The development of Protestant Dissent in the eighteenth century involved discontinuities of a fundamental kind. As Chapter 1 has argued, Dissent was in an advanced state of atrophy in 1740. The radical Puritanism to which it was heir had become less evocative in the more tolerant climate of early Hanoverian England than it had been in the seventeenth century, and the numerical decline of Dissent had been accompanied by a serious expurgation of its Puritan religious culture. While Presbyterians and General Baptists had turned increasingly from Puritan orthodoxy to Socinianism, in those sections of Dissent where orthodoxy had survived it had been muted by quietist tendencies[20]. As early as 1729 it had been possible for a dissenting minister to argue that Puritanism meant neither more nor less than the 'spirit of liberty', although he had been compelled to admit that some early Dissenters had 'had a few oddities mixed with this generous sentiment'[21]. Expurgation so drastic had not been general, but there had been a clear tendency for Dissent to become 'rather political than religious'[22].

This was Dissent at the beginning of the period under review, but the scenario changed rapidly in the second half of the eighteenth century, and became more complicated in the sense that different sections of Dissent began to develop in very different ways. Table 2.3, which disaggregates decennially and denominationally the number of buildings registered between 1691 and 1851 for the purpose of dissenting worship, indicates that the marked decline of dissenting activity during the period before 1740 was followed in some denominations by a major recovery which continued at an accelerating rate until well into the nineteenth century, and in others by stagnation or continuing decline. Registration was mandatory under the provisions of the Act of Toleration, and the detailed statistics presented to the House of Commons in 1853 are illuminating despite serious ambiguities of meaning and categorisation[23], and despite the fact that registration was at best an indirect measure of extra-Establishment religious activity.

A decision to register a building for dissenting worship could reflect a variety of motives. It was not uncommon for a congregation to use and register several places of worship either simultaneously or in quick succession, and soon after the introduction of the Toleration Act, simply as a commemorative gesture, the Presbyterian congregation at Toxeth, Liverpool, registered, in addition to its regular meeting-house, twelve local premises which its members had frequented during the pre-toleration era. The latter kind of idiosyncrasy would have affected only the early figures, but during the entire duration of the series the registration of 'temporary' places of worship, particularly, was not simply a reflection of the growth of Dissent. What was being enumerated in these official statistics was the number of buildings within which Dissenters were able to hold services without contravening the law, and the incidence of registration doubtless varied partly in response to the stringency with which magistrates chose to enforce the legal obligations inherent in religious Dissent. The more intolerant social and ecclesiastical climate of the generation after 1790, for example, was doubtless a factor contributing to the sharp rise in the demand for certification evident between 1791 and 1830. For Wesleyanism it accelerated the trend towards full extra-Establishment status, for much to the consternation of the aged Wesley, around the middle of 1790 justices of the peace in many areas adopted an 'entirely new' policy of harassment designed to force Wesleyan preachers and societies to register as 'Protestant Dissenters'[24]. But as a corresponding sharp rise in the

Table 2.3 Dissenters' places of worship certified by Registrars-General, 1691–1850

Decennial periods	'Protestants' and 'Protestant Dissenters'		Congregationalists		Baptists		Presbyterians		Quakers		Other denominations		Unspecified registrations		Total	
	Temporary	Permanent	Temporary	Permanent	Temporary	Permanent	Temporary	Permanent	Temporary	Permanent	Temporary	Permanent	Temporary	Permanent	Temporary	Permanent
1691–1700	325	13	49	0	66	1	28	0	80	6	3	0	696	12	1,247	32
1701–10	368	14	48	1	71	2	98	7	98	3	1	0	542	14	1,219	41
1711–20	295	9	26	2	63	0	59	2	46	1	3	1	383	6	875	21
1721–30	121	6	38	0	35	2	26	6	30	3	0	0	198	10	448	27
1731–40	121	8	4	0	57	1	55	7	82	3	0	0	105	5	424	24
1741–50	151	8	27	0	51	5	70	4	74	1	25	0	98	9	502	27
1751–60	320	24	51	5	58	6	99	5	27	5	43	1	105	9	703	55
1761–70	409	25	84	17	70	16	39	13	20	5	13	1	66	8	701	85
1771–80	527	55	152	39	55	19	37	19	10	5	77	3	120	20	978	158
1781–90	621	117	180	41	89	30	7	8	10	2	65	15	182	38	1,154	251
1791–1800	1,693	372	516	128	170	74	7	9	12	11	307	85	710	153	3,413	832
1801–10	1,968	580	373	230	216	98	2	21	14	18	438	293	953	230	3,964	1,470
1811–20	4,400	1,271	352	241	258	171	15	13	7	6	483	360	1,977	583	7,493	2,645
1821–30	4,607	1,487	299	248	206	188	7	22	6	8	375	327	2,167	600	7,667	2,880
1831–40	2,712	1,331	153	286	116	170	6	7	9	15	227	454	1,317	521	4,540	2,784
1841–50	1,609	1,084	107	205	110	182	5	6	1	4	271	754	974	426	3,077	2,661

Notes

1 'Temporary' places of worship include houses, rooms, etc., used for worship as well as for other purposes. Chapels and meeting houses were classified as 'permanent' places of worship.

2 The series measure trends over time in the incidence of registration. They indicate neither the absolute strength of a denomination at a particular time, nor the relative strength of any one denomination *vis-à-vis* any other. (During early decennial periods, at least, Baptists and Quakers evidently were more likely to specify their denominational character when registering than were Independents or Presbyterians.)

3 A majority of registrations were never denominationally specific, but as the proportion which were remained more or less constant, the trends (which are in any case corroborated from other sources) presumably are broadly accurate.

number of complaints about magisterial harassment made to the Protestant Dissenting Deputies confirms[25], this new treatment of Methodists was merely symptomatic of a general tightening of the Establishment's interpretation of the Toleration Laws. All non-Anglican bodies permitted the protection of registration were likely to have become more scrupulous about taking out licences after 1790.

But it was the *growth* of Dissent which more than anything else determined the overall pattern of registration from decade to decade, as well as the denominational variations within this pattern. Changes in Establishment attitudes towards Dissenters and variations in other factors influencing the rate registration were secondary. The steep rise in registrations after 1790, for example, certainly was not simply a reflection of the new 'hard line' being adopted by the authorities. Indeed, the hostility of the ruling classes in both Church and State was largely a response to what seemed an ominous growth of extra-Establishment religion[26]. Trends in the registration of Congregational and Baptist places of worship (the decline between 1710 and the middle of the century, the gradual revival thereafter, and the extremely rapid increase from the closing years of the eighteenth century), followed a pattern precisely the same as that which is suggested by available data on the number of congregations (as distinct from places of worship) of these denominations during the period from 1716 to 1850, a pattern also confirmed by evidence about membership. Similarly, the very different pattern of registrations by the Presbyterian and Quaker denominations is corroborated by other evidence of their continuing decline during the period in the late eighteenth and nineteenth centuries when Congregationalists and Baptists, like Methodists, were multiplying rapidly.

There were 1,182 Congregational, Baptist, and Presbyterian congregations in England in 1716[27], and it is a measure of the seriousness of the decline which took place in subsequent decades that in 1773, when Dissent as a whole had begun once more to expand, such congregations totalled only 1,080, over 100 fewer than the figure of half a century earlier[28]. But from the 1770s Dissenting congregations multiplied rapidly. In 1808 the historians Bogue and Bennett counted more than 500 dissenting groups which had not existed thirty-five years earlier[29]. Trends in the registration of Dissenter's places of worship, in short, while they may have been accentuated by mounting judicial and social pressures after 1790, bore a close resemblance to actual growth trends of dissenting communities.

This was true as much of denominational trends as it was of the overall pattern. In the case of the Baptist churches a total of 283 congregations in 1716 was reduced to around 200 by 1751, but the accelerating expansion of the century which followed saw the number rise to 532 in 1808, 1,025 in 1830, and 1,276 in 1840[30]. The establishment of Independent congregations followed a similar pattern: of those extant in 1871, when denominational officials carried out a survey, 252 traced their origins to the period 1650–99, only 95 to the period 1700–49, 269 to the period 1750–99, and 824 to the period 1800–49[31]. But while these sections of Dissent recovered rapidly from the decline of the first half of the eighteenth century, Presbyterianism, which had accounted for about two-thirds of all Dissenting congregations in 1714, continued to decline to the point where in 1808 its congregations were vastly outnumbered by those of both Independents and Baptists[32]. Many Presbyterian congregations had simply died out, and so serious had the Socinian controversy become that while the remaining orthodox groups were tending to drift into independency, heterodox Presbyterianism at the beginning of the nineteenth century was in the process of merging with the new Unitarian movement initiated by Theophilus Lindsay in 1773[33]. The Society of Friends was not, like Presbyterianism, facing virtual extinction at the beginning of the nineteenth century, but it, too, was playing no part in the massive expansion of Dissent taking place within Congregational and Baptist communities. There were about 20,000 Quakers in England and Wales in 1800, only half as many as there had been at the end of the seventeenth century, and a slow decline was continuing[34].

Thus there was discontinuity in the development of eighteenth century Protestant Dissent, not only in the sense that a trend of serious decline before 1750 was reversed emphatically in the second half of the century, but also because within Dissent as a whole and even within individual denominations the century saw a break-up of the old dissenting tradition and the emergence of various new movements, widely divergent in matters of theology, polity, and conversionist zeal. But while the variety within and between the dissenting bodies might be pursued almost endlessly, from substantial controversies to nuances of interpretation, from locality to locality, or from one dissenting academy to another, the fundamental division was between those sections of Dissent which were metamorphosed by the Methodist Revival and those which were not. As contemporary observers recognised, a dichotomy between a 'New Dissent' and an 'Old Dissent' had become an essential feature of the English religious landscape by the end of the eighteenth century[35].

The New Dissent

During the period from the Act of Toleration to the middle of the eighteenth century the various dissenting denominations had followed similar patterns of decline. Series on the registration of Dissenters' places of worship confirm this. But in the decade 1761 to 1770 registrations began to reflect the emergence of the New Dissent. While Congregationalists and Baptists were registering many more places of worship than they had registered previously, Presbyterians and Quakers were registering even fewer. The bifurcation of Dissent quickly became unmistakably apparent. Whereas in 1751 to 1760 Presbyterians and Quakers combined had taken out more licences than Congregationalists and Baptists, by 1781 to 1790 the latter denominations had a combined majority of more than 12:1 (Table 2.3).

Within the dissenting tradition the New Dissent was a phenomenon analogous to that of Methodism within the Anglican tradition. The example and influence of Methodism was, indeed, an essential factor in the metamorphosis of Congregational and Baptist Dissent in the second half of the eighteenth century, despite the fact that the doctrinal issues underlying the New Dissent—Old Dissent division had emerged during the Salter Hall Controversy of 1719[36]. Sometimes, as in the case of the Congregational and Particular Baptist churches, the new, 'methodistical' values and modes of activity gradually won more or less universal approval. But for General Baptists the rise of the New Dissent involved abrupt organisational discontinuity. Motivated by a newfound conversionist zeal, orthodox elements of this Arminian wing of the Baptist movement broke away to form the General Baptist New Connexion in 1770, leaving behind an emasculated Old Connexion which was largely unitarian in theology.

The religious-cultural character of this New Dissent and the relationships between it and the Methodist movement will be explored later in the study. What is relevant in the present context is the similarity between the two phenomena in their quantitative development. Table 2.4 traces the growth of Particular Baptist and General Baptist New Connexion membership from 1750 to 1891, when the two movements were

Table 2.4   The New Dissent
Congregational, Particular Baptist, and New Connexion General Baptist membership, 1750—1914

	Congregational		Particular Baptist		General Baptist New Connexion	
	Members	Density	Members	Density	Members	Density
1750	15,000		10,000		–	
1772	–		–		1,221	
1780	–		–		1,800	
1790	26,000		17,000		2,843	
1800	35,000	0.65	24,000	0.45	3,403	
1810	–		–		5,322	
1820	–		–		7,673	0.11
1830	–		–		10,869	0.13
1838	127,000	1.38	86,000	0.94	13,947	0.15
1851	165,000	1.52	122,000	1.12	18,277	0.17
1863	180,000	1.56	132,000	1.07	20,714	0.17
1870	–		149,500	1.11	20,541	0.15
1880	–		176,500	1.15	24,489	0.16
1890	–		194,500	1.10	26,805	0.15
1900	257,435	1.27	239,114	1.19		
1910	287,952	1.23	266,224	1.14		
1914	289,545	1.21	264,923	1.11		

Notes

1   The Particular and New Connexion General Baptists united in 1891 in the Baptist Union of Great Britain and Ireland.

2   Congregational and Baptist membership and density figures for 1967 were 175,001 (0.5) and 180,750 (0.5) respectively.

amalgamated, and the growth of the Baptist Union thereafter, as well as the growth of the Congregational denomination between 1750 and 1914. It also includes series measuring the density of denominational membership within the adult population throughout this period. In Figs 2.1 and 2.2 these indices of the growth of the New Dissent are juxtaposed with the composite Methodist series of Table 2.2.

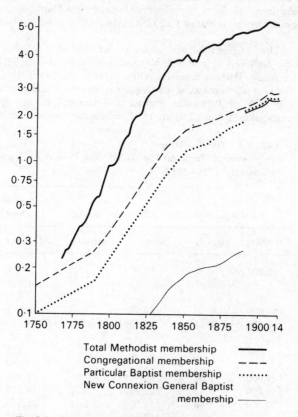

Total Methodist membership ——————
Congregational membership — — —
Particular Baptist membership ....
New Connexion General Baptist
membership ——————

Fig. 2.1 Methodist and New Dissenting membership, 1750–1914.
Scale: Semi-log. Source: Tables 2.2 and 2.4

The basic similarity of Methodist, Congregational, and Baptist growth patterns is unmistakable. While it is true that until the twentieth century neither the Particular Baptist nor the Congregational data were sufficiently complete to identify more than the broad contours of membership growth, these broad contours do provide definite evidence of a common growth pattern which the New Dissent shared with Methodism. In the case of the General Baptist New Connexion, moreover, more detailed corroborating evidence is available in a series which is virtually

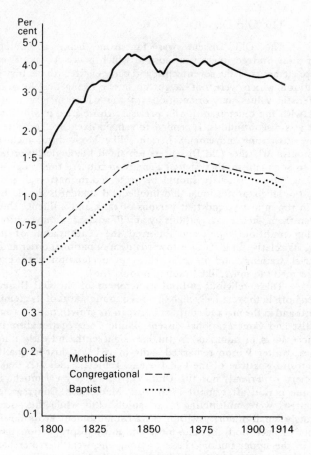

Fig. 2.2 **Methodist and New Dissenting membership as a percentage of the population aged fifteen and over, 1800–1914.**
Note: The Baptist series plotted is an aggregation of Particular and General Baptist density indices. *Scale: Semi-log. Source: Tables 2.2 and 2.4*

unbroken annually between 1772 and 1891. Like Methodism, the New dissenting movements experienced their most rapid expansion before about 1840. Thereafter, not only did the absolute rate of growth slacken in every case, but the various density indices improved only marginally. From the middle of the 1880s Congregational and Baptist membership, like membership in the various Methodist connexions, began to decline relative to the size of the adult English constituency from which it was drawn; and also like Methodism, the New Dissent reached the zenith of its absolute strength in 1906, and thereafter entered a phase of prolonged and continuing decline.

The Old Dissent

The Old Dissent was far from being a homogeneous phenomenon. Indeed, there is a sense in which it was a residual category for those elements of the seventeenth and early-eighteenth century dissenting tradition which were not caught up in the Evangelical Revival. In its characteristic values and orientations to the wider society it was continuous with the older tradition in precisely those areas in which the New Dissent was discontinuous. It tended to remain exclusive and elitest while the new dissenting movements became, like Methodism, inclusive and conversionist. Whether Old Dissenters remained theologically orthodox or turned to Socinianism, they shared a common concern that religion should be 'serious', that regularity should be preserved in matters of polity and liturgy, that high professional and intellectual standards should be maintained in the ministry, and that persons of rank and influence should not be driven from their congregations by any ill-advised popularisation of the dissenting tradition[37]. They abhorred the 'enthusiasm' of the New Dissent, its relative indifference towards denominational order and formal ministerial training, and its evangelical preoccupation with expansion which seemed too much like 'trading in souls'[38].

These religious-cultural preferences of the Old Dissent were reflected both in the relatively high socio-economic status of its members and adherents and in the marked contrast between its growth patterns and those of Baptist and Congregational dissent. While Congregationalism received 'large accessions in numbers' in the late eighteenth and early nineteenth centuries. Walter Wilson remarked sadly in 1814, it 'lost in quality'[39]. The opposite was true of the Old Dissent. Table 2.5 indicates that neither the Society of Friends nor the Unitarian churches grew much, if at all, during the period after about 1790 when Methodists, Congregationalists, and Baptists were multiplying most rapidly. But while they became an increasingly small minority within extra-Establishment Protestantism, the members of each body became more and more disproportionately represented in the upper middle classes, among the wealthier merchants and manufacturers of industrial England, and within the radical municipal oligarchies which emerged after the Municipal Corporation Act of 1835 to challenge the traditional Tory-Anglican urban elites[40].

Table 2.5   Society of Friends membership, 1800—1914

1800	19,800	1881	15,113
1840	16,277	1891	16,102
1847	15,345	1901	17,476
1861	13,384	1911	19,612
1871	14,021	1914	19,942

Note

1   There may have been as many as 55,000 Quakers in England and Wales in 1680. In 1968 Quaker membership was 20,909.

The figures on the quantitative development of the Society of Friends speak for themselves. In the 120 years before 1800 Quaker membership fell by 50 per cent, and there was a further decline of 33 per cent in the period between 1800 and 1860. Despite a century of slow recovery the Quakers, numbering only 21,000, remained extremely weak in the middle of the twentieth century. But while in the case of the Society of Friends the differences in growth between the New and Old Dissent are unmistakable, Unitarian statistics are superficially more ambiguous. Having begun to assume the character of a separate denomination only after Theophilus Lindsay left the Church of England on antitrinitarian grounds in 1773, Unitarianism was capable by 1851 of attracting a total of 50,000 attendants to its morning, afternoon, and evening services on Census Sunday[41]. This was only 14,000 fewer than the combined morning, afternoon, and evening attendances at services of New Connexion General Baptists[42]. Superficially it might appear that similar growth processes had been at work, for both bodies had begun their organisational evolution in the 1770s.

But the rise of Unitarianism reflected a regrouping of the heterodox remnants of the old Presbyterian and General Baptist traditions. It was not the kind of growth being experienced by the New Dissent during the same period: it involved the metamorphosis of existing congregations rather than the creation of new ones. Statistics relating to the first half-century of the movement must be treated with caution because the distinction between Unitarianism and Presbyterianism remained blurred, but it is clear that once the process of metamorphosis was complete the organisation showed little capacity for further expansion. In 1832 the *Unitarian Chronicle* identified 200 Unitarian congregations in England[43], a number only twenty-nine below the total number of Unitarian places of worship in England *and Wales* in 1851[44]. And in a critical comment on the growth of these communities, the *Congregational Magazine* drew a valid distinction between growth by proselytisation and growth by conversion. In its growth, the magazine asserted caustically, Unitarianism was 'like those parasitical plants, which gather not their moisture from the earth, but vegetate by the nutriment they steal from nobler and more ancient stocks'[45]. Certainly it was true that once the original English Presbyterianism (the stock, however noble, upon which the initial growth of Unitarianism had depended), virtually disappeared in the second quarter of the nineteenth century, the Unitarian movement followed a growth pattern comparable with that of the Society of Friends.

The New Presbyterianism

While the original English Presbyterian tradition was in the final stages of dismemberment in the early nineteenth century a new English Presbyterianism was in the process of being born. But while this new movement was destined to become an integral part of the Free Church section of English Christianity in the twentieth century, throughout the nineteenth century it never fitted easily into any of the traditional categories of Protestant Dissent. It was not an indigenous English religious culture. When the Presbyterian Church of England was formed in 1876 by a union between two synodical systems, each linked with a different branch of the disrupted Scottish Presbyterian tradition, a large majority of its members and almost all its ministers were Scottish migrants[46]. During the previous forty years Presbyterianism had grown rapidly in England. From a combined membership of below 10,000 in 1838 the two major organisations had expanded to about 15,000 in 1851, 27,000 in 1860, 38,000 in 1870, and more than 46,000 when they united in 1876[47]. But this had been very much an exogenous growth process, reliant on Scottish immigration. And those elements of the new Presbyterian Church of England of 1876 which were indigenous to England had in many cases been acquired at the expense of Congregationalism[48].

Celtic migration, from Wales and Ireland as well as Scotland, remained a dominant factor in the growth of the English Presbyterianism at least until 1914, despite determined efforts by the new denomination to discard its exotic image. The Church's Statistical Committee reported in 1882 that the bulk of the increase in denominational membership during the previous five years had been due to a continuing influx of Scottish Presbyterians[49]; and in 1914, of 6,124 new members of English Presbyterian congregations (there were others merely transferring membership from one congregation to another), about 40 per cent were from outside England[50]. The denomination only slowly achieved the position within the mainstream of Free Church religious culture which was reflected in its merger, in 1972, with the Congregational Church of England and Wales[51]. In the period covered by this study, certainly, this new English Presbyterianism is to be distinguished from both the New Dissenting and Old Dissenting traditions which had taken shape in the eighteenth and early nineteenth centuries.

Nineteenth- and twentieth-century sectarianism

Methodist and New Dissenting denominations, which had expanded dramatically during the period before 1840, were being outgrown by the end of the nineteenth century not only by the revived Church of England, but also by certain newer, more sectarian movements. The most obvious example is the Salvation Army. Table 2.6 illustrates the immense importance of the period 1877–1900 for the growth of Salvationism in Britain. From below 5,000 in June 1877, Army membership grew rapidly to an estimated 100,000 in 1900 and to 115,000 by 1911[52]. Its centres of activity and the number of full-time officers working for it multiplied accordingly, principally in England.

Other non-Anglican bodies of nineteenth century origin also enjoyed their most rapid growth during the closing decades of the Victorian era. As Table 2.7 confirms, this was true of the Churches of Christ, a small, fairly sectarian body in England, which had begun its history about the time when the expansion of Methodism and of the New Dissent had begun to slacken. It was also true of the Plymouth Brethren movement. Open Brethren 'membership' (a very nebulous concept in Brethren polity) was estimated to be 80,000 in England and Wales in

Table 2.6   The Salvation Army

	Corps	Officers
1878	81	127
1881	251	533
1886	1,006	2,260
1896	1,375	2,600
1906	1,431	2,868
1911	1,316	2,555
1916	1,224	3,049

Notes
1   'Corps' are centres of work.
2   'Officers' include employees in Salvation Army institutions.
3   In 1967 'Corps' numbered 1,158 and 'Officers' 3,302.

Table 2.7   Churches of Christ membership, 1842–1914

1842	1,300	1891	9,511
1852	2,081	1901	12,224
1861	2,528	1911	14,725
1871	3,776	1914	15,228
1881	6,451		

Notes
1   In the United States the Churches of Christ are known as the Disciples
    of Christ.
2   The data relate to Great Britain, but membership is confined very
    largely to England.
3   In 1968 Churches of Christ membership was 5,615.

1951[53], and in 1959 a Brethren publication enumerated 1,862 Open
assemblies in the British Isles[54]. Originating around 1830, the movement
appears to have entered its most expansionist period when there was a
'vast increase' in the number of assemblies between 1880 and 1900[55].
      It is noteworthy that new movements like the Salvation Army,
the Churches of Christ, and the Open Brethren experienced their most
pronounced expansion during the closing decades of the nineteenth
century, when Methodist, Congregational, and Baptist statistics were
beginning to reflect a deepening of the institutional difficulties first
apparent almost half a century earlier. A Baptist historian, Ernest Payne,
has cited the emergence of such movements as 'evidence of the life that

was in the Free Churches during the Victorian epoch, a life difficult to confine within traditional channels'[56]. Decelerating Methodist and New Dissenting growth rates, he has implied, represented an increase in the number of organisational 'channels' rather than a decrease in the demand for the kind of extra-Establishment evangelicalism which these older bodies previously had almost monopolised.

Payne's hypothesis is of a kind which has been adduced frequently to explain the appearance of sectarian movements. Sectarian religion, the theory suggests, often arises in response to the inevitable processes of institutionalisation and organisational consolidation in older movements. In the case of English religion, Martin has argued, applying precisely this sociological assumption, 'the Salvation Army took over from the Methodists and the Pentecostalists from the Salvation Army'; and each new departure followed 'a cooling of religious zeal and an intrusion of formality' into the life of an existing religious culture[57].

There can be little doubt that this analysis does have relevance to the fissiparous development of conversionist and adventist movements in modern English religious history[58], but the available statistical evidence suggests that the creation of new organisational 'channels' has failed to compensate fully for the decelerating growth of established movements[59]. The growth of alternatives to what Payne has called the 'traditional channels' failed, for example, to make up the leeway caused by the reduction of Methodist, Congregational, and Baptist growth during the late Victorian and Edwardian years. Between 1880 and 1911 the combined membership of these major denominations declined as a proportion of the adult English population from 6.6 per cent to 5.6 per cent (Tables 2.2 and 2.4). For the combined density index to have remained steady during this period would have required an additional net gain of more than 220,000 members. But the contemporary growth in England of the Salvation Army, the Plymouth Brethren, and the Churches of Christ, combined with that of the smaller Victorian sects[60], would not have gone half way towards closing such a gap.

Thus while the rise of various sectarian movements during the Victorian era, and especially during its final decades, is evidence of a demand for a kind of organised religion which was not being provided adequately either by the Church of England or by the 'traditional channels' of Methodism and Dissent, it is equally clear from the growth of these new movements that the demand was quite limited. In other words, to the extent that the new sectarianism was heir to a religious-cultural position from which older traditions had departed, or appeared to be departing, it is significant that the response which it evoked was so much smaller than that which had been evoked by Methodist and New Dissenting movements in the eighteenth and earlier nineteenth centuries. An obvious conclusion is that while certain internal institutional and cultural changes, affecting the older movements increasingly as the nineteenth century proceeded, apparently retarded their growth and prompted the emergence of organised alternatives, English society was in any case becoming much less conducive to the kind of extra-Establishment Protestantism which had revolutionised English religious life in the early industrial age.

The Catholic Church

In the period from the late eighteenth century to the present, considered in overall perspective, the religious organisation which has most improved its quantitative position in English society is the Catholic Church. Catholic growth processes have not, however, involved the kind of interaction between a religious collectivity and its wider society which marked either the expansion of the New Dissent and the Methodist movement during the Evangelical Revival or the resurgence of the Church of England during the Victorian era. The latter growth processes depended essentially on the recruitment of new members and adherents from the wider society: on the encroachment of the 'Church' into the 'world'. In contrast, the massive expansion of English Catholicism was dependent primarily on exogenous growth. What the Jesuit, W. J. Amherst, wrote of Scottish Catholicism, that it remained numerically weak 'until God sent the Irish people to swell to large proportions the members of His Church, and to sing the song of the Lord in a strange land'[61], could have been applied equally well to England.

Attracted by the rising demand for labour which English industrial expansion was generating, Irish-Catholic immigrants were entering the country in sufficient numbers even before 1800 to reverse the long and serious decline of English Catholicism which had begun more than a century earlier. And in the 1840s the migratory process was stimulated by the devastating impact of the potato famine on the Irish economy. By the final quarter of the century there were well over half a million Irish-born residents of England and Wales, and they were only a minority within the large Anglo-Irish subculture which was providing English Catholicism with its basic constituency. Despite contemporary alarm about the problem of 'leakage', it is clear that the traditional Irish fidelity to Catholicism survived fairly well into second and third generations of Irish immigrants[62].

Throughout the nineteenth century the Church retained a sprinkling of upper-class lay members, most of them heirs of the old Catholic landed families which had maintained their Catholic commitment during the depressing years of the late seventeenth and eighteenth centuries. There was, moreover, a small flow of English converts from these socially privileged classes, as well as a minor but highly significant incidence of defection by middle-class intellectuals from the Puseyite wing of Anglicanism to the English Catholic Church[63]. But in 1911 new members gained by 'adult conversion' represented only 0.2 per cent of the estimated Catholic population[64]. As a source of growth conversion was of little significance in comparison with immigration from Catholic countries and the natural increase in England of Catholic immigrant communities[65].

Table 2.8 provides data on the estimated Catholic population, the Catholic priesthood, the number of Catholic churches and chapels, and attendance at Mass during the period since 1715. National totals derived from parochial estimates of the Catholic population do not provide a particularly satisfactory index of Catholic growth. The figures are not very precise, and the type of religious commitment being quantified is scarcely

Table 2.8   The Catholic Church

	Estimated Catholic population	Churches and chapels	Priests	Actual mass attendants
1720	115,000	–	–	61,600
1780	69,376	–	–	37,200
1800	–	–	–	–
1840	700,000	469	–	371,500
1851	900,000	597	826	482,000
1861	–	798	1,177	–
1871	–	–	1,551	–
1881	–	1,175	1,979	–
1891	1,357,000	1,387	2,604	726,000
1901	–	1,536	3,298	–
1911	1,710,000	1,773	3,302	915,000
1913	1,793,038	1,845	3,650	960,000

Notes

1   The figures relate to England and Wales.
2   'Priests' include secular and religious clergy.
3   The series on 'Actual Mass attendants' has been derived from the 'Estimated Catholic population' series on the conventional assumption that the ratio between the two has been consistently what it was in 1961–66, when data on both were collected. The series is therefore somewhat artificial, but it provides perhaps the best available Catholic index comparable with indices of participation in other religious organisations.
4   The population of Britain between 1841 and 1961 included the following numbers of Irish born:

1841	290,891	1871	566,540	1901	426,560
1851	519,959	1881	562,374	1931	381,080
1861	601,634	1891	458,315	1961	870,440

comparable with membership or attendance in other religious organisations. Yet the overall trend certainly is clear enough. English Catholicism grew almost as rapidly as the Methodist and evangelical Dissenting communities during the early industrial era, albeit for different reasons, but unlike these Protestant competitors its growth continued unchecked throughout the Victorian era. And in the twentieth century, of all the major religious traditions, it alone has managed virtually to escape a serious decline of manpower and material resources, and an accompanying drastic reduction of popular religious adherence. Indeed, only in data on 'adult conversions' is there evidence that English Catholicism has been affected by the powerful secularising tendencies within the wider society which have undermined other varieties of organised Christianity[66]. The rate of adult conversion fell significantly during the First World War, in the period between 1936 and 1946, and in the 1960s, and although it improved in the 1920s and the 1950s, the overall trend has been one of decline, both absolutely and (even more) in relation to the size and organisational resources of the Church. In other religious bodies, which have had to rely on growth by recruitment from the wider society much more than Catholicism has, precisely the same trend has led inexorably to the serious contraction of membership and to general organisational decay. The capacity of Catholicism to achieve continued expansion in the increasingly secular society of twentieth-century England—a phenomenon of obvious importance for the social as well as the religious historian— clearly has been related to the unusual subcultura cohesion of its major constituency, and to the continued extension of this constituency by immigration[67].

Synopsis

Quantitative evidence provides a basis for identifying various distinctive patterns in the development of organised religion in England, at least since the early decades of the eighteenth century, and the nature of these patterns, and the inter-relationships between them, help to clarify many of the major issues in the history of modern English Christianity. In this chapter the analysis has distinguished seven different growth patterns.

1 *The Church of England*

In the period from 1740 to the 1830s Anglicanism rapidly lost much of the national constituency to which, in theory, it had exclusive access; and in 1914, despite rapid growth in the Victorian and Edwardian eras, it remained merely the largest of three major religious-cultural systems in England, the others being the Catholic and Free Church systems.

2 *The Catholic Church*

Catholicism was a small and diminishing stream of English religiosity until the closing years of the eighteenth century, but in the nineteenth and twentieth centuries, aided by massive immigration from Ireland particularly, it has increased in volume more than any other variety of organised religion.

3 *The Methodist movement*

Beginning as a reform movement within the Church of England in the 1730s, Methodism grew with extreme rapidity during the early industrial period. But its growth rate had begun to slacken by the early Victorian era, and before 1914 Methodist membership actually had begun to decline.

4 *The New Dissent*

A new variety of Protestant Dissent emerged during the second half of the eighteenth century as the original Dissenting tradition reached a parting of the ways. This New Dissent, comprising Congregationalists, Particular Baptists, and New Connexion General Baptists, followed a pattern of growth paralleling that of Methodism.

5 The Old Dissent

The Old Dissent took its character from the continuation of trends apparent in the original dissenting tradition before its fragmentation between 1719 and 1770. It stagnated or actually declined during the late eighteenth and early nineteenth centuries when the New Dissent was growing rapidly. Old Dissent included Quakers, most General Baptists, Presbyterians, and the Unitarian movement which gradually usurped the original English Presbyterian tradition.

6 The New Presbyterianism

Initiated by a steady influx of Scottish immigrants from the early nineteenth century onwards, new Presbyterian organisations were established in England, and in 1876 they merged to form the Presbyterian Church of England. Throughout the period before 1914 this new Church continued to rely on Scottish expatriots as its major social constituency.

7 The Victorian sects

New sectarian movements sprang from several of the older religious traditions which began to reach organisational and cultural maturity during the Victorian era. While some of them, such as the Salvation Army or the 'Open' Brethren, were to move quite close to the mainstream of Free Church Christianity as the twentieth century progressed, in 1914 they remained quite distinctive religious-cultural phenomena.

Part two

Religion in early industrial England

The rise of Evangelical Nonconformity

As the statistical series of Chapter 2 have indicated, the religious life of early industrial England was dominated by the deteriorating position of the Established Church and by the rise of a large competing religious culture based on the Methodist movement and the New Dissent. Even without other evidence, the essential similarity of Methodist, Congregational, Particular Baptist, and New Connexion General Baptist growth patterns during the period would suggest that these bodies were linked in a single, if multiform, social and religious phenomenon. Non-statistical evidence confirms this conclusion. The second half of the eighteenth century saw a confluence of these separate streams of English Protestantism, a confluence produced as the Evangelical Revival cut through the organisational and cultural traditions of English religiosity. The purpose of this chapter is to emphasise the essential homogeneity of the new, expansionist, chapel-based movement, described here and in subsequent chapters as 'Evangelical Nonconformity', and to analyse the underlying beliefs, values, and social characteristics which Evangelical Nonconformists shared.

Ecclesiastical history frequently is written from a denominational perspective, a perspective which tends to emphasise denominational differences irrespective of whether they represent the most important divisions within the religious life of a society. A denominational approach to religion in early industrial England, for example, tends to distort the reality of a situation in which a broader distinction between 'Church' and 'Chapel' was of fundamental importance. This is not to imply that denominationalism was irrelevant. In Evangelical Nonconformity, a turbulent religious culture, a variety of denominational currents diverged around obstacles of polity, dogma, and sociopolitical outlook. But each current was flowing in the same direction, and each drew upon a massive human catchment area which was responsive to social functions and religious values common to them all.

The Evangelical consensus

The impact of Evangelical Nonconformity on English society in the early industrial period was determined partly by the basic evangelical and conversionist values which gave the movement its underlying homogeneity. As Bogue and Bennett pointed out in their history of

Dissent between 1760 and 1808, Congregationalists and Baptists shared with Methodists not only an insistence on high standards of piety and personal morality, but also a primary emphasis on 'the necessity of conversion'[1]. The Baptist Union defined itself officially in 1832 as a union of ministers and churches 'who agree in the sentiments usually denominated evangelical'[2]; and a year later the Congregational Union made a similar affirmation in its 'Declaration of Faith and Order', endorsing what the *Eclectic Review* had described earlier as a theological consensus within the denomination[3]. Thus while it is true of contemporary Free Church religion in England that evangelicalism is only part of a wide theological spectrum, and outside the Baptist churches not a dominant part[4], it was not true of the Methodist or New Dissenting movements of the period before 1840. Evangelical belief was completely normative.

It is possible, of course, for evangelical theology to coexist with religious-cultural priorities which do not produce aggressive evangelism or rapid organisational growth. But conversionist zeal was as characteristic of the New Dissent in the early industrial era as it was of Methodism. Walter Wilson, with evident disappointment, remarked in 1814: 'the Independents have gone over to the Methodists. Indifference [towards theological issues once regarded as vital] and enthusiasm have thinned the ranks of the old stock, and those who remain behind are lost in a crowd of modern religionists'[5]. One indication of the change had been the lapsing of academic standards in the old dissenting academies. The typically learned minister of seventeenth and early eighteenth century Dissent had been superseded in the New Dissent by what have been called 'illiterate enthusiasts'[6]. Describing new criteria of selection for the ministry, the *Protestant Dissenters' Magazine* (by this time a reactionary journal), explained in 1794 that the great object was 'to find a man of popular talents ... who can make the most noise, or tell the most entertaining stories'[7]. Like the various Methodist communities of this period, Congregationalists and Baptists offered potential converts a 'religion of the heart'[8], and for those whom they recruited, the religious-cultural consequences of commitment were broadly similar from one branch of Evangelical Nonconformity to another.

There were differences within and between the various denominations which often seemed to obscure from Evangelical Nonconformists the essential homogeneity of the movement as a whole. 'Jews had no dealings with the Samaritans', a leading Victorian Congregationalist wrote in his autobiography, recalling relations between Methodists and other Dissenters in Prescot in the 1830s. 'We used to visit each other's chapels on the occasion of an anniversary', he continued, but 'Interchanges of occasional visits, however, like these, did not mean any active co-operation in public work'[9]. Prescot cannot be regarded as typical of denominational relations generally during the period of rapid Nonconformist expansion before 1840. In some areas a high degree of cooperation was normal. But lack of cooperation was not, in any case, evidence of fundamental religious-cultural differences.

Deep divisions within the evangelical consensus did arise in the case of certain doctrinal issues. There was a significant breach between Baptists and other Evangelical Nonconformists over the doctrine of

Baptism, as well as a dour dispute between Arminian and Calvinistic inter-pretations of the doctrines of Election, Atonement, and Grace. But deep though these divisions were, they were not fundamental. 'The centre of gravity of the Baptist conception of the Gospel and the Church was not, and is not, baptism, but conversion', a Baptist writer insisted in 1914, rightly emphasising the ultimacy of evangelicalism in the Baptist tradi-tion[10]. Similarly John Wesley, the most famous proponent of Arminian-ism in English ecclesiastical history, regarded disagreements about predestination as secondary. The Calvinist position, he believed, was 'not subversive of the very foundations of Christian experience, but compatible with a love to Christ and a genuine work of grace'[11]. 'If any doctrines within the whole compass of Christianity may properly be termed funda-mental', Wesley explained in his often-repeated sermon on 'the New Birth', 'they are doubtless these two, the doctrine of justification, and that of the new birth; the former relating to the great work which God does *for us* in forgiving our sins; the latter to that great work which God does *in us* in renewing our fallen nature'[12]. This was the theological foundation not just of Methodism but of Evangelical Nonconformity generally.

The mobilisation of the wider society

Evangelical ideology alone would not have distinguished the Methodist and New Dissent movements from the rest of English Christianity in the century after 1740. A minority evangelical movement existed within the Established Church throughout this period, increasing in strength in the late eighteenth and early nineteenth centuries; and ideo-logical differences between the New Dissent and the older dissenting orthodoxy which it had superseded were in any case matters of emphasis and application rather than of essence. The character of a religious culture depends as much on the norms and values with which it operates as on its belief system. Evangelical Nonconformity was above all a *popular* religious movement, geared to achieving the widest possible support in a society where commitment would be nothing if not voluntary. Emphasis on the popularisation of the evangelical ideology by aggressive evangelism was as important a defining characteristic of the movement as was the ideology itself.

Within Evangelical Nonconformity the basic modes of conver-sionist activity differed little from one denomination to another, although differences of polity certainly affected the *scale* on which recruiting could be coordinated. The connexionalism of Methodism provided a much better basis for systematic evangelistic planning than did the independency of the Congregational and Particular Baptist traditions, and such differences obviously effected the growth potential of a denomination at a national level. But at a local level it mattered little in practice whether the popular evangelicalism was mediated through a Methodist, Congregational, or Baptist channel. Three common features stood out: the priority ascribed to conversionist endeavours, in practice as well as in theory; the centrality of itinerancy and village preaching in the recruitment process; and the heavy reliance of each denomination on the activities of laymen.

The conversionist priority

The primacy of conversionist values in the Evangelical Non-conformity of the early industrial age is perhaps most evident when the demands of evangelism are considered in relation to other priorities. The desire to grow by recruitment from the wider society often was paramount in the allocation of finance. Chapel-building, for example, and even more the quality of the chapels built, were emphasised much less than they would be in Victorian Nonconformity, and the critical caricature of the 'religion of barns' was literally true in many cases. Ironically, however, the criticism highlighted a strength of the movement rather than a weakness[13]. Unimpressive physical facilities for worship were normal, not simply because congregations were relatively poor but also because they were committed to expansion rather than consolidation. Individual congregations supported itinerants, or contributed to regional associations of churches which did so, and in many cases continually depleted their own resources in order to establish satellite congregations in surrounding areas. The Heptonstall Chapel in Yorkshire, for example, initiated a succession of new societies from 1764 onwards, and by the constant expenditure of financial and human resources eventually became 'the mother church of all the Calder Valley Methodists'[14]. In the *class meeting*, in fact, a Methodist society possessed an internal cellular structure ideally suited to growth by fission; and in some areas the evolution of classes into separate societies became a normal growth process[15].

But Congregational and Baptist churches, which lacked any formal equivalent of the Methodist class meeting, also succeeded in initiating denominational expansion by channelling manpower and finance into the establishment of satellite congregations. In a typical case history the *Baptist Magazine* described how two Baptist congregations had been established in the Wye Valley, near Monmouth, during the 1820s. A group of Cardiff Baptists, learning in 1821 that the village of Llandogo was populated by 'poor, . . . numerous, and much neglected inhabitants', had contributed sufficient money to support effective evangelism there. They had organised itinerant preaching in the district, rented a room for religious services, opened a Sunday School, and offered material assistance to cottagers who were 'poor and distressed'[16]. The result was the rapid formation of a congregation in Llandogo, and the building of a meeting house in 1824, financed with help from Cardiff. An arrangement was made for the Baptist pastor from Penallt, five miles away, to visit the village twice a week.

Once established, the Llandogo Baptists had taken an early opportunity to become themselves the sponsors of further denominational extension. In 1829, in consultation with their Cardiff colleagues, they had decided that the nearby village of Whitebrook would repay evangelistic endeavours. Whitebrook had 'no place of public worship of any description', except a small Methodist chapel which had the twin disadvantages of being one-and-a-half miles away and 'on the summit of a high hill'. The same process of evangelisation, rewarded again by a ready response from 'poor cottagers', had culminated in 1831 in the opening of the third Baptist chapel involved in this chain of growth[17].

Accounts such as this were standard fare in the Evangelical Nonconformist press of the late eighteenth and early nineteenth centuries because they described the kind of activity valued most highly in Evangelical Nonconformist religious culture at this stage of its evolution. They were celebrations of expansion. A generation or so later a newly formed congregation might aspire rather to the possession of its own chapel: an edifice architecturally satisfying and fully paid for. A Wesleyan minister complained in 1866 that the new symbols of success were memorial stones 'laid with silver trowels, in stately ceremony'[18], and Victorian Nonconformists who supported the new emphasis on consolidation rather than expansion which he was deploring were equally ready to see it as a departure from the past. They argued simply that 'the temporary use of a borrowed or hired building' had 'ceased to be the appropriate material assistance required'; that the concentration of denominational resources had become 'a new and necessary form of Christian enterprise'[19].

Itinerancy and the Sunday School

If the primary goal of early Evangelical Nonconformity was growth, the primary instrument of growth was itinerancy. Wesley was adamant that where itinerant preaching declined so did the capacity of a religious society to recruit from the surrounding population[20]. But while it originated as a Methodist institution, itinerancy became an institutional hallmark of Evangelical Nonconformity generally during the era of optimum expansion in early industrial society. By its very nature, it demanded an acceptance of the priority of *expansion* over *consolidation*, for it required the expenditure of local resources on the extension of the work elsewhere. It was, in the nomenclature of the period, an 'aggressive system', enabling Evangelical Nonconformity to be taken where the response was likely to be greatest. Whereas the open doors of a chapel might invite outsiders to enter, there to join an existing congregation, the principle of itinerancy was to carry the movement *to* prospective recruits, and frequently to form new congregations where previously there had been none.

Itinerancy was, of course, used to sustain existing networks of religious associations as well as to extend the networks into new areas. It fulfilled pastoral as well as evangelistic functions. Indeed, even before 1800 it was becoming in certain respects fairly institutionalised. For Wesley itinerancy had remained more or less synonymous with 'field-preaching', but by the end of the century it was becoming normal practice for itinerants (like those in Llandogo in 1821) to rent or borrow premises and to register them as 'Dissenting Places of Worship'. The increasing formality of the full-time itinerant ministry in Wesleyanism obscured, however, a spontaneity which had survived in the application of the itinerant principle. By the 1790s Evangelical Nonconformity had entered an era in which short-distance, part-time itinerancy by laymen of all denominations had become the primary instrument in the mobilisation of the wider society.

From Whitefield in particular, according to Bogue and

Bennett, but also from the initial successes of Methodism generally, the New Dissent had adopted in its evangelism the 'straight forward, and pointed address to the consciences of men', which reiterated the basic evangelical doctrines of Sin, Repentance, and Salvation by Faith. The fervent, unsophisticated approach, effective 'both in attracting hearers to the dissenting places of worship, and in fixing them there'[21], was ideally suited to the exploitation of lay talents in itinerancy. The basic message of Evangelical Nonconformity, in short, was simple enough for propagation by almost anyone zealous enough to offer his services for the work. Apart from ministerial itinerancy, explained John Rippon, a leading Particular Baptist and editor of the *Baptist Annual Register* in the 1790s,

> Multitudes of other brethren are employed, according to their abilities, in village services—reading, praying, expounding—two or three brethren from some churches, seven or eight from others; in one church seventeen persons, and in another no less than thirty offered their assistance in these services[22].

Such lay workers, having been told which village to visit on a particular Sunday, would scatter in twos and threes into the surrounding countryside at the conclusion of the afternoon service at their own chapels. Some would lead their village audiences in singing, others would preach or read specially written 'village sermons', and all would pray[23]. Once a village community showed signs of response, prayer meetings and 'village readings' would be organised, often to be held on midweek evenings in the cottage of some person who had displayed special interest[24]. These cottage meetings formed the basis of numerous Nonconformist congregations.

'Almost the whole country', Rippon wrote, was 'open for village preaching' in the 1790s; and the massive, popularly sustained 'sales campaign', without which Evangelical Nonconformity could not have exploited the obvious receptivity of the wider society, was being carried virtually into all areas[25]. Methodists, of course, had been engaged in the work for half a century by 1790; and from the 1760s onwards, as regional associations had been formed or reconstituted for the purpose of co-ordinating evangelism, the older denominations had begun to emulate them[26]. It was the period from the mid-1780s to the second quarter of the nineteenth century, however, which for Evangelical Nonconformity as a whole was the age of itinerancy[27].

In the example of Baptist expansion examined earlier in this chapter, the Cardiff Baptists who evangelised the Monmouthshire village of Llandogo in 1821 opened a Sunday School almost immediately. In so doing they were conforming to an established pattern of Evangelical Nonconformist growth as surely as when they engaged in itinerancy. From as early as 1737, when Griffith Jones had founded the Circulating Schools movement for which he is famous in Welsh educational and religious history, education and religious instruction carefully tailored to evangelical requirements had been associated with the development of Nonconformist evangelicalism. But except in Wales, where the Sunday School was designed for adults as well as for children, its role as a recruiting agency for chapel membership was an indirect one.

This point is worth emphasising because it illustrates the fact that in the eighteenth and early nineteenth centuries Evangelical Nonconformist communities did not have to rely for their growth on the religious socialisation of juveniles, as most modern English denomination do[28]. Significantly, the notion that the Sunday School scholar was *ipso facto* a potential Nonconformist member was described as 'new' at the Autumnal Congregational Union Assembly of 1848. Previously, when the Sunday Schools had lost contact with scholars so had the churches, except in cases in which the scholars had been children of church-going families. 'It has always been assumed that they will go, and they have gone', said J. L. Poore, a Salford minister, explaining the previously-dominant attitude of Congregational churches to their Sunday scholars[29].

By 1848 this attitude had been under challenge for almost a quarter of a century, but it represented the original conception of the work. In an era of high receptivity to Evangelical Nonconformity, the setting up of a school created a context for the recruitment of an adult population: associational patterns emanating initially from the instruction of children were exploited for the purpose of evoking adult commitment to Nonconformist membership. The Sunday School, like the prayer meeting, was recognised as an invaluable training-ground for aspiring laymen[30]; it was regarded as a means of diffusing the 'first principles' of religion among the young (and perhaps preparing them for conversion in adulthood); and it was valued for its civilising and socialising functions[31]. It was, in short, an adjunct to itinerancy during the period of optimum Nonconformist growth in early industrial society, not a major alternative mode of recruiting. But its importance in determining relations between Evangelical Nonconformity and the wider society was nevertheless immense, for it placed the movement in significant contact with a social constituency including elements not reached by any of its other activities.

Ministers, laymen and religious-cultural spontaneity

Heavy reliance on lay workers and lay initiative in itinerancy and Sunday School teaching made for religious-cultural informality and spontaneity in early Evangelical Nonconformity. It was a popular religious movement, sensitive to the understanding, taste, and outlook of its rank-and-file members, partly because it was heavily dependent on their day-to-day involvement in its affairs. The itinerant, if a minister, could serve a plurality of congregations, but only by leaving each congregation a good deal to its own devices; and where itinerancy was in the hands of laymen the 'popular' element in the religious beliefs and values communicated obviously was immense. In other words, spontaneity and lay initiative in the liturgical, devotional, theological, and social aspects of the movement were characteristic of this initial phase in its development when the mobilisation of the wider society was a primary concern.

Countervailing tendencies towards institutionalisation, increased formality, and greater professionalism were ever present, of course. Like all social entities, denominational organisations and chapel communities could not escape domination by minorities, and the minorities tended to be biased in favour of the ministry and the more socially prestigious sections of the laity[32]. But not only did the leaders, local or connexional[33], frequently share the religious attitudes of the rank and file: they were often powerless even when they did not. Wesley himself was able to exercise only limited control over the Methodist laity in local societies. He failed, for example, to alter the opposition of the Epworth Methodists to the local Anglican parson. 'If I cannot carry this point even while I live,' he wrote in 1788, 'who then can do it when I die?'[34]. The question was of course rhetorical. In a voluntary association the members, if their commitment is more than perfunctory, exercise a powerful influence on the associational culture. In early Methodism the tension arising inevitably from the dual demands of society and Connexion tended to be resolved at the local level with engaging practicality. In a face-to-face confrontation with a society Wesley could impose his will; and after his death, although rarely achieving an ascendancy over the laity comparable with his (except at the cost of schism), the Wesleyan ministry continued to wield paramount authority. *In absentia*, however, both Wesley and the travelling preachers could be respectfully ignored: they came and they went, the chapel community persisted.

Feeling that the popular movement had not been controlled properly, Jabez Bunting, whose religious and political conservatism was to dominate the Wesleyan hierarchy for almost forty years, observed in 1813 that 'the progress of Methodism in the West Riding of Yorkshire has been more swift than solid; more extensive than deep'[35]. He was worried by many aspects of the situation, but the essence of his criticism was the relative lack of denominational order and ministerial control in an area which had seen rapid Methodist expansion. Bunting's perception in linking the spontaneity of Wesleyanism with its rapid growth was accurate. A year later Walter Wilson would be acknowledging and deploring precisely the same tendency in New Dissenting communities throughout England[36]. 'Sunday Schools, village preaching, and the labours of irregular preachers', which were turning the Congregational and Baptist denominations into large religious communities, were also producing theological superficiality, 'popular' rather than 'serious' preaching, and lack of concern for the distinctive doctrines of Independency[37]. In Evangelical Nonconformity as a whole the formalisation of denominational institutions, the routinisation of liturgical and evangelistic modes, and the emergence of role differentiation between ministers and laymen would occur only as the bulk of the laity, whether because of diminished commitment or because of ministerial encroachment, accepted reduced responsibility. And as these trends set in the growth potential of the movement would decline, for their effect would be to alter a religious culture finely adapted to the goal of mobilising the wider society.

Popular ecumenism

The age of itinerancy in Evangelical Nonconformity was an age of popular ecumenism. Both the logistics of widespread itinerancy and village evangelism, and the emphasis on a basic, uncomplicated message able to be expounded and propagated by laymen, tended to encourage local interdenominational cooperation and solidarity. These effects were not universal, as the experiences of J. G. Rogers in Prescot in the 1830s (cited earlier in this chapter) clearly indicate. But they were common enough. Another leader of Victorian Congregationalism, R. W. Dale, recalled with mixed feelings that the 'evangelical passion for saving men' had not only transcended denominational barriers in the late eighteenth and early nineteenth centuries, but had threatened them with oblivion. 'It emphasised the vital importance of the Evangelical creed, but it regarded almost with indifference all forms of Church polity that were not in apparent and irreconcilable antagonism to that creed', he wrote. Evangelical Nonconformity, Dale perceived, was an essentially spontaneous movement, 'satisfied with fellowship of an accidental and precarious kind'[38].

The Sunday Schools of the period between the 1780s and the 1820s, for example, were usually undenominational in their teaching and often interdenominational in their organisation[39]. Except in areas where Methodism virtually monopolised Nonconformist evangelism, moreover, itinerancy was often organised, or at least coordinated, on an interdenominational basis. The Baptist Society in London for the Encouragement and Support of Itinerant Preaching was constitutionally committed to the principle of sharing its work with other Nonconformist bodies[40]; Congregationalist itinerancy was organised on the same principle[41]; and in many areas, especially in the south and across the Midlands, 'General Unions' involving all the Nonconformist bodies (and occasionally evangelical Anglicans as well) became the main instruments for coordinating village preaching[42].

Ecumenism in the twentieth century has been a concomitant of organisational decline in religious bodies. 'Lateral growth', expansion by amalgamation with other bodies, has become increasingly attractive as the prospect of 'frontal growth' has receded[43]. But this modern ecumenism of decline, which very often has been initiated by the professional elements in the religious organisations concerned[44], stands in sharp contrast to the ecumenism typical of the era of rapid Evangelical Nonconformist expansion. Yet the latter phenomenon was equally a concomitant of particular circumstances of organisational growth. The receptiveness of early industrial society to the new popular evangelicalism encouraged the evolution of modes of evangelism which maximised the manpower available in Nonconformist communities. The operation of the resulting lay agencies not only created a religious-cultural climate in which subtleties of theology, liturgy, and ecclesiology (on which denominational distinctions rested), were regarded with relative indifference, but also facilitated interdenominational cooperation in many areas. For cooperation meant that each of the bodies concerned could reap a larger share of a profuse harvest, a harvest sufficiently extensive to minimise the need for denominational competition.

The Evangelical Nonconformist constituency

A typical Methodist or New Dissenting community in early industrial England was not a microcosm of the wider society within which it operated. It drew its members from a restricted range of socio-economic groups. This was inevitable. As a sub-cultural phenomenon religious deviance could not be expected to have universal appeal. Earlier forms of extra-Establishment religion had had their own specific social constituencies outside of which their appeal had been negligible. Indeed, one of the most important respects in which Methodism and New Dissent differed from the seventeenth and early eighteenth century Dissent which preceded them was in the size and social character of the social constituency which they shared. The discontinuity obvious in a comparison between the numerically weak and declining Dissent of 1740 and the rapidly expanding Evangelical Nonconformity of half a century later reflected the success of Methodist, Congregational, and Baptist recruiting among social groups previously uninfluenced by extra-Establishment religiosity. The rise of the new popular evangelicalism, in short, saw a broadening of the social basis of religious deviance in England.

Early Methodist converts were 'a low, insignificant people'[45], according to John Wesley, who is known to have kept records of the occupational structure of at least some early Methodist societies[46]. They were 'poor, almost to a man'[47]. Wesley and his evangelical colleagues were committed to reaching the maximum number of people possible, irrespective of their social status. It was part of the Wesleyan itinerant's task to recognise localities and social groups in which receptivity to Methodism was likely to be high, and to 'send more labourers than usual into that part of the harvest'[48]. The best places to preach, Wesley taught, were where there was 'the greatest number of quiet and willing hearers', and where there was likely to be 'most fruit'[49]. These criteria oriented Methodism towards the lower strata of an hierarchical society, because it was there that the movement evoked the greatest response.

The meticulous reporting in Wesley's *Journal* provides a clear picture of this social constituency of early Methodism. Societies sprang up particularly among the artisan and labouring classes of manufacturing districts in the north-east, among workers in the textile industries of the north Midlands and the West Riding, in the Potteries, among the Cornish tin miners and the domestic craftsmen of the West Country woollen trade, in seaports and fishing villages, and in agricultural areas characterised by extensive freeholding. Tradesmen, soldiers, and small manufacturers were potential Methodist recruits. But representatives of the very lowest strata of society (paupers and vagrants, for example) rarely were; and as the Duchess of Buckingham told the Countess of Huntingdon, Methodism, even in its somewhat less plebian Calvinistic form, was 'much at variance with high rank and good breeding'[50].

While there was a perceptible rise in the economic and social status of Methodist society even during the lifetime of its founder[51], the same socio-economic groups and broad geographical areas continued to provide the bulk of Methodist membership at least until the beginning of the Victorian era. Typical observers throughout this early industrial period were impressed with the outstanding success enjoyed by Methodists among the 'manufacturing population'[52], with the significance of the new urban proletariat as the 'very social material Methodism was wont to lay hold upon'[53], and with the general rule that 'where there is little trade there is seldom much increase in religion'[54]. W. J. Warner's conclusion that in the late eighteenth and early nineteenth centuries Methodists 'dealt mainly with industrial labourers like the miners, the iron-workers, weavers, skilled artisans, and the day-labourers of the towns', has not been challenged seriously in the social history of Methodism[55].

Early Methodists were exploiting this rapidly expanding social constituency at a time when Dissent, heedless of the advice of men like Philip Doddridge, continued to ignore it. The declining Dissent of the period around 1740, heir to a religious culture which only a generation or so earlier had attracted the socially and economically privileged in considerable numbers, was preoccupied with maintaining its heritage, not with propagating it among 'the plain people of low education and vulgar taste'. But with the emergence of the New Dissent the situation rapidly changed. As Congregational and Baptist communities adopted the aggressive conversionist values of the Evangelical Revival, not only did their growth patterns begin to parallel that of Methodism, but there was an increasing similarity between these two streams of non-Anglican Protestantism in the class and occupational composition of their communities. In 1809, in writing the third volume of their *History of Dissenters*, Bogue and Bennett suggested that as early as 1760 'mechanics of all descriptions' in the towns, and 'labourers in husbandry in country villages' were constituting a 'large proportion' of those being recruited by the expanding Dissenting bodies; and that tradesmen, and in some areas farmers, were also prominent[56]. Three years later they attributed to 'neglect of the poor, ignorant, perishing multitude' the failure of the Old Dissent to match the rapid expansion of Congregational and Baptist churches[57]. The growth of the New Dissent, in short, had been dependent on a downward shift in the social basis of recruiting.

This fact was recognised most clearly by those who deplored it. The old-style Dissenter who in 1766 likened Methodist influences on independency to some 'desperate consumption', was concerned partly with the growing tendency of local churches to adapt their character and ministry to the task of mobilising 'numbers of ignorant people'[58]. And when Walter Wilson reviewed the same phenomenon half a century later he observed rather snobbishly that preachers who were 'usually such as have been in trade' were active in most parts of England gathering congregations from among 'the lower orders'. By exploiting the undoubted receptiveness of such people to Evangelical Nonconformity they were 'trading in souls', Wilson wrote[59]. The truth was that by adopting the character and *modus operandi* of Methodism the New Dissent was building up a clientele resembling that of the Methodist societies, and that Wilson regretted the passing of an age in which 'men of rank and influence were not ashamed to patronise the nonconformists'[60].

Many analyses of the social structure of the Evangelical Nonconformist denominations have dwelt on the nuances of social differentiation from denomination to denomination rather than the underlying social homogeneity of the total phenomenon. This approach is inevitable in studies organised around denominational subjects. But while the nuances could be significant, especially in localities where several varieties of extra-Establishment Protestantism were represented[61], the notion that particular denominations served their own distinctive social constituencies was false, despite its evident attraction for contemporary denominational leaders who liked to rationalise sectarian differences in terms of specific denominational missions to particular social groups. Thus while Primitive Methodists could claim to be a 'distinct denomination' in the sense of having a special mission to 'the lowly working classes of English society', and while Congregationalists could claim an equally distinctive mission to the middle classes, neither claim was sociologically accurate[62]. Indeed, both claims were inspired more by rhetorical goals and denominational strategies than by a desire to describe social reality.

Solid confirmatory evidence that the social basis of Evangelical Nonconformity was essentially homogeneous exists in occupational data contained in extant registers of births, deaths, marriages, and baptisms in Methodist, Congregational, and Baptist communities in early industrial society. Several thousand of these *Non-Parochial Registers* were deposited with the Registrar-General following the passage in 1836 of legislation providing for the national civil registration of births, deaths, and marriages. In many Nonconformist congregations records had been preserved for several generations before 1836 which contained not only the kind of information legally required, but also additional data on the occupations of persons registered (or in the case of children born or baptised, the occupations of the fathers). Such data, which provides a clear picture of the occupational structure of particular chapel and circuit communities, has been used profitably in many local histories. It is equally useful for the analysis of the national picture, although in the past it has not been exploited in nationwide studies.

Table 3.1 summarises occupational data from a sample of *Non-Parochial Registers*. Some of these registers were opened before 1800, but most of the registrations relate to the period from the beginning of the nineteenth century to 1837. None relates to the period after 1837. The picture provided, in other words, is that of Evangelical Nonconformity during the years of its optimum strength in early industrial society. Despite certain problems in using the *Registers*, notably problems of sampling, no other source permits as clear, comprehensive, and quantifiable an answer to questions about the social structure of the movement during this period, and none indicates more conclusively the nature of the constituency from which Nonconformist communities drew their members.

Table 3.1 indicates that the success of Evangelical Nonconformity in the early nineteenth century depended largely on its appeal to the artisan classes. 'Artisan', in this analysis, inevitably is a broad category. The labels used in *Non-Parochial Registers* rarely were specific enough to permit classification into important subgroups such as 'outworkers', 'skilled factory workers', 'self-employed craftsmen', or 'skilled employees'. Weavers, for example, usually failed to disclose whether they were power-loom rather than handloom weavers, and many other occupational labels obscured equally important distinctions. 'Artisan', then, is to an extent a residual category covering a wide range of prestige, wealth, and skill. It includes men who were independent craftsmen, and perhaps employers of

Table 3.1 The occupational structure of Evangelical Nonconformity in England, *c*. 1800–37

Occupations	All Nonconformists		Wesleyans		Primitive Methodists		Baptists and Congregationalists	
	Total	%	Total	%	Total	%	Total	%
Merchants and manufacturers	245	2.2	76	1.7	13	0.5	139	5.4
Shopkeepers	796	7.1	253	5.8	93	3.9	213	8.2
Farmers	579	5.3	239	5.5	135	5.6	183	7.1
Artisans	6,531	59.4	2,750	62.7	1,149	47.7	1,629	63.0
Labourers	1,192	10.8	415	9.5	387	16.1	101	3.9
Colliers, miners, etc.	726	6.6	334	7.6	301	12.5	55	2.1
Other occupations	928	8.5	318	7.2	329	13.7	263	10.3
Total	10,997	100	4,385	100	2,407	100	2,583	100

Notes

1   The above data have been drawn from a sample of *Non-Parochial Registers*. All these *Registers* had terminated by 1837. They recorded occupational details covering all or much of the period 1800–37, although some had been opened several decades earlier.

2   The sample is not random in a scientific sense. Selection of *Registers* was determined partly by the availability of occupational data, which were not included in every *Register*. As the table suggests, Methodists tended to be more assiduous than Congregationalists or Baptists in recording occupations. But on the assumption that the inclusion or exclusion of occupational data was a neutral factor (in the sense of being unrelated to the actual occupational structures of particular congregations or circuits), the sample may be taken as an approximate cross-section.

3   'Farmers' include freeholders and tenant farmers; 'artisans' include all skilled workers, whether employed in factories or in domestic industry; 'labourers' include industrial workers in unskilled occupations and agricultural workers.

4   'Other occupations' include registrations which were illegible or otherwise unclassifiable in any of the other categories. The largest occupational groups not categorised were the *professions* (schoolteachers, lawyers, doctors, etc.), *fishermen*, and *seamen*.

5   In some instances registrations may be repetitious, e.g., a father's occupation was registered with the birth of each child.

labour, as well as men who were employees. The wages, conditions, and status of the 'artisan' varied considerably from trade to trade and area to area[63]. Yet even as a broad residual category the classification is useful. Indeed, it was precisely in the general sense of the present analysis that

Algernon Wells used the term to define the social character of Congregationalism in 1848. Quite wrongly (in the light of evidence in *Non-Parochial Registers*), Wells suggested that 'artisans', like unskilled workers, were 'not converted by Romish zeal, or any longer gathered by Wesleyan energy, or drawn by the more intellectual discourses of Independent or Baptist preachers'[64].

It may have been Wells's London-based perspective, providing as it did a misleading view of the social reality of Congregationalism in the Midlands and the north, which caused him to err about the importance of artisans in Congregational communities. The London leaders of the denomination were accused of myopia often enough[65]. Yet in another section of this same paper to the Assembly of the Congregational Union of 1848 Wells acknowledged that there was 'probably a larger proportion of poor' among Congregationalists than there had been in 1800[66]. Possibly he may have been making a hyperbolic statement about changes he perceived in the social character of mid-century Congregationalism. Whatever inspired his analysis, however, his clear definition of the term 'artisan' as 'all who pursue skilled handicraft labour', whether within factories or outside factory industry[67], is evidence of the contemporary usage of the concept in its most inclusive sense.

The average Congregational or Baptist community was in fact marginally more artisan in its composition than its Wesleyan or Primitive Methodist counterpart, and there does not appear to have been any major variation from denomination to denomination in the type of artisan recruited. Representation from more prestigious crafts, such as those of carpenters, tailors, curriers, hatters, masons, and (early in the nineteenth century at least) shoemakers, varied little denominationally; and weavers, a less prestigious group, constituted the largest single artisan element in every denomination. The type of artisan recruited clearly depended more on the locality of a Nonconformist community than on its denominational character. In textile areas weavers and spinners constituted a large majority of all Nonconformist congregations, for example, just as in the nail-manufacturing areas of the Black Country nailers provided the bulk of all chapel communities.

In any case, the artisan, whatever his prestige or status in relation to other artisans, was separated emphatically from the lower strata of society. It is this fact which makes so broad a classification useful for analysing the social basis of Evangelical Nonconformist recruiting. To know that the largest social element in each denomination was composed of artisans is to know that the bulk of Nonconformity's constituency in English society, in terms of conventional notions of social status, lay between the trading and professional classes above, and the various unskilled occupational groups below. Stressing the importance of the latter social boundary, E. P. Thompson has explained that:

> The distinction between the artisan and the labourer—in terms of status, organization, and economic reward—remained as great, if not greater, in Henry Mayhew's London of the late 1840s and 1850s as it was during the Napoleonic Wars . . . 'In passing from the skilled operative . . . to the unskilled

workman . . .', Mayhew commented, 'the moral and
intellectual change is so great, that it seems as if we were in a
new land, and among another race'[68].

But although its quantitative strength depended primarily on
its appeal to artisans, Evangelical Nonconformity reached downwards into
the ranks of the unskilled labourers and miners (almost one in every five
registrations were associated with such occupations), and upwards to
include a small but significant element of shopkeepers, merchants, manufacturers, and professional men. It was at each of these extremities of the
social spectrum of the movement that important social differentiation
between the denominations occurred. The older bodies were both better
represented in the shopkeeping, merchant, and manufacturing occupations
than either Wesleyans or Primitive Methodists, and significantly less
successful among labourers, miners, and colliers.

Geographical distribution doubtless influenced the occupational structure of a denomination, although probably not to the extent of
explaining why Primitive Methodism had almost twice the average Evangelical Nonconformist representation among the unskilled, or why the
number of Congregationalists and Baptists from the upper sections of the
Nonconformist social spectrum (although a relatively small proportion of
the total following of each body) was proportionately larger than the
number in either of the larger Methodist Connexions. There was social
differentiation along denominational lines, but it should not be overemphasised.

For contemporary observers, and especially for those likely to
record their opinions, analyses of the social character of a denomination
were often more concerned with the *qualitative* importance of the various
social groups represented than with their quantitative strength. Thus Wells,
in his paper to the 1848 Assembly of the Congregational Union, followed
up his passing acknowledgement of the increasing numerical importance of
the poorer classes in the Congregational communities of the previous half-
century by assuring his middle-class colleagues that 'their access, as yet,
has had little influence in changing that paramount impress of the middle
class, so obvious on our denomination'[69]. In significant contrast was the
tendency of Primitive Methodism, a denomination lacking the kind of
cultural leadership provided by the Metropolitan 'aristocracy' of Congregationalism, to exaggerate its plebian qualities[70]. In other words, both the
ethos of a denominational leadership, and the natural tendency for
denominational organisations to justify their separateness in terms of
social functions for which they could claim to be uniquely fitted,
influenced contemporary stereotypes of Evangelical Nonconformist bodies
as social entities.

The stereotypes consequently reflected religious-cultural
nuances within Evangelical Nonconformity as much as actual differences
of social structure. This remained true at the end of the Victorian era, in
London at least. Writing about Wesleyans in the metropolis, the sociologist
Charles Booth concluded: 'The congregations are drawn fron the same
classes that support the Baptists and Congregationalists, but it is a somewhat different temperament that is appealed to'[71]. The point is that

throughout Nonconformist history cultural characteristics, real or imagined, often have been mistaken for evidence of differences in the social composition of Nonconformist communities. In the case of the social structure of Evangelical Nonconformity in early industrial society, however, no resort to indirect evidence is necessary. In every denomination, data from *Non-Parochial Registers* show, a majority of the adherents during this era of optimum expansion came from a common, if variegated, social constituency of skilled and semi-skilled artisans, and in each case the majority was augmented by significant recruitment from shopkeepers and tradesmen, small farmers, and urban and rural labourers.

If this Evangelical Nonconformist constituency is compared with the social structure of English society as a whole, the problem of explaining the rapid increase of religious deviance in early industrial society can be defined more precisely. The clearest picture of English society in the early nineteenth century is that provided by Patrick Colquhoun's estimate of income distribution by occupational group, published in 1806[72]. Distinguishing between the 'aristocracy', the 'middle ranks', and the 'lower orders', and within these broad class categories between forty-seven occupational classifications, Colquhoun estimated the number of families, the income per family, and the aggregate income of each occupational group in 1803. His figures provide a quantitative basis sufficiently accurate for a general comparison of the occupational structure of the wider society with that of the Evangelical Nonconformist bodies dealt with in Table 3.1.

Such a comparison emphasises the extent to which the popular evangelicalism was concentrated in the upper echelons of the 'lower orders' and the lower income groups within the 'middle ranks' of the society. The summary in Table 3.2 shows that whereas the proportions of tradesmen, merchants, and manufacturers in Evangelical Nonconformist communities was about the same as the proportions in the wider society, and the proportions of farmers and labourers considerably lower, the proportion of artisans was between twice and three times as high. Miners, colliers, and quarrymen, a much smaller social group, were also heavily over-represented. It is noteworthy that all but 8.6 per cent of Evangelical Nonconformist adherents were drawn from occupational categories which accounted for only 67 per cent of the whole society. Above the middle classes English society was virtually impervious to Protestant religious deviance; and at the bottom of the social scale, among the lowest income groups and those without employment, there was another, much larger segment of the population grossly under-represented in Evangelical Nonconformist communities.

But while the social constituency of the movement in early industrial society can be characterised generally in the language of class—with reference to horizontal divisions within a stratified society—it cannot be defined exhaustively in such terms. Traversing the horizontal layers of wealth and status in English society there were vertical social boundaries based on the continuing solidarity of functional interest groups and the social and cultural peculiarities of particular occupations. Readiness to embrace Evangelical Nonconformity evidently varied with the vertical divisions as well as with the horizontal. It is clear, for example, that certain

Table 3.2 **The social basis of Nonconformity and the occupational structure of the wider society in England in the early nineteenth century**

Occupation or status	Percentage distribution	
	The whole society	Nonconformist adherents
Aristocracy	1.4	0.0
Merchants, manufacturers	2.2	2.2
Tradesmen	6.2	7.1
Farmers	14.0	5.3
Artisans	23.5	59.4
Colliers, miners, etc.	2.5	6.6
Labourers	17.0	10.8
Other occupants	33.2	8.6

Notes

1 The order of accuracy and the specificity of the Nonconformist data extracted from *Non-Parochial Records* is not sufficient to permit a more detailed occupational breakdown of the social structure of Nonconformity.

2 The Nonconformist data refer to England only; and while the data on the whole society refer to England and Wales, the picture they provide is dominated by the occupational structure of English society.

types of artisans (handloom weavers, for instance) [73], and certain occupational groups, such as miners, quarrymen, and fishermen, were mobilised much more easily than others by Nonconformist evangelism. But personal and domestic servants, who made up about 10 per cent of the total work force at the end of the Napoleonic Wars [74], provided almost no Evangelical Nonconformist members or adherents. In general, whether occupational groups were connected with the 'landed interest' [75], rather than with commerce or manufacturing, appears to have been significant in determining receptiveness. Rural labourers and tenant farmers tended to be under-represented in Evangelical Nonconformist communities in comparison with non-agrarian occupational groups of comparable status, although there were interesting regional exceptions to this rule.

The history of religion in early industrial England was dominated both by the Church of England's failure to retain any semblance of a religious monopoly in an expanding and increasingly pluralistic society, and by the success of the new popular evangelicalism of Methodism and New Dissent in capitalising on this Anglican decline and on the societal context which was producing it. This chapter has examined aspects of the social and religious-cultural character of Evangelical Nonconformity, and identified broadly those sections of the wider society which it affected directly. The major task of explanation remains unresolved, however. The Evangelical Nonconformity of the eighteenth and early nineteenth centuries was an aggressively conversionist movement, but commitment to it was voluntary and involved social disadvantages which would have militated against growth unless considerable incentives for membership had accompanied Nonconformist conversionist activities. The Established Church, on the other hand, retained many of its prescriptive rights over English religious behaviour, and much of its traditional 'influence', yet in the space of a century it lost control over half of that section of the population which continued to practise Christianity. By looking at social, geographical, cultural, political, and religious relationships between Church and Chapel in early industrial society, the next two chapters will ask what it was about the nature of the religious Conformity, about the character of Evangelical Nonconformity, and about the *Zeitgeist* of the early industrial age, which generated hostility or apathy towards the religious Establishment within many sections of English society, and which at the same time created a widespread demand for socially deviant religiosity of a particular kind. Neither problem can be solved by focusing in isolation on either Anglicanism or Nonconformity.

4   The functions of 'Church' and 'Chapel'

It is appropriate for the social historian to consider churches as service organisations attracting adherents because of spiritual, social, cultural, psychological, or other functions which they appear competent to fulfil. Indeed, it is a truism to say that the 'functions' of a religious movement—those things which the movement does for a society and for individuals within it—form the basis of its existence and of its growth. People associate themselves with religious organisations because they, or those who influence them, value at least some of the consequences of the associational commitment involved. Viewed in these terms the relative decline of the Church of England in the early industrial age, and the unprecedented demand for extra-Establishment religious alternatives which accompanied it, can be explained with reference to changing perceptions of the utility and relevance of the religious Establishment within English society, on the one hand, and on the other with reference to the capacity of Evangelical Nonconformity to satisfy widespread individual and communal needs.

Another factor must be adduced to complete the explanation. Alienation from the Established Church and receptiveness to Nonconformity were not everywhere the results of religious or social preferences. Supply as well as demand was important in the religious 'market situation' which had begun to emerge in early industrial England. A later section of the analysis will explore this supply factor by focusing on the ways in which the increasing inadequacy of the human and material resources of the Church in an expanding and industrialising society influenced the religious history of the period. But it is important first to recognise that for many Englishmen an affiliation with 'Church' or 'Chapel' represented a definite option for one of two very different religious and social value systems.

Church, Chapel and popular religiosity

The functions which religious bodies perform may be divided into various categories. Obviously some of the satisfactions inherent in religious commitment are specifically religious or spiritual. By its putative capacity for invoking supernatural support, consolation, and reconciliation in this world, and through the prospect of other-worldly salvation, religion can satisfy basic human aspirations for transcendental meaning, emotional security, or spiritual assurance; and for some of its adherents, although certainly not for all, this primary *religious function* is paramount. The spiritual utility of belonging to a religious body is the major factor inducing such people to make and maintain an associational commitment. However at a secondary level religion exercises *cultic functions* which, while they arise out of its primary religious or spiritual functions, can for some participants provide satisfactions of a more or less autonomous kind. Through rites and ceremonies, authoritative disciplines and practices, religious commitment may contribute to the emotional security or aesthetic needs of individuals and social groups even where there is only token dependence on its primary spiritual or religious utility. But whether they merely reinforce some basic spiritual satisfaction or whether they are in themselves of primary religious significance, the cultic aspects of religion clearly contribute to the utility of a religious body for many of its adherents.

It is evident that many inhabitants of early industrial England, like the fictitious Adam Bede whom George Eliot created, found in the Established Church complete religious satisfaction. Equally, however, there clearly were others who, like Adam Bede's brother Seth, turned to Methodism precisely because it exercised religious and cultic functions with which Anglicanism appeared unable or unwilling to compete. Especially as a pastoral institution, the eighteenth-century Church has been given a bad press by ecclesiastical historians. Even those who have come to its defence have sounded fairly ambivalent in their conclusions. Like the famous reappraisal of the much-maligned eighteenth century episcopate by Norman Sykes, who stressed the 'diligence' of the bishops 'in the face of many obstacles'[1], the best attempts to defend the pastoral work of the eighteenth-century parochial clergy remain somewhat damning in the faintness of their praise. After a careful study of parochial returns submitted to Archbishop Herring at his Visitation of the Diocese of York in 1743, S. L. Ollard wrote: 'On the whole the strong impression left by the returns is that of a body of conscientious and dutiful men, trying to do their work according to the standard of their day'[2]. There was a 'large amount of quiet spiritual life and work' carried on in the diocese, J. H. Overton and F. Relton had concluded earlier in response to the same body of evidence, 'an amount which would not be credited by those who look upon the Church of that time as wholly, or almost wholly asleep'[3].

Apart from small Evangelical and High Church minorities the Church of the eighteenth century was not one in which specifically religious and cultic functions were prominent. The eminent lawyer who set out to sample the preaching of all the notable clergymen in London, and who claimed at the end of the experience to have heard not a single sermon 'which had more of Christianity in it than the writings of Cicero', was not telling the whole truth. But in a retrospective judgment about published sermons which have survived from the period, S. C. Carpenter has concluded:

> Some of them might be described as sub-Christian, and many
> are content to deal for the most part with points of morality

and moral duties. . . . The preachers aimed at pleasing the
more cultured part of the congregation, and did little for the
simple. Hogarth's 'Sleeping Congregation' is no doubt a
caricature, but caricatures must have some verisimilitude[4].

'At all events', Carpenter has observed, such sermons 'met the
desire of those who heard them'[5]. Certainly many Anglicans, then as
now, owed their allegiance to the Church primarily as a social institution,
and their expectations were centred on its exercise of its social functions
as the religious Establishment. Latitudinarian theology, muted piety, and
the somewhat perfunctory performance of ecclesiastical duties by the
clergy would be of little concern to such people. Indeed, the absence of
'enthusiasm' within the Establishment religious culture in most areas
seemed a decided blessing to those many Englishmen who shuddered at
the excesses of Methodists and Dissenters. Yet there is evidence to suggest
that the Church of the eighteenth and early nineteenth centuries did lose
support partly because for some of its constituents it failed to provide
spiritual and religious satisfactions to match those available elsewhere.

The rise of Evangelical Nonconformity during the century
after 1740 was an aspect, and quantitatively the most important aspect, of
the Evangelical Revival. It was what has been called a 'revitalisation movement', and as such was essentially ideological, not simply in the broad
sense of being 'a deliberate, organised, conscious effort by members of a
society to construct a more satisfying culture', but also in the sense that it
adhered to certain explicit ideological (and in its particular case, theological) premises[6]. One reason for the response it evoked among considerable sections of the English population was the existence of a demand
for the kind of religious and cultic satisfactions arising out of the evangelical worldview.

Reflecting on rough estimates he had made of the relative
strengths of the various forms of organised religion in England in 1794,
Edward Williams, a leading Congregationalist, decided that what distinguished the expanding sections of Dissent from those which were dormant
or in decay was their evangelicalism[7]. This was not a novel conclusion.
Indeed, emphasis on the religious and spiritual functions of Evangelical
Nonconformity was present in most contemporary explanations of its
progress in early industrial society. When Wesley in his old age looked back
on the religious revolution which had begun more than half a century
earlier in the Holy Club at Oxford he felt that the essence of Methodist
success had lain in the revival of 'grand truths' which before the 1730s had
been 'little attended to'. Outlining the tenets of evangelicalism he recalled
that

> when these truths, justification by faith in particular, were
> declared in any large town, after a few days or weeks, there
> came suddenly on the great congregation . . . a violent and
> impetuous power, which . . . frequently continued, with
> shorter or longer intervals, for several weeks or months. But
> gradually it subsided, and then the work of God was carried on
> by gentle degrees[8].

The more detailed and more immediate reports in Wesley's *Journal* confirm that this was a fair summary of the initial impact of Methodism in many areas. What is significant is that people could be mobilised, often on a massive scale, by evangelical preaching, well before the social and cultural functions of Methodism became apparent. This is not to say that the movement could have survived apart from these other functions, or without its organisational coherence, but it does suggest that there was an important ideological dimension to the demand which Methodists exploited.

The same was true of Evangelical Nonconformity generally. Presbyterianism declined as it abandoned orthodoxy, Socinianism never acquired popular appeal, but the New Dissent grew rapidly. The reason was not simply that there was popular demand for the latter, and general disinterest in the former ideologies. An obvious supply factor came into operation. As Chapter 3 has argued, conversionist zeal was a hallmark of Evangelical Nonconformity, particularly in the late eighteenth and early nineteenth centuries. Its adherents were much more concerned to propagate their faith than were, for example, Unitarians, and their greater concern was partly responsible for their faster growth. The fact remains, however, that evangelical beliefs found a ready market among large sections of the population. 'Almost the whole country is open for village preaching', John Rippon, the Particular Baptist editor, proclaimed in 1798, and the reports of receptivity to Baptist evangelism which filled the pages of his *Baptist Register* supported his optimism[9]. Like other contemporary reports of Evangelical Nonconformist progress, they showed that for Baptists and Congregationalists as well as Methodists, the initial impact of the movement frequently was associated with the adumbration by itinerant preachers of the evangelical ideology. The 'straight forward, and pointed address to the consciences of men', which appealed 'to impenitent sinners to seek the salvation of their souls', was the 'grand cause' underlying the growth of Evangelical Nonconformity, Bogue and Bennett insisted in 1812[10].

Contemporary opinions about the motives of religious converts cannot, of course, be accepted without question. In utilising the concept of the 'purposes' of religion to describe 'what people intend in their religious behaviour', sociologists of religion sensibly have distinguished between 'manifest' and 'latent' purposes[11]. It is an important part of the religious historian's task to identify the latent purposes underlying commitment: to recognise that however primary his theological position might appear to the evangelist himself, the primary motives of his converts might be more mundane, oriented to some of the non-ideological functions of the collectivity in which they have been induced to seek membership. Even among members of long standing, fundamental doctrines often are grasped in a confused and theologically unsatisfactory fashion. Despite constant teaching, Wesley reminded his preachers, many eighteenth-century Methodists were 'almost as ignorant as if they had never heard the gospel'. 'I study to speak as plainly as I can', he said, 'yet I frequently meet with those who have been my hearers for many years, who know not, whether Christ be God or man; or, that infants have any original sin'[12]. The same was doubtless true of all denominations.

But if it is a mistake to assume that Evangelical Nonconformist membership *necessarily* involved a definite theological commitment, it would be equally fallacious to assume that only the latent purposes of its adherents were really important in inducing and maintaining their allegiance. For secular men in a secular culture it is difficult to feel empathy for the popular religious *Weltanschauung* of the eighteenth and early nineteenth centuries. The early industrial age was a time when, as H. R. Murphy has put it, 'men did not argue that this world is but a vale of tears that must be passed through on the way to eternal bliss or eternal damnation; they felt it and took it for granted'[13].

Such people could easily be mobilised by the evangelical doctrine of salvation, especially at times of crisis. The presence or the threat of cholera epidemic, for example, 'produced a considerable excitement in favour of religious observance'[14], both in 1832 and 1849. In the Redruth Circuit of Cornwall (to cite a single case) Wesleyanism experienced an 'extraordinary revival' at the approach of 'that awful messenger of God' in the autumn of 1849. The circuit in fact escaped rather lightly, but while the threat remained, 'domestic engagements and matters of worldly business seemed to be suspended, that the people might seek the salvation of their souls'[15]. Such 'breaking-points' in the routine of social life had the effect of magnifying an ever present demand for the 'salvation' which evangelicalism offered. The demand was more difficult to stimulate at normal times. But as Wesley realised, it could be exploited by 'workers' skilled 'to deal with men ... with a holy mixture of seriousness, and terror, and love, and meekness, and evangelical allurements'[16]. The spectre of terror beyond the grave, and the 'evangelical allurements' of justification and eternal life, were particularly potent weapons in the religious arsenal in an age when even normal times brought constant reminders of the poverty, powerlessness, and contingency of human existence for the great mass of the population.

In the Church of England, however, there was still little concern for popular religiosity. Paternalistic, and still dispensed on monopolistic principles in many English parishes, Anglicanism remained less sensitive to popular tastes and popular religious demands than did the Methodist or New Dissenting movements. And as its attitude towards Methodists and other dissident 'enthusiasts' began to harden—a trend particularly evident from about 1790 onwards—the religious Establishment exhibited increasingly negative attitudes towards popular religious tendencies within its own ranks. The reaction against religious deviance encouraged Churchmen to rely on their residual monopolistic advantages rather than to compete with the new popular movements for the voluntary allegiance of the society. Indeed, the activities of the evangelical minority among the parochial clergy often were positively discouraged. Only one clergyman in ten was an evangelical in 1800, according to the Nonconformist historian, Herbert Skeats, who said of the non-evangelical majority that 'their opposition to the more zealous members of their own profession was equal to that encountered by the Dissenters'[17]. Skeats probably exaggerated the opprobrium attaching to evangelicalism, but there is no doubt that in the ecclesiastical climate of the late eighteenth and early nineteenth centuries those Anglicans who tended to be most diligent in discharging the specifically religious functions of the Establishment were neither encouraged nor emulated by their fellow Churchmen.

Hannah More learned this in the Cheddar district of Somerset in the 1790s. In Cheddar Parish in 1789 she founded the first of her famous Sunday Schools, a voluntary agency exploiting the talents of lay helpers; and at the same time she initiated visitation work and tract and Bible distribution. Within a decade church attendance in the parish had risen from 50 to 700, and the number of parishioners who received communion had risen from 15 to 120[18]. In adjacent parishes similar spectacular recoveries of rates of religious practice followed the introduction of the same popular religious services[19]. The achievement proved that in certain areas, at least, Anglicanism could have a religious-cultural impact on a previously neglected community comparable with that which Methodism and New Dissent achieved in many early industrial communities. But it was an impact which could be achieved within the Establishment only at the price of estrangement from the mainstream of Anglican society. Not only had Mrs More been forced to turn to 'a methodist' to find assistance in starting her first school[20], but by the beginning of the nineteenth century her work was under severe criticism within the Church for being 'Methodistical'[21].

Because 'Methodistical' Anglicans like Hannah More tended to be ostracised by most of the clergy and by most influential laymen, their efforts often unintentionally contributed more to Nonconformity than to the religious Establishment. After only six years of 'irregular' evangelical ministry in Farnham, Surrey, for example, an evangelical parson, the Rev Gunn, could point to 'great numbers of the inhabitants of Farnham, as well as those of the adjacent villages', who had begun to participate in the services of the Church[22]. But it was the year 1792, and on the grounds that his 'irregular' methods were alienating 'the opulent people', Gunn was forced out of the living and replaced by an incumbent 'of very different sentiments'. The result (typical of many similar situations which had occurred throughout the Evangelical Revival period)[23] was the secession of the congregation from the Church. Aided by a group of opportunistic Nonconformists from London, the seceders purchased land, built a chapel, and set themselves up as a substantial independent community[24].

The functions of the unreformed Establishment

Ordination as an Anglican clergyman obliged a man to be more than just a minister of the Gospel. Indeed, the suggestion that a parson was committed more to the 'secular' responsibilities of his office than to his spiritual and priestly functions would not necessarily have been regarded as a criticism in the eighteenth- and early nineteenth-century Establishment. 'The object of the national Church', Samuel Taylor Coleridge wrote in his very influential essay *On the Constitution of Church and State according to the Idea of Each*, was 'to secure and improve that civilization, without which the nation could be neither permanent nor progressive'[25]. Coleridge went so far as to suggest that

Christianity, and *a fortiori* any particular scheme of theology derived and supported by its partizans to be deduced from Christianity', was 'no essential part of the being of the national Church, however conducive or even indispensable it may be to its well-being'[26].

The responsibility 'to secure and improve' the civilisation of its English constituents had by the eighteenth century become institutionalised in many aspects of the Church's life. Anglicanism was part of the political and legal system of the nation, most conspicuously because its bishops sat in the House of Lords, but also in a host of more minor or less formal ways. The parochial system provided the basic structures of local government, social control, education, and poor relief in England well into the second quarter of the nineteenth century, and in some cases beyond it. Granted such a diversity of social, political, and economic roles, it is clear that the Establishment's utility within the society did not end with its specifically religious concerns, and did not necessarily depend on these concerns at all.

Less tangible but no less important than its utility as a welfare and administrative institution were the communal functions which the Establishment exercised. It has become a commonplace in the sociology of religion that, as Thomas O'Dea has put it, 'religion *sacralises the norms and values* of established society, maintaining the dominance of group goals over individual impulses', and that a religious system 'thereby reinforces the legitimation of the divisions of functions, facilities, and rewards characteristic of a given society'[27]. The unreformed religious Establishment gloried in its task of functioning in this way in English society. Its non-recurrent rites—baptisms, confirmations, marriages, and funerals—contributed to the maintenance of communal solidarity at times of individual and social crisis; the annual rituals or festivals which it sponsored or legitimated helped bind a local society together in the natural cycles of rural existence; and its recurrent rites and services were seen, in true Durkheimian terms, as 'means by which the social group reaffirms itself periodically'[28]. Such conservative social functions were recognised explicitly by Establishment theorists. 'It is certain', Addison wrote early in the eighteenth century,

> the Country-People would soon degenerate into a kind of Savages and Barbarians, were there not such frequent Returns of a stated Time, in which the whole Village meet together with their best Faces, and in their Cleanliest Habits, to converse with one another upon indifferent Subjects, hear their Duties explained to them, and join together in Adoration of the Supreme Being[29].

Thus religious conformity at once symbolised and reinforced the cohesion of an established social order. Symbolically it was a person's affirmation of the basic moral values, social conventions, and cultural mores of his community; and it symbolised, too, his own acceptance by that community and his integration within it. In this way the Establishment performed important identity functions for individuals and social groups. But as Addison implied, its role was equally one of social control. The parson, like his lay counterpart, the gentleman landowner, in theory was an exemplar to the lower orders of morality, propriety, and patriotism; and even when theory and practice coincided only imperfectly, the alliance of squire and parson, operating through the informal 'influence' of rank and status, through a variety of parish officers and institutions, or through the immense authority of the local magistracy, was able to exercise a clear leadership role in local societies. The preservation of the existing order, the maintenance of social harmony and social tranquillity: this was the *raison d'être* of the Church of England as a religious Establishment.

> Very few in the Church of England before the eighteen-thirties [G. F. A. Best has pointed out] thought that the church, in its function as an established church, could have any higher aim than complementing the work of the civil power and—what it alone could do—toughening the fabric of society [30].

The behaviour of marginal elements within the social order provided clear evidence of the Church's function as a guardian of the *status quo* in an hierarchical and deferential society. Rejection of the Establishment was an obvious act of defiance for the socially deviant: for people at loggerheads with the norms and values of their community, people who were rebels against established authority and resistent to the 'influence' of their social superiors. As early as 1682, for example, when Oxfordshire clergy were asked by their bishop to account for the stand taken by Dissenters, their replies in many cases implied that the recalcitrance was socially rather than ecclesiastically motivated. Dissenters from the Church were 'wilful', the incumbent of Drayton parish explained: they were the kind of people who also refused to pay rent to their landlords. Freehold farmers and cottagers living on common land (both members of socio-economic groups which were socially atypical in the extent to which they were independent of the influences of landed society), were mentioned frequently in the returns as the kinds of people who refused to conform [31]. In the relatively stable societal context of pre-industrial England religious deviance was unusual, however. For the vast majority of the population the Establishment was functional, if not for the specifically religious services it offered then because of its social and cultural utility as a conservative, integrative influence within the nation.

The dysfunctions of the unreformed Establishment

The functions of upholding and legitimating the *status quo*, and of bringing individuals to terms with their prescribed roles in a fairly rigid social system, were of paramount importance in the theory and practice of the Establishment in the eighteenth and early nineteenth centuries. It is therefore a measure of the seriousness of the crisis which confronted the Church in early industrial England that precisely these functions were being called into question by the speed and direction of social and political change. For increasing numbers of Englishmen in the period from about 1760 onwards, and especially in the forty years after 1790, the Anglican affirmation of the norms and values of the dominant culture, with its paternalism, its expectations of deference from the lower orders, and its intrinsic conservatism, was becoming either irrelevant or positively dysfunctional.

After a careful study of particular cases of social and structural change in early industrial Lancashire, Neil Smelser has found it illuminating to 'contrast the *relative* stability and institutional calm of the era preceding the industrial revolution with the storm and confusion of the period of the industrial revolution itself, and again with the *relative* stability of the prosperous and optimistic Victorian period'[32]. The same contrasts were characteristic of English society generally, and recognising their existence is vital to an understanding of the fluctuating fortunes of Anglicanism in the eighteenth and nineteenth centuries. In the unsettled era of early industrialisation traditional authority structures began to disintegrate, social cohesion began to break down, and for individuals and families the personal security which came from integration in a stable community often gave way to anomie in the new and relatively unstructured world of the industrial shanty town or the industrial city. In such a situation the Church's identification with the old order, and with the traditional ruling classes striving to maintain control of a changing society, became divisive. Upholding the social fabric had been a popular enough function while the seams of the fabric had remained relatively unstrained: there had been apathy but not much Dissent in the early Hanoverian Church. But as the strains imposed by rapid social change grew, what once had been an integrative role took on an obviously partisan character.

The revolutionary changes of the early industrial era had a variety of sources, not all of which had any close association with the Industrial Revolution itself. There was a revolution on the land. The period from the late 1750s to the beginning of the Victorian era witnessed the overthrow of the traditional agrarian economy in much of England, for the processes of enclosure and tithe commutation, which accelerated rapidly during this period, altered fundamentally the settlement patterns, patterns of land tenure, and class relationships of rural society. There was at the same time a trend towards the popularisation of politics. Opposition to hereditary privilege, unrepresentative government, and the political hegemony of the landed interest—resentment against the whole prescriptive basis of the traditional society—was not new in the late eighteenth century. Indeed the evolution of a democratic and pluralistic English society had its origins deep in the history of the pre-industrial past. But in the half-century after about 1790, intensified by the spectacle of revolution in France and by the unsettled domestic situation in England, popular radicalism increased dramatically to the point where it appeared seriously to threaten the existing social order. It was as a concomitant of these agrarian and political trends that the Industrial Revolution had its initial impact on the social and institutional structures of English society, and on the values and expectations of the English people.

The compound dislocation of English society in the early

industrial period presented the unreformed religious Establishment with an inescapable dilemma. Its foundation in law, its traditional social alliances and functions, and the social origins, affiliations, and values of its clergy tended to make it an increasingly reactionary institution, while at the same time the apparent radicality and intransigence of its opponents militated against effective reform. Reform might seem to legitimate radicalism, secular as well as religious. There was a case, from the conservative standpoint, for construing attempts to modernise the Establishment as at best a waste of time, at worst an unpatriotic concession to enemies of society. Perhaps the clearest evidence of this reactionary tendency in the late eighteenth century was the definite hardening of Anglican attitudes towards Methodism and Dissent.

By the close of the 1780s Methodists were being subjected to a new form of harassment which forced them into *de jure* Nonconformity. Attempts were made in many areas of the country to curtail the activities of Methodist preachers and societies by invoking the penal provisions of the Uniformity Laws[33], and in 1791 this reactionary policy was endorsed by an Act of Parliament affirming that earlier legislation prescribing regular Anglican practice 'should still be in force and executed'[34]. In a typical case (cited by Wesley in an attempt to have the anti-Methodist campaign halted), magistrates at a Lincolnshire Quarter Sessions in 1790 unanimously upheld a £20 fine against a society member who had permitted a meeting to be held in his home. 'The Methodists', they ruled, 'could have no relief from the Act of *Toleration*, because they went to church; and . . . so long as they did so, the *Conventicle* Act should be executed upon them'[35]. Whatever its validity as a legal judgment, as a basis for defending the religious Establishment this policy could scarcely have been more ill-conceived. Yet it typified the response of mainstream Anglicanism to religious deviance during the period from 1790 to the end of the Napoleonic Wars, and even during the postwar era it was a policy which died hard. Not until the 1830s, and then only with reluctance, did the Church reconcile itself to the inevitability of reform.

Methodism was thrust out of the Church, there to exploit, together with the older Nonconformist bodies, the real, if limited protection of the Toleration Act. The Anglican-Tory reaction to the spread of popular extra-Establishment religiosity never quite achieved the strength to carry retrograde legislation through Parliament, although during the first decade of the nineteenth century the Government was known to be interested in curtailing the licensing of Dissenting preachers[36], and in 1811 Viscount Sidmouth actually introduced into the House of Lords a Bill which, had it succeeded, would have imperilled the further expansion of Nonconformity[37]. As it was, however, the legal guarantees of toleration remained intact. While Nonconformity was harassed and forced onto the defensive (in the twenty years after 1790, for example, the number of legal battles fought by Congregationalists and Baptists, as well as by Methodists, increased sharply in response to widespread petty persecution[38]), it enjoyed during the 1790s and the early nineteenth century the most rapid growth of its entire history.

The Establishment, exemplified in the alliance of squire and parson, had always been able to resort to coercion in situations where 'influence' alone had seemed inadequate, and so long as the deferential relationship between the ruling elite and their social subordinates had been more or less taken for granted by both parties, the suppression of deviant behaviour had received fairly general support in a community. The crucial change which was becoming apparent before the end of the eighteenth century was the destruction of this 'dependency system' from below. Instead of being accepted and even welcomed as socially useful, the paternalism of the squire–parson alliance, and especially its functions of social control, were provoking resentment from communities whose confidence in the traditional social orthodoxy had vanished.

An interesting index of this change was the tendency for 'the mob' to become an enemy of the ruling classes, a variety of collective behaviour directed against the *status quo*. Previously it had been an instrument of the 'dependency system', a conservative force. Wesley had learned this often enough, as his *Journal* records. Admitting the relative failure of Methodism in North Molton, Devonshire, for example, he had expressed sympathy in 1755 for the few stalwarts who had remained faithful to the local Wesleyan society. The local gentleman had 'threatened them much', Wesley wrote, and had not only 'turned many out of their work, or farms', but had 'headed the mob in person'[39]. Other instruments were also available, of course. A clergyman and some local squires once used huntsmen and hounds to disrupt one of Wesley's outdoor sermons[40]. But far more common was opposition from some 'senseless, insolent mob'[41].

The mob, like the hounds, was functioning on behalf of a hostile local establishment. Its members usually had been 'encouraged by their betters, so called', as Wesley put it[42]. After thirty years' experience he was adamant that 'wherever a mob continues any time, all they do is to be imputed, not so much to the rabble, as to the Justices'[43]. The fact remains, however, that the 'rabble' and the gentry were working together against what they perceived to be dissent from the established social order. The 'Church and King' mob and the anti-Methodist riot reflected the existence of a conservative consensus which transcended the major barriers of social status in the traditional society. The decline of such popular reactions after the 1790s was therefore a significant measure of the growing social isolation of the Church in many parts of England. The last serious manifestation of the 'Church and King' mob was in the notorious Birmingham riots of 1791, when the Unitarians, in particular, suffered for their political and religious radicalism. Thereafter the phenomenon gradually became a thing of the past[44], and the religious Establishment was forced to rely increasingly on overt legal and economic pressures to curb religious deviance. The Nonconformist press, from the early nineteenth century onwards, carried numerous reports of magisterial refusals to supply chapels and meeting houses with the protective licences guaranteed under the Act of Toleration; and it reported at the same time the widespread prosecution of the unlicensed, the dismissal of tenants and employees for refusing to conform to the Church, the raising of chapel rents to the point where extra-Establishment communities became insolvent, and the withdrawal by leading Anglican laymen of 'the common offices of good neighbourhood', including the refusal to deal with Nonconformists in business[45].

In the new industrial areas, where the Church of England lost physical contact with large sections of the population of early industrial England, the great problem was lack of *proximity* to potential adherents. But in many rural parishes where proximity was no problem the Establishment faced the problem of widespread *alienation* among its nominal constituents. In one context the Church was able to function scarcely at all, in the other its most important social functions were becoming increasingly unacceptable to much of the population. Through its direct involvement in land enclosure and tithe commutation schemes, and because of its role in the maintenance of social control in communities united no longer by a common social orthodoxy, the Church, once an integrative influence, was seen to be taking one side of an increasingly polarised situation.

During the late eighteenth and early nineteenth centuries there was a strong economic motive for the role of many clergymen in the Agrarian Revolution. The period saw a sharp rise in the power of the clergy as a landowning class, partly as a result of general agricultural prosperity, but primarily because of land enclosures and (what usually accompanied an enclosure agreement) the commutation of tithes for land on terms extremely generous to the tithe owners. In parishes which had escaped earlier impropriations, commutation for land raised many incumbents securely into the ranks of the independent landed gentry. The independent status and authority so acquired did not reduce the dependence of the Establishment on landed wealth and influence, of course. It reinforced it. The squire—parson alliance did not disappear, it merely became personified in certain localities in a new phenomenon: the 'squarson'.

Enclosure had the effect of perpetuating the power of the landlord while destroying the softening elements of the older paternalism. Instead of being a more or less spontaneous expression of respect for superiors, deference had become something which increasingly had to be extorted. W. R. Ward has explicated these social and cultural changes with particular reference to the clergy. The incumbent of an unimpropriated parish not only rose considerably in wealth and status as a result of the new land tenure arrangements, but was seen to do so partly 'at the expense of the peasant proprietors'. Commutation of tithe, in short, alienated rural labourers and small farmers from the clergy. This was sometimes true even in a strictly literal sense, for 'the old mud and wattle parsonage in the village, which had been good enough when the parson was simply a peasant with a university degree, would do no more'; the gentleman parson often moved 'out of the village, sometimes out of the parish altogether'[46].

The result was that when the Establishment engaged in the conservative social functions which once had seemed to buttress the cohesion of a rural community, it did so from the 1790s onwards (in many parts of the country) as an obviously partisan institution. As gentlemen and landowners the clergy were welcomed on to the county bench in large numbers. Once ineligible for magisterial duties, by the early decades of the nineteenth century they accounted for at least a quarter of all justices of the peace, and possibly for a much higher proportion[47]. Clerical magistrates, moreover, were notoriously active in the dispensation of justice as they saw it[48]. As late as 1834 at least one beneficed clergyman in eight exercised magisterial authority, and in many parishes, according to William Cobbett, incumbents were 'better known as Justices of the Peace than as clergymen'.

Cobbett, with his intimate knowledge of rural England, was ideally placed to assess the damage suffered by the Church as a result of its involvement in the dislocation of agrarian society during the early industrial period. 'I cannot conclude my remarks on this Rural Ride without noticing the *new sort of language* that I hear everywhere made use of with regard to the *parsons*, but which language I do not care to repeat', Cobbett wrote after a tour of Hampshire, Berkshire, Surrey and Sussex in 1823. He went on to stress that anticlericalism represented a virtual consensus of opinion among farmers[49]. A few months later he made similar remarks about rural labourers. 'It is true', he observed, 'that the *labouring* people have, in a great measure, ceased to go to Church. . . . I can remember when they were so numerous, that the parson could not attempt to begin, till the rattling of their nailed shoes ceased'[50]. The reason, he suggested, was 'that their way of thinking and feeling with regard to both church and clergy are totally changed; and that there is now very little *moral hold* which the latter possess'[51].

This was the crux of the serious religious-cultural crisis which confronted the unreformed Establishment. The moral imperatives which had inspired popular conformity in the past, the deferential compliance with prescribed authority characteristic of pre-industrial society, the consensus between the rulers and the ruled that the social harmony symbolised and defended by the Church was worth preserving: these things were disappearing. People in increasing numbers turned from the Church to the voluntary associations of Nonconformity not merely because the Church was inefficient, not only because it continued to behave like a monopoly in a competitive 'market situation', but also simply because it *was* the 'Establishment'. It became an axiom of English radicalism that, while religion itself was intrinsically 'kind and benign', an established religion was a pernicious thing. As Thomas Paine put in his seminal *Rights of Man*, written in the early 1790s: 'By engendering the church with the state, a sort of mule-animal, capable only of destroying, and not of breeding up, is produced, called *The Church established by Law*'[52].

The functions of Methodism and Dissent

Because of the sometimes intense opprobrium attaching to 'the Church established by Law', extra-Establishment religion of one kind or another was, for particular social groups (such as artisans, labourers, miners, small freeholders, tradesmen, and merchants and manufacturers), and in particular cultural contexts, the obvious choice for those interested in religious associations in early industrial England. A situation which in some respects is analogous has been analysed by the Brazilian sociologist, Emilio Willems, in a study published in 1964. The establishment status of

Brazilian Catholicism, he has argued, is a serious handicap to the maintenance of the Catholic religion within certain social groups. Conversion to
Protestantism

> constitutes one of the many ways in which hostility and
> rebellion against a decaying social structure may be expressed.
> . . . The Catholic Church is often perceived by the masses as a
> symbol of the traditional order or as an ally of its supreme
> exponent, the landed aristocracy. . . . The farther removed the
> ideology and structure of a particular denomination are from
> those of the traditional society, the stronger the appeal it
> holds for the common people[53].

Similarly, the ideology, the structures, and the communal functions of
extra-Establishment movements in early industrial England, especially
those which have been classified in earlier chapters within the broad
category of 'Evangelical Nonconformity', made them uniquely attractive
to a wide cross-section of 'the common people'.

The element of protest

The other-worldly incentives of justification and eternal life,
together with the obverse fear of terror beyond the grave, were very
important elements in the ideological appeal of Evangelical Nonconformity. But the beliefs and values which attracted people to the movement were not exclusively other-worldly. The social and even political
implications of a theological system can be as important as the basic
doctrines themselves. And as the history of Wesleyanism, in particular,
illustrates, these secondary ideological functions of religion can operate
even when religious leaders do not recognise fully either their character or
their importance. For example, the ruling classes who connived at anti-
Methodist rioting, and later attempted to check the spread of Evangelical
Nonconformist itinerancy, may have been labouring under misapprehen-
sions about the kind of social deviance with which they were faced. They
may, Wesley conceded in 1745, wrongly have suspected Methodists of
'carrying on some sinister design', and have doubted Methodism's 'inviol-
able attachment' to the Crown and the Constitution[54]. Yet there is a
sense in which they had recognised, more clearly than Wesley himself, the
latent antagonism between the value system implicit in the new popular
evangelicalism and the dominant values of eighteenth- and early nineteenth-century society. While charges of Papistry, Jabobitism, and, later,
of Jacobinism, were unfounded; the Duchess of Buckingham, in her blunt
reaction to the preaching of George Whitefield, had grasped the truth (if
not the whole truth) about the broad ideological and social implications of
Methodist doctrines when she described them as 'strongly tinctured with
impertinence and disrespect . . . towards superiors, in perpetually
endeavouring to level all ranks, and do away with all distinctions'. It was
monstrous, she considered, 'to be told that you have a heart as sinful as
the common wretches that crawl on the earth'[55].

The 'common wretches', for their part, were less likely to take offence at this emphasis on the natural equality and essential moral inadequacy of all men before God, which was so central in the Evangelical Nonconformist ideology. Methodists, Congregationalists, and Baptists, in short, propagated a spiritual status system which, while not radical in any political sense, cut across the hierarchical structures of the contemporary society. 'Worldly' values did influence the internal ordering of their communities (wealth and social status were never effectively obliterated at any stage, despite the repeated dire warnings of denominational leaders), yet the belief that the most important division in human society lay between those who were 'truly converted to God, and travelling towards heaven', and those who (whatever their class or social status) were 'without God in the world' and bound for perdition[56], clearly could be of more than spiritual comfort to men whose social position placed them on the least desirable side of most conventional social divisions.

The fact that receptiveness to Evangelical Nonconformity was located chiefly in the lower and lower-middle ranks of early industrial society was related partly to the ideology of the movement. There has been serious disagreement among historians about the precise nature of this relationship, however. E. P. Thompson, for example, has admitted with some reluctance that there was an ideological dimension to the appeal of Methodism, for his admiration of the good sense of the working classes is equalled by his distaste for Methodist beliefs and values. In his important and provocative analysis he has concluded, therefore, that 'many working people turned to religion as a "consolation"'. 'There is a sense', he has argued, 'in which any religion which places great emphasis on the after-life is the chiliasm of the defeated and the hopeless'[57].

But this chiliastic function, while it doubtless operated in the case of individuals, was of relatively minor importance in the total ideological impact of Methodism. The same could be said of the New Dissent. What should be stressed is that Evangelical Nonconformity echoed the *aspirations* rather than the *despair* of the working classes. Purely as a theological system, of course, evangelicalism might be expected to have appealed most to the lower strata of a society, at least if it is true that wealth and status on earth tend to blunt concern about a possible future existence. But to account for the success of the popular evangelicalism of the early industrial age as 'the chiliasm of despair' is to beg the question why it was not the most 'defeated' and 'hopeless' sections of the society which were mobilised by the movement, and to minimise its obvious and widespread appeal among individuals and social groups whose economic and social positions were not only adequate, but were actually improving.

Thompson has partly anticipated these questions by calling Methodism 'the religion of both the exploiters and the exploited'[58]. But while the social basis of Evangelical Nonconformity was broad enough to reproduce within chapel communities most of the social tensions characteristic of early industrial society, it was at the same time narrow enough for Evangelical Nonconformists to share a common set of social as well as religious values. For apart from the 'manifest' purpose of gaining salvation, for the prosperous merchant and the factory operative alike, becoming a Nonconformist could be a symbolic rejection of the mores and values of a social system which ascribed status largely in terms of inherited advantages of landed wealth and family background.

It is worth recalling that even John Wesley, Tory and autocrat though he was, was a hostile, albeit ultimately impotent critic, of any tendency for secular criteria of status to influence social relationships within Methodist societies. 'We regard no man according to his . . . country, riches, power, or wisdom', he said: 'We consider all men only in their spiritual state, and as they stand related to a better world'[59]. Indeed, by the end of his life he was convinced that he should have insisted on a standard form of dress among Methodists as a means of preventing ostentation and suppressing perhaps the most obvious index of social differentiation in a congregation or class[60].

But while Wesley's efforts to check the emergence of a social hierarchy within Methodism were in vain, there were many aspects of his attacks upon the dominant values of the wider society which, although motivated by concern for the spiritual welfare of his hearers, often echoed their social prejudices. The poor, pious Christian was better than the rich heathen; the 'child of the devil' who owned an estate was inferior to the 'child of God without one'; the converted tradesman was superior to the unconverted lord or gentleman[61]. The rich were culpable for their pride, luxurious living, ostentation, sloth, and dissipation[62]. These were not occasional themes in Wesley's sermons, they were extremely prominent.

Wesley was not playing the role of social critic, but in a society built on deference his implicit rejection of the life style, the values, the status symbols, and the recreational pursuits of the dominant classes made him an unwitting agent in the dissolution of the dependency system. As Everett E. Hagen has stressed, in the transition from the prescriptive society of pre-industrial England to the modern industrial society which succeeded it, a crucial social process was the erosion of the feelings of deference and dependence among the 'lower orders' which had been essential to the maintenance of the old system[63]. During the eighteenth and early nineteenth centuries there occurred what he has called the 'withdrawal of status respect'[64].

The demand for extra-Establishment religion during this period was in part a reflection of the functionality of religious deviance both as an ideological legitimation of 'status withdrawal', and as a symbolic expression of 'independence'. One of the chief reasons why Methodists were a target for the resentment of their social superiors, so Wesley told his followers, was their apparent immunity from the influence conventionally associated with 'power, and money, and wisdom'[65]. Dissent, as the Baptist leader, Robert Hall, put it in 1791, provided an 'asylum' for those willing to affirm their social emancipation from the hegemony of squire and parson[66].

The Industrial and Agrarian Revolutions, and the political radicalism of the period after 1789, were in different ways solvents of the 'dependency system' of pre-industrial society, and as such they combined to create an ideological vacuum which religious deviance was able to fill, in company with other more radical, and sometimes specifically political movements. People in the process of gaining emancipation from the system of paternalism and deference which traditionally had enabled the ruling classes to influence, among other things, the religious behaviour of their social inferiors, found in extra-Establishment religion a legitimation for their aspirations. Significantly, the concepts 'status withdrawal' and 'emancipation' both connote transition; and the connotation is apposite, for it is clear that in some respects, at least, the distinctive utility of religious deviance was a passing phenomenon.

Once the 'dependency system' was dead—once it had given way to the more complicated, less personal socio-economic structures of a mature industrial society—the ideological function of legitimating aspirations for 'independence' would become less relevant. But while the system was dying commitment to some extra-Establishment body often represented an important assertion of autonomy by individuals whose social and religious behaviour previously had been prescribed by a squire or a parson. As a this-worldly value system, in other words, Evangelical Nonconformity was peculiarly well adapted to the social and cultural needs of the early industrial age. During this 'period of disturbed transition', as Smelser has called it, while the traditional society was under intense pressure but before 'new social forms began to find a solid place in the social structure'[67], the element of social protest in commitment to a 'chapel' rather than a 'church' was vitally important.

The legitimation of 'improvement'

As well as legitimating their emancipation from the 'dependency system', and providing artisans, freeholders, merchants, manufacturers, and related social groups with a fairly acceptable form of social protest, both Methodism and Dissent inculcated values which endorsed the socio-economic aspirations which such people were acquiring during the early industrial age. Agricultural innovations, the introduction of capitalistic modes into the agrarian economy, and most of all the Industrial Revolution itself, were precipitating a 'revolution of expectations' in English society in the century before Victoria came to the throne, This period saw a major watershed in the nation's history: one which separated an era of slow economic growth, in which for the mass of the population economic expectations had been static and poverty more or less normal, from a new era of widespread wealth, rapid and more or less continuous economic growth, and reasonable expectations of genuine economic improvement for most members of the society. This was true in spite of the suffering, dislocation, and hardship which the process entailed, and in spite of the fact that for particular social and occupational groups it was nothing less than catastrophic. Whereas in previous generations it had been realistic for a man to expect to pass his life without significant change in his socio-economic position, it now was becoming realistic for most men to aspire to 'improvement'[68].

But in a society just emerging from a situation where the *maintenance* of a standard of living not far above the subsistence level had been a realistic economic goal, men who would 'improve' had to embrace new values. They had to learn to value the profit motive as opposed to the motive of subsistence. They had to be acquisitive. They had to accept the novel concept of work, not as a necessity for survival, but as an avenue to socio-economic advancement. If from the perspective of a modern industrial society these values seem self-evident, then it is salutary to remember the problems that early industrial manufacturers experienced in inculcating a capitalistic work discipline into the new industrial work force, problems with parallels wherever industrialisation and modernisation have taken place in economically undeveloped societies. In such situations those who acquire the new outlook earliest make the most successful adjustment to the new societal context.

Values which Evangelical Nonconformity shared with the Old Dissent, and especially the Society of Friends, made the religious culture of the Chapel highly functional for people intent on 'improvement' in early industrial England. Negatively, by eradicating wherever possible the recreational habits of pre-industrial society, habits incompatible with the strict discipline of factory production; and positively, by esteeming the pursuit of this-worldly success as a Christian duty, these extra-Establishment bodies facilitated the adjustment of their members to the emerging industrial society. While riches ill-gotten, unearned, or extravagantly used were abjured in chapel communities, money itself was regarded as 'an excellent gift of God, answering the noblest ends'[69]. Methodists, for example, were not only told to gain all they could by diligence, and to save all they could by frugality; they were encouraged to improve their economic status by being innovative in business and industry[70]. The same was true of both the Old and the New Dissent[71].

W. J. Warner, writing in 1930, argued that there was a direct link between the economic implications of the Wesleyan ideology and the recruiting power of Wesleyan societies. Some people joined Wesleyanism, he suggested, primarily *because* it appealed to them as a socio-economic value system[72]. In the majority of cases, however, the link was doubtless much less direct. The socio-economic implications of chapel membership contributed to the growth of the Methodist movement largely as part of a total religious culture which proved particularly hospitable to the temporal circumstances of artisans, tradesmen, and manufacturers. Certain social groups, in other words, exhibited a very high degree of cultural congruity with Evangelical Nonconformity. Until the demoralising impact of the powerloom on handloom weaving after the Napoleonic Wars, for example, handloom weavers exemplified a receptiveness based not simply on the specifically religious satisfactions inherent in chapel membership, but also on an overall congruity between the religious culture and the world they took for granted[73]. Handloom weavers were able to perceive a clear relationship between the economic rewards which they received and their own industry, ingenuity, and skill. Their economic position, as an historian of the cotton industry pointed out in 1823, 'depended mainly on their own exertions', and as a result they were characterised by 'a spirit of freedom and independence' and 'a consciousness of the value of character and of their own weight and importance'[74]. It was no accident that between 1740 and 1820 the 'great mass' of weavers had become 'deeply imbued with the doctrines of Methodism', and that by 1823 they formed 'a great proportion of the whole number of persons who professed that religion'[75]. Data on the occupational structure of Congregational and

Baptist communities located in cotton manufacturing areas indicates, moreover, that the demand for Methodism among handloom weavers was part of a more generalised demand which the New Dissent could satisfy equally well.

There are many ways of looking at a single phenomenon, and the final picture presented by an analysis can vary widely according to differences of perspective and emphasis. Evaluations of the role of Methodism and Dissent in early industrial England have differed significantly because different historians have been impressed by different aspects of the same social or ideological functions. For example, Thompson has emphasised the repressive 'utility' of Methodism in inculcating a 'work discipline' rather than the more attractive obverse aspect of its legitimation of self-improvement and economic endeavour; he has stressed its 'all-enveloping "Thou Shalt Not"' rather than the security adherents derived from its doctrine of salvation[76]. An emphasis cannot be regarded as either right or wrong, but it can be challenged on the grounds of being misleading. In evaluating Thompson's picture of Methodism, which, arguably, is the most perceptive available, it is important not to lose sight of the voluntary nature of the popular evangelicalism. Like all associational commitments, it involved 'costs' as well as 'benefits'; but hundreds of thousands of people in early industrial society valued the 'benefits' highly enough to tolerate the 'costs'.

The amelioration of anomie

An area of Evangelical Nonconformist life well explicated by the 'cost—benefit' analogy is the complex of functions associated with the chapel community as a cohesive social entity. The cost of membership, measured in terms of personal freedom, was high. The chapel community was a cohesive and totalitarian religious subculture: totalitarian not least when it was at its most democratic. There was no aspect of a member's life which was not implicated in his commitment to membership. Religious practice was obligatory, for persistent non-attendance meant expulsion. Honesty, chastity, sobriety, and moderation in dress and behaviour were normative. The performance of even the most secular duties could be subject to the scrutiny and disciplinary action of a local congregation or of the local denominational leadership. Idleness, for example, could lead to expulsion from a Wesleyan society, sloth being regarded as 'inconsistent with religion'[77].

Work, in fact, was one of the few areas of interaction between the subculture and the wider society. The belief that 'the world' was 'a rebellious province against the King of Heaven'—the conviction, resolutely inculcated, that there was 'evil in its company, in its spirit, in its pleasures, its maxims, and its course'[78]—tended inevitably to insulate individual congregations, and on a wider scale the popular evangelicalism itself, from the secular culture. Converts were won *from* the 'world'. Baptism in infancy made a man an Anglican, but becoming a Methodist, a Congregationalist, or a Baptist involved thorough integration into a 'gathered church' which contrived to keep to a minimum primary relationships with outsiders. A comparable exclusivism existed in the Society of Friends, which made marriage to a non-member automatic grounds for expulsion. The significant difference, of course, was that while the subcultural position of Methodist and New Dissenting communities was maintained *in spite of* a constant influx of recruits from the wider society, the exclusivism of the Quakers was preserved partly *by* policies which militated against recruitment.

If the 'world' was hostile—and opposition was regarded as a proof of genuine commitment[79]—it followed that chapel communities had to fashion for themselves a system providing social as well as spiritual satisfactions. Methodists, an angry but accurate observer wrote in 1813,

> consider themselves as a chosen and separate people. The expressions by which they designate their own sect are, 'the dear people',—'the elect',—'the people of God'. The rest of mankind are 'the carnal people', 'the people of this world', etc., etc. Not satisfied with salvation, they must have everything exclusive. They have not only their own chapels, their own schools, their own madhouses, and their own magazine, but they have their own Bible, their family Shakespeare, their newspaper, their review, their pocket-book[80].

In his 'Rules for the Methodist Societies', drawn up in 1743, Wesley had declared that members of a society were obliged to do good

> especially to them that are of the household of faith, or groaning so to be: employing them preferably to others; buying one of another; helping each other in business: and so much the more, because the world will love its own, and them *only*[81].

Even in the matter of work, then, interaction with the wider society was to be restricted wherever members of the subculture could conduct business relations between themselves.

Wesley's use of the familial image of Methodism as 'the household of faith' reflected his unwavering conception both of his own role within the movement, and of the primacy among Methodists of in-group relationships. In his supervision of the 'household' he neglected no aspect of personal or social behaviour, whether religious, moral, political, recreational, or economic; and on each subject he declared his mind with a confident assurance of 'fatherly' authority. Indicative of the exclusivism for which he strove was his explicit warning against close relationships even with parents, brothers, or sisters who were 'of the world'. The concession that it was permissible to 'be civil and friendly at a distance' served mainly to emphasise the degree to which faithful Methodists were to be 'separate'[82].

The father of Methodism was a shrewd sociologist. While he fashioned the movement to exercise wideranging social and communal functions partly because his followers simply lacked adequate alternative agencies, he was motivated also by the desire to reinforce the subcultural insularity which he valued for religious reasons. Anglicanism might prosper by making minimal demands upon its adherents; the extra-Establishment sect cemented the allegiance of its adherents by making the kinds of demands which accentuated their alienation from the 'style and manner of living' of the wider society[83]. For this reason, its pronouncement of anathema on the 'profane' culture was no mere symbolic gesture during the early industrial age. As rules drawn up in 1816 to govern membership of the Congregational church at Aylesbury, Buckinghamshire, put it, it was 'the indispensable Duty of a Church to purge ... by a solemn Act of Excommunication', members failing the test of 'separation'[84].

Why then did people value the benefits of participation in chapel communities highly enough to accept the stringency of a sectarian discipline? The answer lies partly in the ideological and religious-cultural satisfactions which have been examined already, but perhaps the most important of the latent functions of Methodism and New Dissent involved the capacity for satisfying the profound associational and communal needs of people experiencing anomie[85] and social insecurity in a period of rapid social change and dislocation. Technological changes, and changes in settlement patterns and socio-economic relationships which they dictated, placed increasing numbers of people in unfamiliar, unstructured, and largely normless environments in early industrial England. Whatever industrialisation did to the standard of living of particular social and occupational groups, it acted fairly generally as a solvent of traditional institutions and forms of social organisation. In this respect, at least, the 'First Industrial Revolution' was prototypical of later Industrial Revolutions in other countries and social contexts. It is 'typical', Wilbert Moore has written, 'especially of the first impact of new economic patterns, that they threaten or disrupt the previous social relationships, while not immediately supplying new security devices in their place'[86]. Industrialisation, in short, produces an initial phase of anomie.

The obverse of anomie is a heightened demand for new associational and communal foci to replace those which have been lost. It has become a commonplace in the sociology of industrialisation that an industrial revolution 'brings in its wake a proliferation of interest groups and associations', particularly among the artisan, manufacturing, and entrepreneurial classes most affected during its initial stages[87]. The success of Evangelical Nonconformist recruiting in England in the booming industrial villages of the late eighteenth and early nineteenth centuries—a success reflected in the occupational lists in *Non-Parochial Registers*—was a phenomenon which has been repeated by later sectarian movements among new industrial populations elsewhere. Such populations are composed mainly of migrants, an American authority on church growth has pointed out recently discussing the contemporary situation in several Latin American countries. They have been 'so pounded by circumstances', he has written,

> that they are receptive to all sorts of innovations, among
> which is the Gospel. They are in a phase of insecurity, capable
> of reaching out for what will stabilize them and raise their

spirits. It is no accident that the tremendous growth of Pentecostals in Brazil has taken place largely among the migrants flooding down from the northeast to the great cities of the south[88].

The social functions of a religious organisation are usually an important element within the complex of satisfactions which it offers its constituents, but their significance is increased greatly within a constituency experiencing anomie. Receptiveness to extra-Establishment religion was heightened in early industrial England because the exigencies of rapid social change made more pressing and more widespread fundamental social demands which Evangelical Nonconformist organisations, particularly, were well adapted to satisfy. Chapel communities were able to meet associational, recreational and communal needs which in many cases would otherwise have gone unfulfilled; and they were able to provide a degree of economic protection and social security rarely available elsewhere. In the late eighteenth and early nineteenth centuries, in short, religious deviance was often the only form of associational commitment open to the lower-middle and working classes, especially in new industrial areas. Alternative institutions, secular or religious, sometimes took years to develop, even in populous communities, and in their absence the chapel was the obvious focus of social activity. In a situation of dissolving allegiancies and values, the chapel community provided its own microcosm of status, leadership, and authority. Even when an Anglican alternative was available, moreover, the Methodist, Congregational, or Baptist association was often more attractive to certain classes. A shopkeeper or an artisan was 'an unheard-of unit' in an Anglican congregation, the Secretary of the London Diocesan Church Building Society told a House of Lords Select Committee in 1857; but in a chapel community he might be 'looked upon as somebody', whether in the capacity of deacon, visitor, tract distributor, or as the holder of some other office. In comparison with the Church, the Rev Thomas Stooks continued, the Nonconformist bodies excelled in the exercise of socially integrative functions: 'They have tea meetings and prayer meetings; they bring their people more together, and they are able to carry out the spirit of union more fully in a dissenting chapel than we have yet the secret of doing in the church'[89]. If these associational factors were attracting people to Nonconformity in the 1850s, it is clear that they would have been even more significant a few decades earlier, when alternative associations were less frequently available.

Nonconformity, as Thompson has pointed out with regard to Methodism, rejected 'the older, half-pagan popular culture, with its fairs, its sports, its drink, and its picaresque hedonism'[90]. Howell Harris, one of the fathers of Calvinistic Methodism, was typical of Nonconformity generally in making 'alehouse people, fiddlers, harpers, etc. (Demetrius like) sadly cry against him for spoiling their business'[91]. But in place of the 'worldly pleasure' which they excluded from their communities, Evangelical Nonconformists provided alternative recreational and communal activities. In many social contexts, moreover, the recreational satisfactions available in the chapel community did not have to compete with secular alternatives, at least of an organised kind. In the new settlements of the early industrial era the cultural equivalents of the wakes, fairs, or sports of pre-industrial society were often monopolised by the new popular religious organisations.

The 'camp meeting', for example, one of the hallmarks of Primitive Methodism, fulfilled obvious cultural and social functions in addition to exercising its manifest religious function. 'We proceeded in a body to sing through the streets, which had a very good effect', a Congleton Primitive Methodist reported in May 1822, describing the beginning of a Camp Meeting. People from as far afield as Burslem and Tunstall 'kept falling in on every side' as the procession wended its way into the countryside for a day of preaching, praying, and general gregariousness[92]. There was an obvious demand for such services, as there was also for love feasts, watch nights, and those even more routine occasions in a chapel when preaching and hymn singing were the order of the day. Spiritual fervour they evoked, and excitement, and camaraderie. Anglican critics might write savagely of 'the tossing of heads, the ogling of eyes, the laugh and jest, the catches and glees' which seemed characteristic of meetings of chapel folk, and imply that the motives of many participants were far from spiritual[93]. But the associations of the chapel community were the foci around which the subculture created its alternatives to the world of public houses, sports, gambling, theatrical entertainments, and other secular amusements. Indeed in many areas, for considerable periods, they were simply the only forms of organised recreation available.

In addition to these fundamental communal and recreational functions, the utility of Evangelical Nonconformity in early industrial society included the contribution of the chapel community to the material welfare and security of its members. As early as 1827 the young Primitive Methodist movement, aware that membership had in certain cases been used as a pretext for gaining financial assistance and accommodation, decided that it had to formulate rules to exclude religious charlatans. The class ticket had become an object of the forger's art[94]. Yet this was merely a misuse of one of Nonconformity's most important social functions. Membership of a chapel community often provided the best means of access to such basic necessities as housing, clothing, food, credit, or employment in times of crisis. In a society bereft of adequate systems of social security, integration in a cohesive community was one of the best forms of insurance, particularly for socio-economic groups at the mercy of the emerging trade cycle.

During the postwar depression after 1816, for example, the Baptists of Brettell Lane Chapel in the Black Country opened soup kitchens and provided clothing for those of their members worst affected; and during a subsequent slump in the early 1840s the pastor of the nearby Congregational chapel at Stourbridge reminded his flock to maintain their traditional practice of 'mutually aiding each other in their secular employments by dealing with one another'[95]. More formally, Wesleyan and other Methodist bodies worked on the same principles. Indeed, as early as 1744 Wesley not only had ruled that each member of the Methodist societies should contribute weekly all he could spare 'towards a common stock', but had suggested that the scheme should operate only 'till we can have all things common'[96]. By 1748 he had abandoned this vision of a primitive communism in Methodism, but the principle of mutual aid remained.

In a comment on Methodist growth, an anonymous critic of the movement wrote in 1813 that 'the immediate temporal advantages which people of the lower classes feel as soon as they enter the society, must be numbered among the efficient causes of its rapid and continual increase'[97]. There was a link between receptiveness to chapel-based religion and the material satisfactions which membership of a chapel community was believed to provide. But in recognising this connexion it is necessary to come to terms with the fact that growth tended to be adversely affected by economic depression. Superficially these two facts appear to be in contradiction.

An examination of Nonconformist growth rate series confirms what contemporary observers frequently noticed about the association of economic trends and organisational growth in Nonconformity. 'Trade has been very bad', Joseph Taylor told Thomas Jackson in the spring of 1812. 'This hurts Religion sadly. Many will not come to their Classes nor take their Tickets'[98]. Comments of this kind generally accompanied periods of economic depression. The problem was partly a reflection of increased 'removals' as members of chapel communities were forced to move elsewhere in search of employment[99]. But disillusionment was also present. 'Well, we went to church', Mark Rutherford wrote in 1887, characterising one of the attitudes underlying lapsing from Congregationalism in 'Cowfield' in the 1830s, 'but when the business dropped we left off going, for nothing much seemed to come of it'[100].

The implication of such evidence is not that Nonconformity failed to perform valuable socio-economic functions, but rather that it failed to perform them adequately during periods of *general* economic strain. Indeed, disillusionment set in precisely because the expectations of members evidently exceeded what the actual economic advantages of membership turned out to be during a widespread economic recession. The chapel community could cope with crises suffered by individual members under normal circumstances, but as a community it suffered when the pressures of recession were general. Samuel Jackson recognised this in his Annual Address to the Wesleyan Societies in 1847. Periods of 'general temporal distress' were unfavourable for growth, he explained, 'while personal affliction, and the dangers of pestilence, have been the means of awakening thousands'[101].

When Nonconformist congregations sung together the words of Charles Wesley,

> Help us to help each other, Lord,
>   Each other's cross to bear,
> Let each his friendly aid afford,
>   And feel his brother's care,

they were describing an ideal of the chapel community which drew many members of the lower and lower-middle classes of the century after 1740 into the popular evangelicalism of Methodism or New Dissent. Encompassing all its specific cultural and social functions, the religion of the chapel offered community sense: the feeling of belonging to a cohesive social group, of being integrated into a complex network of primary relationships which stretched, in many cases, outwards from a local chapel into most parts of the country. It was a popular form of collective behaviour partly because as well as offering 'salvation', as well as providing an ideological legitimation of the world-taken-for-granted by particular social groups, it provided an institutional framework within which primary human relationships were possible.

The pattern of Nonconformist
        encroachment

There were more than 10,000 parishes in England during the
early industrial period, and probably as many nuances of parochial life and
conformist behaviour as there were parishes. Yet the Church of England
was more vulnerable to the encroachment of Nonconformity[1] in some
areas than in others; and although the geography of religious deviance was
highly complex it is possible to identify certain major factors which, singly
or in various combinations, determined the overall effectiveness of the
parochial system from area to area, and by so doing created a definite but
complex geographical pattern of Anglican strengths and weaknesses
throughout the country. Chapter 4 has argued that Evangelical Nonconformity, and to a much lesser extent the Old Dissent, were able to perform
religious and social services more attractive to large sections of the population than were the alternatives available within the Established Church.
But such services could be 'marketed' only where the Church was either
too weak or too negligent to defend its traditional monopoly of English
religious practice. There was an important inverse relationship, in short,
between the decline of 'Church' religiosity and the proliferation of
'Chapel' communities in the period preceding the Anglican reforms of the
1830s. To explicate this relationship, the present chapter will analyse the
factors underlying the partial breakdown of the parochial system in early
industrial society.

The quality of pastoral care

An obvious, and in a sense overarching factor in the operation
of the parochial system was the marked variation in the pastoral effectiveness of the parochial clergy. Not directly accountable to their congregations or dependent on them, as were Independent pastors, and free from
the unrelenting scrutiny and discipline built into the Methodist ministry,
Anglican clergymen could, if they chose, neglect the cure of souls almost
with impunity[2]. What is more, a parish became unworkable as a religious
entity (in a way in which a Methodist society or a Congregational or
Baptist community did not) in the absence of a resident minister or
qualified curate. The parochial system, in short, was only as effective as
the vocational commitment of its individual parochial incumbents.

Among the most important reasons for the spread of Nonconformity, according to many early nineteenth century advocates of Church

reform, was the 'lukewarmness' and negligence of many parish clergymen. The Vicar of Axbridge (to take an extreme example) resided in his Mendip parish in 1789, but he was 'intoxicated about six times a week' and was often prevented from conducting services by 'two black eyes, honestly earned in fighting'[3]. Such gross behaviour was atypical. More common, and therefore more serious, was the alienation of many clergy from the bulk of their parishioners: the presence in parishes of men whose discharge of their liturgical functions was perfunctory, and whose pastoral endeavours were nil. The anonymous author of *The State of the Established Church*, an important reformist pamphlet addressed to Spencer Percival, then Chancellor of the Exchequer, went as far as to claim in 1809 that a 'majority' of clergymen were 'wrapt up in secular pursuits, with a total indifference to the spiritual duties of their calling'[4]. It was because the eighteenth-century Establishment had responded with complacency to the steady erosion of its monopolistic advantages, the pamphlet explained, that the nineteenth-century Church was in danger of becoming a minority religious organisation. Had the clergy laboured with 'half the zeal and diligence' of their opponents something approaching religious uniformity could have been preserved, by consent if not by prescription. It had been lack of competition, 'the lukewarmness of the established clergy', which had been the main reason for the success of Nonconformity. The remedy, therefore, lay in thoroughgoing Church reform; in putting to an end the clerical neglect which had abandoned parishioners to 'revelling and drunkenness, or what is more common now, to the itinerant enthusiast'[5].

Hyperbolical as these claims were, there can be no doubt that one of the ways in which the parochial system compared unfavourably with the voluntary organisations of Nonconformity was in its overall effectiveness as a pastoral institution. The fault, of course, lay as much in the nature of Anglican religious culture as in the laxity or secularity of its professional ministry. In an age in which religion had increasingly to be 'marketed', the Church often seemed constitutionally less able than Nonconformity to cater for the devotional and communal religious demands of the people whose allegiance it claimed. Thomas Arnold made this point emphatically in 1832. Even when it was functioning properly, he said, the machinery of the unreformed parochial system was 'stiff and feeble':

> Ministers could only officiate in a church, and were compelled to confine themselves to the prescribed forms of Liturgy; while the Dissenters, free and unrestricted, could exercise their ministry as circumstances required it, whether in a mine, by a canal side, or at the doors of a manufactory; they could join in the hymns with their congregations, could pray, expound the Scriptures, exhort, awaken, or persuade, in such variety, and in such proportions, as the time, the place, the mood of their hearers, or their own, might suggest or call for[6].

When he wrote this famous treatise on Church reform Arnold was one of a growing number of Anglicans who had realised that parochial effectiveness depended on more than the regular and conscientious provision of the ancient services of the Church in the canonically appointed way. The opposite attitude was epitomised in the advice Bishop Samuel Butler of Lichfield gave one of his curates in 1837:

> If the inhabitants will not take the trouble to come . . . to hear your sermons, and much more to hear the beautiful prayers of our Liturgy, which are superior to any sermons that were ever written, I am sure they do not deserve to have them brought to their doors[7].

The problem, of course, was that while the inhabitants did not 'take the trouble' to practise Anglicanism, Nonconformist itinerants did bring popular evangelicalism virtually 'to their doors'. Except in parishes where religious conformity could still be prescribed, the conventional machinery of the parochial system was intrinsically vulnerable to Nonconformist exploitation. 'It is obvious that "the aggressive system" is practised by Dissenters to a much greater extent than by Churchmen', the editor of the *Congregational Magazine* wrote in 1832, attempting to explain the capacity of Nonconformity to outgrow the Church[8]. The explanation was far from complete. It ignored, for example, the significance of Establishment status as a social and political impediment to the success of Anglicanism among the classes from which Nonconformity recruited most of its members. But it correctly observed a connexion between the relatively faster growth of Nonconformity and the kinds of pastoral and evangelistic exertions typical of Nonconformist ministers and parochial clergymen respectively.

In the nomenclature used by Nonconformist evangelists there was a tendency to equate areas of parochial ineffectiveness with areas 'destitute of an evangelical ministry'[9]. The equation was understandable, granted the theology of Nonconformity, and reasonably accurate during the era of optimum Nonconformist growth, when evangelical incumbents tended as a group to show the greatest dedication to the cure of souls. But the crucial variable was pastoral rather than theological. As Puseyite clergy were to demonstrate from the 1840s onwards, dedicated incumbents from the opposite end of the theological spectrum could be as successful as evangelicals in providing parishioners with devotional and communal satisfactions to rival those available in Nonconformists chapels.

But as long as such satisfactions were unavailable, and wherever the parochial clergy did not actively and 'aggressively' propagate the Anglican religion, there was scope for Nonconformist growth. It was not a theological preference, nor an unavailability of Anglican facilities, which induced both of James Guiness Rogers's parents to leave the Church of England and join an Independent congregation early in the nineteenth century. They made the commitment 'simply because they were attracted to the churches where they had received spiritual benefit'. The change, Rogers recalled later, was a typical one[10].

But if, whether because of the personal deficiencies of incumbents or the institutional deficiencies of the system, Nonconformist agencies were able to exploit 'spiritual destitution' and 'neglect' even in parishes where Anglicanism ostensibly was secure, the potential for Nonconformist growth was obviously greater in parishes without resident incumbents. The strenuous efforts by Church reformers from 1800 onwards to eradicate pluralism and non-residence indicated a recognition of the significance of these problems in the spread of Nonconformity and the increase of irreligion. Throughout the first half of the nineteenth century a recurrent complaint of parsons taking up residence in previously vacant parishes was to draw attention to the legacy of apathy and Dissent which they had inherited from their absentee predecessors. A typical response from such a parson was expressed with evident feeling by the Vicar of Enstone, in Oxfordshire, a month after he took up residence in 1831. He reported to Bishop Bagot: 'I find myself set down in a wild, uncultivated and neglected village, the church deserted, the conventicles filled'[11].

'Non-residence' was an ambiguous concept, technically describing the failure of an incumbent to occupy the official residence located in his parish, but usually denoting physical absence from a living. Many non-resident clergymen actually lived close enough to the borders of their parishes to be able to perform their prescribed duties, and others provided for qualified curates. Non-residence, in other words, did not necessarily imply neglect. But neglect through absenteeism was widespread. In 1812 more than 1,000 parishes—almost one parish in ten—had no pastoral supervision at all, good, bad, or indifferent[12]. Such parishes were exposed to Nonconformist encroachment by what Best has called the 'material inefficiency' of the parochial system: by the economic problems which 'made it impossible or cruel, in practice and theory alike, to expect each benefice to support a resident clergyman without other assistance'[13].

The breakdown of the 'dependency system'

Granted the importance for the effectiveness of the parochial system of the local religious establishments operated jointly by squires and parsons, there was an obvious connexion between areas susceptible to Nonconformist encroachment and areas in which a significant proportion of the population had achieved emancipation from the 'system of dependency'. Oddly enough, perhaps the least significant factor in this social equation was the specifically religious zeal of the parson. Clerical negligence in pastoral matters might produce religious apathy or ignorance, but it would not create a context for Nonconformist growth if the parson or the squire discharged his conservative social responsibilities with vigilance and determination. As a barrier to extra-Establishment religiosity the effectiveness of the squire—parson alliance varied ultimately with the extent to which the social power of landed property—'the immense prestige attaching to wealth and acres, the awe which the way of life of the aristocracy inspired, and the respect in which most country squires were held'[14]—continued to evoke deference in local communities and to circumscribe the 'independence' of individuals in matters of social and religious behaviour. Emancipation from this prescriptive system could occur in a variety of ways.

The non-residence of the gentry

Clerical absenteeism could facilitate Nonconformist encroachment into a parish, but the absence of the lay partner in the squire—parson alliance was sometimes of comparable importance. 'I observe a great improvement since the Squire's house has been inhabited by a resident family', the incumbent of East Claydon, Buckinghamshire, told Bishop Wilberforce in 1854, his relief evident. He added, by way of acknowledging that further improvement was possible, that 'one great lack is the Power and Presence of the Holy Ghost'[15]. Few clergymen would have made so abrupt a progression from the Church's reliance upon the squirarchy to its reliance on the Holy Ghost, but (in Visitation Returns at least) it was the former prerequisite of parochial effectiveness which received most attention.

In this 1854 Episcopal Visitation of Oxford Diocese, for example, typical complaints came from the Parish of Granborough, Buckinghamshire, which was described as never having 'had the advantages of the tone given by a few resident gentry'; from the Vicar of Hillesden, in the same county, who considered his pastoral work deficient mainly because, as he put it, 'the owner of the Parish resides at a distance, and takes no interest, and exerts no influence in the parish'; and from the parson at Knowle Hill, Berkshire, who told of wealthy laymen failing to assist the clergy by 'urging their labourers to attend Church'. In some cases such complaints were made specifically in explanation of Nonconformist encroachment. Admitting that all but about twenty of the inhabitants of South Stoke Parish in Oxfordshire were Nonconformists, the incumbent blamed an 'entire want of cooperation and assistance from the largest landed proprietor', whose estate had been leased to 'a violent opposer of the Church'[16]. This kind of explanation of Nonconformist growth was, for obvious reasons, popular particularly among clergymen, but its significance can scarcely be doubted[17].

Structural weaknesses in the parochial system

In many areas, however, it was not the non-residence or apathy of the squirearchy which weakened the element of social control on which parochial effectiveness depended: it was the fact that economic and settlement patterns rendered populations unamenable to 'influence' based on landed property. The dependency system was best adapted to the rural communities of what Joan Thirsk has called 'lowland' England, where arable farmlands, and traditional, nucleated villages were prevalent[18]. But it broke down partially or completely in communities where freehold tenure and smallholdings were prevalent; in isolated or scattered communities, especially those in remote parts of outsized parishes or in extraparochial districts; in communities wholly or partly dependent on rural industries or other non-agrarian occupations; and in urban communities.

In elaboration of these claims it is worth noting the obvious correlation between the overall effectiveness of the parochial system and the broad dichotomy between 'highland' and 'lowland' regions adumbrated by Thirsk. As early as 1603 returns of the number of communicants in each diocese of England showed that allegiance to the Church was strongest in the Home Counties, and that throughout southern England, with the notable exception of Cornwall, a high percentage of the population supported it with 'firmness'. But in Cornwall, in the west Midlands, and throughout the north, Establishment loyalties were much less secure[19]. This bias of Anglican strength in favour of the south, the south Midlands, and the south-east remained essentially unaltered almost 250 years later when Horace Mann conducted the official Religious Census[20].

Thirsk and other agrarian historians have observed that the parochial system functioned best in the small, compact communities of pre-industrial society which depended economically on the agriculture of arable 'lowland' regions. In such regions, most of which were confined to southern and eastern England, it was generally true that 'forms of society were ... deeply rooted, social classes were relatively stable and distinct, manorial customs fairly rigid, political habits comparatively orderly, and the labourer's outlook deeply imbued with the prevalent preoccupations of church and manor-house'[21]. Domestic industry was not a feature of such communities. Throughout 'lowland' England it was a rarity characteristic of atypical areas like the Weald of Kent, the forest areas of Northamptonshire, and the Isle of Axholme in Lincolnshire. Nor was smallholding typical. Although small freehold farms were common in such places as the Chilterns, the market-gardening districts around Biggleswade in Bedfordshire, the Fenlands of Lincolnshire and Norfolk, and the rural areas of south-eastern Suffolk, largescale landholding (and consequently powerful landlord influence) was much more characteristic of 'lowland', south-eastern England, than of the West Country, the north and west Midlands, and the north[22]. For to the north-west of a line running roughly from Teesmouth to Weymouth, moorland and mountain, and soils suitable for pastoral rather than arable use, were prevalent, and minerals more plentiful than in 'lowland' regions. Here scattered communities combining pastoral farming with domestic industry, or engaged in mining or quarrying, had been characteristic of pre-industrial society, and they survived alongside the new industrial complexes which sprang up in the eighteenth and early nineteenth centuries.

Not only did the pastoral agriculture and domestic industry of 'highland' regions encourage more diffuse settlement patterns than were normal in arable farming areas, but the relative weakness of the landed interest in such regions, and in mining and quarrying districts, reduced both the influence of the clergy and the basis of their financial support. Tables and Figs 5.1 and 5.2 indicate the broad correlations existing between Thirsk's lowland–highland division and the size and economic viability of the average Anglican parish. Parishes tended to be larger in 'highland' areas partly because populations were more scattered, and partly because there was not an adequate economic basis for increasing the number of benefices. Even although north Midland and northern benefices

Table 5.1 Regional variation in the average size of an Anglican parish in 1811

Region	Total number of parishes	Area in acres	Average size of parish in acres
East	1,634	3,240,000	1,980
South-east	1,048	2,594,000	2,475
South Midlands	1,379	3,558,000	2,580
North Midlands	1,236	3,517,000	2,840[1]
South-west	940	2,703,000	2,880
South	873	2,541,000	2,910
West Midlands	1,253	4,021,000	3,200
Cornwall	205	868,000	4,230
Yorkshire	630	3,898,000	6,190
North	290	3,419,000	11,790
North-west	156	1,852,000	11,860

Notes

1 Within the north and west Midlands regions there was considerable variation in the average size of parishes from area to area. Within the Diocese of Lichfield and Coventry, which straddled both regions (including the counties, Derbyshire, Staffordshire, Shropshire, and Warwickshire) the average size of a parish was 4,275 acres.

2 The composition of the regions is as follows: *East*: Essex, Suffolk, Norfolk; *South-east*: Middlesex, Surrey, Sussex, Kent; *South Midlands*: Berks., Bucks., Beds., Cambs., Hunts., Herts., Oxon., Northants; *North Midlands*: Derby., Leicester, Lincs., Notts., Rutland; *South*: Dorset, Hants., Wilts; *South-west*: Devon, Somerset; *West Midlands*: Hereford., Glos., Salop, Staffs., Warwick., Worcestershire; *North*: Cumberland, Durham, Northumberland, Westmorland; *North-west*: Cheshire, Lancs.

were fewer and farther between than their southern counterparts, significantly more of them were inadequate to support an incumbent in 1836.

The higher ratio of inadequate benefices in the 'highland' sector meant that pluralism was more often an economic necessity, and non-residence more widespread[23]. While it was true until the second half of the eighteenth century that the distribution of the English population was consistent with the concentration of Anglican resources in the south and south-east, this did not alter the fact that large parishes and scattered populations were not amenable to the religious influences of either parson or squire. For however low its population, a large parish was unworkable unless its inhabitants happened to be concentrated in a single locality near the parish church. By the second quarter of the nineteenth century (far too late for the good of the Church) it had become a commonplace in clerical *post mortems* of Anglican failure that a major reason for the growth of irreligion and Nonconformity had been the spatial isolation of

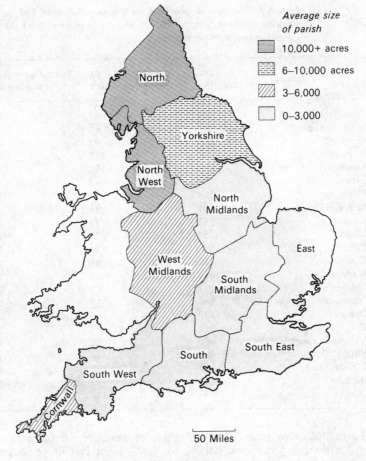

Fig. 5.1 Average size of Anglican parishes in acres in 1811. *For sources and explanations see Table 5.1*

many parishioners from the church, the parsonage, and the manor house. During the 1831 Visitation of the Diocese of Oxford parish clergy were asked whether the church was 'conveniently situated for the greater part of the Parish'; and in 1852, during a parliamentary inquiry into the need for church-building, witnesses indicated that in many cases a mile was considered about the limit people could be expected to travel to worship, and that bad weather or poor roads could reduce this distance[24].

In certain cases the consequences of spatial isolation had been recognised long before any attempt was made to restructure the parochial system. The vicar of Bampton, explaining to Bishop Secker in 1738 that Baptists had built a chapel in his Oxfordshire parish, pointed out that the parish was huge (twenty miles in circumference) and that the Dissenters had secured their foothold in a border village distant from the parish

Table 5.2 Number of benefices with a population of 300 or over requiring augmentation in 1836 expressed as a percentage of the total number of benefices per diocese

Diocese	Total Benefices	Benefices requiring augmentation	Percentage requiring augmentation
Rochester	94	13	13.8
Peterborough	290	44	15.2
Hereford	256	42	16.4
Norwich	1,021	172	16.8
London	635	107	16.9
Bristol	254	47	18.2
Salisbury	386	75	19.4
Bath and Wells	441	96	21.8
Canterbury	343	76	22.2
Lincoln	1,234	276	22.2
Exeter	632	142	22.5
Winchester	416	94	22.6
Worcester	212	51	24.0
Chichester	267	65	24.3
Gloucester	281	71	25.2
Oxford	209	60	28.7
Ely	149	47	31.5
Lich. and Coventry	606	252	41.5
York	891	380	42.6
Carlisle	127	62	48.8
Durham	146	79	54.0
Chester	554	348	62.9

church[25]. Five years later the curate of Bradford offered a similar explanation to Archbishop Herring of York. 'In yt Part of ye Chapelry which more immediately concerns me there are about 423 Families in a very wide and dispersed neighbourhood', he wrote, adding that most of the ninety Dissenting or Recusant families among them were clustered in 'a remote corner' of the chapelry[26]. Many Anglican ministers faced similar difficulties, but the problem of defection from the Establishment was destined to get far worse before moves would be made to subdivide such outsized parishes.

Yet even in 1743 Methodists were beginning to exploit the strained condition of the parochial system in northern England. Methodism was present in eight Yorkshire parishes, Herring discovered, each of them exceptionally large and containing several townships. The new movement had taken root in out-townships, moreover, not in the centres of parish life. In head-townships, where parochial administration tended to be at its most effective, Methodist progress had been minimal. Further Visitation Returns in 1764 indicated that this trend had continued: while 'small groups had formed Methodist societies in most

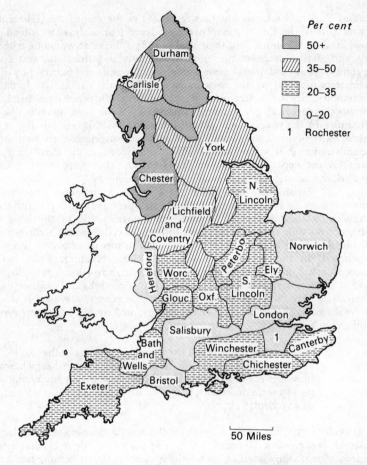

Fig. 5.2 Number of benefices with a population of 300 and over requiring augmentation in 1836, as a percentage of all benefices. *See Table 5.2*

out-townships within the huge parishes', growth in the head-townships had been slow[27].

Unamenable land tenure patterns: freeholding

Archbishop Herring might have discovered serious problems of religious deviance in outsized and overpopulated parishes, but in the compact 'lowland' villages of the Vale of York, where the average parish was small and the influence of squire and parson formidable, the problem was virtually non-existent. The strength of the 'dependency system', and consequently the existence of an Anglican paternalism, would long defy the forces of social change in such areas. Landlordism was so powerful around York, a Wesleyan itinerant remarked at the end of the eighteenth century, that the local farmers were as dependent as 'vassals', dreading their local squire more than their 'Maker'[28] . The same would be true in this and similar areas at the end of the early industrial era, and even beyond it. 'Lowland' parish boundaries generally followed natural physical perimeters dictated by the agricultural requirements of a single farming community. Such parishes were small and their inhabitants resided in a compact village[29]. A resident squire or parson was thus in close proximity to the people under his jurisdiction. But this was not the only reason why typical 'lowland' parishes were susceptible to parochial administration and squirearchic control. They formed the ideal environment for the dependency system partly because they were characterised by a relative absence of smallholding and rural industry.

Parishes in which there was a significant incidence of freehold tenure, or in which smallhold farming was prevalent and the ratio of labourers to farmers relatively low, were unamenable to the kind of influence possible in 'closed villages' (sometimes called 'squire's villages' or 'manorial villages') where the entire population was more or less directly dependent on the economic power of a single landlord. What David Thompson has discovered in a study of Leicestershire—that 'open villages' tended to have significantly lower rates of Anglican religious practice than 'squire's villages'[30]—appears to have been true generally. A sample study of rural areas of Lincolnshire, Leicestershire, and Kent has led Alan Everitt to the conclusion that

> at least three-quarters of the Dissenting groups in the
> countryside were to be found in freeholders' parishes; whereas
> in 80 per cent of the estate parishes, or wherever squire and
> parson were dominant, there was no organised Nonconformity
> of any kind[31].

It is evident that one of the reasons for the association between 'highland' pastoral regions and Nonconformist religiosity was the fact that such regions were distinguished by smallholdings and scattered farming hamlets.

The farther one travelled into the West Country, for example, the fewer and farther between became the nucleated, landlord-dominated villages so characteristic of the south-east. They gave way to dispersed farmsteads, smallholdings, and a dearth of resident landed gentry[32]. Similarly in Wales, a Nonconformist stronghold *par excellence*, a feature of rural settlement patterns was 'the prevalence of a large number of small, separate farms of what may be described as the peasant and family type'[33]; and in the north of England hamlets and small farms, not compact villages, constituted the most characteristic form of rural settlement[34].

The spread of Nonconformity in rural areas in the eighteenth and early nineteenth centuries correlated highly with these 'highland' land tenure and settlement patterns. In Wales the success of Nonconformist evangelism among the farming population was part of a general Nonconformist domination of the Principality. In Cornwall 'yeomen' (freehold farmers) were prominent in Wesleyanism, and it was from the scattered farmsteads that the Bible Christians drew a substantial proportion of their recruits[35]. It is significant that the geographical limits of the Bible Christian Connexion (the Nonconformist body most exclusively rural in social character) coincided with the fringes of the pastoral agricultural zone stretching from Cornwall, Devon, and western Somerset, through the 'highland' parishes of central Dorset, and into the forest and heathland districts of southern Hampshire and the Isle of Wight[36]. And in Yorkshire, while Anglicanism was firmly in control of 'lowland' parishes like Tadcaster, Knaresborough, York, Thirsk, and Northallerton, all compact arable farming parishes in the Vale of York, it had by 1851 been overtaken by Nonconformity among the scattered rural populations of the Pennine moorlands, the North Yorkshire Moors, and the Wolds[37].

Cornwall and Yorkshire, of course, were areas in which the parochial system faced many difficulties, some of them more serious than the problems raised by smallholding and scattered settlement patterns. In Yorkshire it was in industrial rather than rural areas that the crisis facing the Established Church was greatest; in Cornwall the most serious problems were in mining districts. The effects of unamenable land tenure arrangements were therefore most obvious in areas where such arrangements were atypical: where nucleated settlements and squirearchic authority were normal. The incumbent at Ambrosden, near Otmoor in Oxfordshire, was plainly aware of a link between religious practice in his parish in the middle of the nineteenth century, and the unusual land tenure patterns of the Otmoor district[38]. It was because land ownership was 'very much divided', he told Bishop Wilberforce, that Nonconformists were strong in Ambrosden[39].

Another atypical area in the predominantly 'lowland' south Midlands was the Lambourn district of the Berkshire Downs, where Wesleyanism had attracted the support of certain freehold farmers. A local preacher, Thomas Bush, was remembered at his death in 1849 not only for his tireless efforts to carry Methodism into the 'lowland' parishes of the Vale of the White Horse, but also because as an independent freeholder he had led a successful resistance against an 'influential combination' of landlords seeking to deny employment to all farm labourers who failed to attend Anglican in preference to Nonconformist worship[40]. Similar examples of the relationship between landholding patterns which fostered independence from the 'influencing classes', and receptivity to Nonconformity, have been cited by Chalklin, Everitt, and Finberg[41].

Unamenable land tenure patterns: extra-parochial settlements

Nucleated 'lowland' parish communities still accounted for much of the English population in the period immediately before the Industrial Revolution. But it is evident that settlement patterns unamenable to the proper functioning of the parochial system had gradually become less anomalous during the sixteenth, seventeenth and eighteenth centuries. The startling pace of population growth after about 1740 tends to divert attention from the much slower rate of increase which, nonetheless, had produced a doubling of the total English population during the previous 300 years[42]. The larger population had to be accommodated. But, ironically for the Church, the 'lowland', common field districts of England—the strongholds of rural Anglicanism—had positively resisted population growth. In nucleated, highly manorialised communities, 'manorial control had considerable effect in discouraging the immigration of outsiders and squatters on the waste, and the partitioning of land by tenants'[43]. Thus the economic interests of the landlord, who was in other respects becoming the main ally of the parson, had the effect of isolating the parochial clergy from an increasing proportion of the rural population.

The parochial system had been made for communities of men, and where no such communities had existed in medieval England and Wales there were usually no parishes during the following five-and-a-half centuries. Large tracts of country, as well as numerous small pockets of land adjacent to parish boundaries, were 'extraparochial' in status. If settlements sprang up in such areas they were technically and very often actually isolated from the religious and civil controls and services associated with the parochial system[44]. Clearly, extraparochial land had acquired its status because, for one reason or another, it had discouraged settlement. The largest tracts were in forest and marshland areas, and on heaths and moors, which light, poor soil placed below the margin of viable cultivation until the introduction of agricultural improvements and new crops in the eighteenth and early nineteenth centuries[45].

The pressures of population growth, combined with the social pressures limiting population density in established farming regions, made these extraparochial tracts the foci of the most rapid rural population expansion during the period from the sixteenth to the early nineteenth century. Throughout this period there was constant encroachment of settlement into what remained of the Midland forests of Arden, Charnwood, Knaresborough, Rockingham, Sherwood, Wychwood, and Wyre; into the forest areas of Essex, Kent, and Sussex in the south-east; and into the New Forest, the Forest of Dean, and the forest areas of Cranbourne Chase, Savernake, and Bere in the south. Under the Stuarts the great freshwater marshes of the Norfolk, Lincolnshire, and Cambridgeshire Fens, and the Isle of Axholme, were reclaimed by arterial drainage: where there once had been extensive, thinly populated parishes and much extraparochial land, there was by the late eighteenth century intensive agriculture and domestic industry. The problem, as far as the Church was concerned, was that while the population had grown enormously the extensive parishes and the extraparochial lacunae remained[46].

In an important article on rural Nonconformity Everitt has explored various examples of the association between receptiveness to Nonconformity and the existence of isolated or extraparochial settlements which had been established in the seventeenth and eighteenth centuries by the annexation of forest and heathland areas[47]. These settlements, and those which had grown up on unstinted commons, could rarely be assimilated fully into the 'dependency system', and were therefore without effective pastoral oversight even when technically within parochial jurisdiction. The 'cottagers' who inhabited them were commonly regarded as 'sauntering', 'indolent', and less deferential than other social groups 'in the same rank of society'[48]. These traits were noted especially when negotiations about enclosure schemes were in hand, because, like freeholders, cottagers proved less subject to social 'influence' or economic coercion than tenant farmers or day-labourers. 'Many of the commoners', W. E. Tate has written, 'were, and could fairly well afford to be, independent of day labour for an employer'[49]. They were *ipso facto* more open to Nonconformist mobilisation than most rural populations.

Their independence reflected not only their removal from the centres of parochial life, but also their marginal position within the occupational structure of rural society. For a frequent characteristic of the new settlements was some kind of domestic industry. Thus a typical extraparochial community, Lye Waste in Worcestershire, 'consisted chiefly of nailmakers, and of cottagers employed in the local iron and coal works'; and Walton, in Leicestershire, a classic example of an isolated boundary settlement, contained during the reign of George III 'a number of shopkeepers and craftsmen among its inhabitants, and probably many more framework-knitters than farm workers'[50]. Both these communities had strong Nonconformist traditions by the late eighteenth century, as did the relatively recent industrial villages of the Weald of Kent, the Isle of Axholme, and the Northamptonshire forests.

The manufacturing or mining settlement in an extraparochial or isolated district, or on an unstinted common, illustrated a tendency for the various factors undermining the dependency system to reinforce one another. Spatial isolation from the hegemony of squire and parson weakened the social pressures towards religious conformity; but this very isolation was in many cases partly a consequence of the tendency for marginal socio-occupational groups to eschew the cohesive agrarian communities in which the Church was strongest. Thus in many instances the threats to parochial effectiveness posed by the spatial isolation of parishioners on the one hand, and the cultural insulation of particular occupational groups from Establishment 'influence' on the other, were mutually reinforcing.

The 'independence' of marginal occupational groups

But even where the socio-occupational factor operated alone, it could create a context for Nonconformist encroachment. Indeed, involvement in a trade, or in manufacturing, mining, or commerce, represented perhaps the most obvious avenue of emancipation from the dependency system even before the full impact of the Industrial Revolution was felt. Non-agrarian occupations did not guarantee emancipation, of course. In a 'squire's village' (to take the extreme example) the cobbler, wheelwright, blacksmith, miller or shopkeeper was closely integrated into the local economy, and dependent on it. His house, workshop, or store, or the land on which they stood, belonged ultimately to the squire; and his livelihood rested on the patronage of the squire, the squire's tenants, and the local rural labourers. He was thus enmeshed in the web of deferential relationships almost as completely as everyone else in such a village.

Village society was not always so cohesive, however, even in predominantly agricultural areas; and it was no accident that the typical 'village politician' was an artisan[51]. Throughout the eighteenth century artisans had been over-represented in movements of popular economic and social protest, as had miners, and indeed all occupational groups which, for whatever reasons, were relatively free from 'the revenges of village paternalism'[52]. Similarly, when Nonconformity gained access to an agricultural village it was the artisan and trading element of the population which usually showed the greatest willingness to court the displeasure of squire and parson by religious deviance[53].

George Eliot made this point in a perceptive comment on the social basis of Methodist support in a fictional agricultural village in the Midlands around the close of the eighteenth century. A stranger to 'Hayslope' remarked to the local tavern-keeper:

> But you've not got many Methodists about here, surely—in this agricultural spot? I should have thought there would hardly be such a thing as a Methodist to be found about here. You're all farmers, aren't you? The Methodists can seldom lay much hold on *them* [54].

But although in reply the tavern-keeper pointed out that Methodism had made a significant impact in the village, he nevertheless confirmed the assumptions underlying the question. 'Why, sir, there's a pretty lot o' workmen round about, sir,' he said, pointing out that the village possessed a timber yard, that it was close to a stone quarry and a market town, and that the two Methodists actually resident in it were a carpenter and a wheelwright[55].

Increasing the verisimilitude of the account, Eliot cast the visiting Wesleyan preacher as a factory worker from a populous district thirty miles away (not in 'Loamshire' but in a barren, hilly area of 'Stony-shire'), where outwork villages had sprung up around a cotton-mill[56]. The contrast between 'Loamshire' and 'Stonyshire' was significant. For if the artisan in a predominantly agricultural village often had greater freedom within the traditional authority structure than did most of his fellow villagers, he had considerably less than the typical inhabitant of a manufacturing, mining, or fishing village.

The tendency for non-agrarian occupational groups to be more receptive to Nonconformity than groups involved in arable farming was evident to churchmen and Dissenters alike, and both parties recognised its connexion with the strength of the dependency system. In the summer of 1796, accompanied by a young probationer minister, John Saffery and William Steadman (two of the leading Baptist ministers of the generation after 1790), left their home churches in the basically agricultural county of Hampshire on a preaching tour of the West Country[57]. They were struck by the fact that most Cornishmen, being either miners or fishermen, were 'more in a state of independence, and less subject to the influence of superiors, who may be hostile to itinerant preaching', than the inhabitants of counties which depended 'wholly upon agriculture'[58]. Similar remarks characterised the reports of many Nonconformist itinerants throughout the era of rapid expansion[59], and in Wales, during the bitter sectarian and political confrontations of the late 1850s and the 1860s, while both tenant farmers and quarrymen were subject to pressures exercised by Conservative Anglican employers, the latter stood firm *en bloc* while the former generally succumbed to 'the screw'. 'The men in the quarries are independent', a local Nonconformist leader explained to a Parliamentary Committee in 1869, 'much more independent than the farmers'[60].

With comparable certainty but with none of the Nonconformist satisfaction, an Anglican incumbent wrote in 1807 of the impact on parish life in the Midlands of the proliferation of domestic industry in weaving and framework knitting. The parish populations were no longer communities, he complained. Gone was the common economic dependence on a landlord by which 'the proper influence of the clergy' had been 'backed and supported', and in its place was a new dependence on 'a master tradesman in a town at some distance'[61]. As another churchman, Robert Southey, explained in 1820, industry, even in rural parishes, created a network of economic and social relationships which cut across those on which the parochial ideal rested[62].

The problem of urban parishes

However great the difficulties were elsewhere, it was in urban areas that the parochial system was most consistently unworkable. The various factors which acted as solvents of parochial effectiveness—the pastoral problems arising from inadequate endowments and absenteeism, the logistics problems associated with overpopulated parishes, and the socio-cultural conditions which contributed to the breakdown of the dependency system—united in large towns and cities to isolate the clergy, physically and culturally, from their putative parishioners.

Ironically, the urban parishes of England and Wales had been better provided for before the Reformation, when they were less populous, than they were between the Reformation and the beginning of the Industrial Revolution. The decline of personal tithing as a source of ecclesiastical revenue in the sixteenth century had impoverished urban benefices. In London, for example, the actual number of parishes had been reduced from 140 to 108, in Norwich there remained thirty-seven parishes where once there had been seventy, and in each city many of the parishes which survived had been left with an endowment too meagre to support a resident incumbent[63]. Smaller urban centres had faced similar problems. In 1634 Archbishop Laud had complained that 'the vicars in the great market towns, where the people are very many, are for the most part worst provided for'[64]. Significantly, during Nonconformity's rapid expansion in the period after 1740 market towns were conspicuous as regional centres in the propagation of the movement. But Laud need not have singled out market towns, nor the specific problem of inadequate endowment, to exemplify the vulnerability of the Church in urban settlements. Indeed, market towns, because they owed their existence to localised trading networks rather than large-scale manufacturing or commercial concerns, were more closely implicated in the dependency system than most urban settlements.

There was an 'ideological cleavage' between town and country well before the Industrial Revolution[65]. Townspeople valued their relative freedom from the authority and influence of aristocratic and landed society, a freedom sometimes guaranteed by Royal Charter and sometimes resting simply on the social realities of commercial and industrial power, and on the cultural peculiarities of urban life. In urban parishes the alliance of the Church with landed wealth and power could be a positive disadvantage. As Malcolm Thomis has explained in his study of the growth of Nottingham, once a town had achieved the size and independent economic power which enabled it to throw off the shackles of 'aristocratic influence' (around the middle of the eighteenth century in the case of Nottingham), 'the Established Church and its clergy had but little influence'[66].

Ominously for the parochial system, Nottingham was only one of many northern and Midland towns which, around the middle of the eighteenth century, achieved the size and the independent economic importance which rendered them virtually impervious to the traditional social forces of influence and dependency. Previously the problem of urban gaps in the parochial system had been fairly limited and more or less constant. In 1695, apart from the Metropolis with its 500,000 inhabitants, only Norwich and Bristol had populations exceeding 25,000; and besides them, Birmingham, with 12,000 inhabitants, was the only town containing more than 10,000 people[67]. By 1750 Liverpool, Birmingham and Manchester had populations approaching or exceeding 25,000, and the expansion of smaller towns (like Nottingham), together with the spread of virtually contiguous industrial villages in certain areas, represented the early stages of what was to become a dramatic process of urbanisation.

The demographic and Industrial Revolutions

It was no coincidence that the 'demographic revolution' (the rapid and sustained growth and geographical redistribution of the population which began around 1740)[68], and the Industrial Revolution, both made their initial impact upon English society during the era of optimum Nonconformist growth. The foregoing analysis has identified typical situations in which the parochial system became vulnerable to Nonconformist encroachment. Significantly, none of these situations was *peculiar* to the period of intense industrialisation, urbanisation, and rapid population expansion. The demographic and economic revolutions damaged the parochial system, and enlarged the context for Nonconformist growth, not by creating but by proliferating the kinds of situations in which the machinery of the religious Establishment broke down.

In summary terms, the parochial system in pre-industrial society had been considerably stronger in the south, the south Midlands, and the south-east than elsewhere in England; it had been stronger in agricultural areas than among populations engaged in manufacturing or commerce; it had been stronger where it had been able to function in close alliance with the 'landed interest'. It had, in short, been best adapted to those regions, occupational groups, and cultural contexts which contained the bulk of the population. Apart from those caused by pastoral negligence, as late as 1740 the gaps in the parochial system could, with a certain justification, either be attributed to atypical socio-cultural conditions, or ignored because they were confined to the underpopulated fringes of the Church's jurisdiction.

But in 1740 the pre-industrial social order was on the point of becoming, in Laslett's phrase, 'the world we have lost'. A century later, demographic and industrial processes had gone far towards reversing pre-industrial patterns of population distribution and occupational structure, the urban—rural balance was tilting in favour of urban settlement, and the traditional economic basis of political power and social influence was in danger of being engulfed. The proportion of the population engaged in non-agricultural occupations had risen from around 20 per cent at the end of the seventeenth century to well over 50 per cent by the beginning of the nineteenth[69]. It was 65 per cent in 1811 and over 70 per cent in 1831[70]. Similarly, urbanisation had proceeded apace. The inhabitants of settlements of over 5,000 people, a small minority of the population in 1750, accounted for one person in three by 1801, and by 1851 for half the population[71].

The Church of England increased its physical and manpower resources scarcely at all during the period between 1741 and 1821, and only slowly thereafter until the end of the 1830s[72]. Meanwhile, the population of England and Wales had risen from 6,013,000 in 1741 to 15,914,000 in 1841: an increase of almost 10 million or 165 per cent[73]. Yet such stark figures actually minimise the extent of the crisis facing the religious Establishment. For not only was the most rapid population growth occurring in urban settlements and among the kinds of occupational groups least amenable to parochial supervision, but there was a pronounced bias of population growth in favour of the northern counties and the north and west Midlands. As Tables and Figs 5.1 and 5.2 have indicated, these were areas in which the parochial system was particularly ill-equipped to cope with increased pastoral responsibilities.

Industrialisation may not have become a 'revolutionary' process until the 1780s, but for several decades previously new population foci had been emerging with the expansion of various mining and manufacturing industries in the Midlands and the north. A massive demand for labour had accompanied the tremendous growth of cotton production in Lancashire, Cheshire, Nottinghamshire, and Leicestershire, especially from about 1770 onwards. By the final quarter of the eighteenth century, after a series of crucial technological innovations, iron and coal industries were expanding rapidly in Northumberland and Durham, in the east Pennine field stretching from Yorkshire into Derbyshire and Nottinghamshire, and in the Lancashire, Warwickshire, and Staffordshire field on the western side of the Pennines. The rise of manufacturing villages in the woollen and worsted industrial areas around Halifax, Huddersfield, Wakefield, Bradford, and Leeds was contributing to a rapid increase in the population density of the West Riding during the second half of the century; and on a smaller scale the same demographic process was being repeated in the Potteries of northern Staffordshire. 'Since the potteries were introduced', Wesley wrote in 1781, reviewing the previous twenty years in the Burslem area, 'inhabitants have continually flowed in from every side. Hence the wilderness is literally become a fruitful field. Houses, villages, towns, have sprung up'[74].

In comparison, population growth in the older manufacturing and mining counties of Worcestershire, Somerset, and Devon, and in the older woollen centres of the West Country and East Anglia, had been slow[75]; and between 1701 and 1831, while the population of the primarily agricultural counties had more than doubled, in counties where industry and commerce predominated it had tripled or quadrupled[76]. The trend, in other words, had tended to transfer the population balance from agrarian to manufacturing and industrial areas, and from southern and south-eastern England to the Midlands and the north.

Up to 1840, in these latter areas, the expanding population was absorbed less by the growth of large industrial and commercial cities than by the proliferation of industrial villages and small factory and mining settlements. Large towns and cities did develop, of course. Towns of more than 20,000 inhabitants in 1850 had grown at twice the rate of the total population during the Industrial Revolution[77]. But this was a rate slower than that of the *industrial* population generally. The modern conurbations of the north-west, the west Midlands, the West Riding and north Midlands, and the north-east, were products of a later stage of Britain's economic development. Before 1840 the characteristic settlement pattern in such areas was determined by the survival of capitalistic out-work as the predominant form of industrial organisation. It was a system which encouraged the spread of semi-urban industrial villages which were dependent on mines, factories, and manufacturing towns.

Domestic industry, in fact, provided a social and economic bridge between pre-industrial and modern industrial society. The geographical location of industrial development was determined by pre-industrial settlement and occupational patterns as well as by the availability of resources and commercial outlets. Thus it was in forest and woodland areas of Warwickshire, Worcestershire, and Staffordshire, which displayed the interconnected characteristics of late settlement, widespread freehold tenure, and minimal manorial control, that the craft industries of the west Midlands emerged, initially in conjunction with pastoral farming, but by the eighteenth century increasingly independent of it[78]. It was these industries, and others like them, which technological innovation transformed into major centres of the English Industrial Revolution. In assessing the failure of the Church of England to cope with the social consequences of the Industrial Revolution, it is important to recognise that the very social and demographic factors which had tended to weaken the parochial system in pre-industrial society were instrumental also in encouraging industrialisation.

Domestic industry was itself in the long run a casualty of the Industrial Revolution. But the effect of early industrialisation was to expand it immensely. Significantly, of the artisans attracted to Nonconformist communities, most were involved in one or another of the outwork industries which reached their zenith in the late eighteenth and early nineteenth centuries. Handloom weavers (to consider a single category of outworker) increased in number from about 50,000 in 1769 to 240,000 in 1820, mainly in response to increased employment opportunities created by the impact on the spinning side of the industry of the spinning-jenny and the water-frame[79]. Their numbers decreased thereafter—rather earlier than those of other types of outworker—because the adoption of the powerloom had the effect of transforming weaving into a factory industry. But in the intervening period they had provided a large and highly receptive catchment area for Nonconformity.

In a study of Nonconformist growth these related, and essentially transient phenomena, the boom of domestic industry and the proliferation of small-scale industrial settlements, are of immense importance. Domestic industry was transient because it was a rudimentary phenomenon in the evolution of the factory system; and the industrial village was transient because its almost inevitable fate was to be engulfed as the boundaries of a neighbouring city crept steadily outwards. But it was in the early industrial society of which both phenomena were characteristic that Nonconformity enjoyed its maximum success. As the 1851 Census revealed, huge cities might have contained more Nonconformists than Anglicans, but they generally defeated the evangelistic efforts of Church and Chapel alike[80]. It is imprecise to conclude simply that Nonconformity thrived most where the parochial system had broken down, for in certain circumstances Anglican failure reflected the triumph of social forces hostile to organised religion *per se*.

In an early explication of the link between urbanisation and institutional secularisation, Horace Mann argued that the 'new cities' of the Industrial Revolution were destructive of community sense. They had been 'erected more for business than for residence', and were 'mere aggregates of offices and workshops and overcrowded dwellings of the subordinate agents of industry'. Their inhabitants did not form coherent communities which could be mobilised to sustain a local church. In the industrial city, Mann explained, 'the influence of community' was dead: the area of undifferentiated settlement was 'too extensive', the multitude was 'too vast', to encourage the kinds of circumscribed social and cultural groupings which, elsewhere, provided readymade catchment areas for local religious associations[81].

The statistical evidence plainly required some such explanation, and subsequent attempts to interpret both the census data and mounting confirmatory evidence about religion and urbanisation have tended to endorse Mann's hypothesis (which was itself not new in 1853)[82]. Community sense collapsed in the industrial city, E. R. Wickham has concluded after a case-study of Sheffield, 'leaving man a stranger to his neighbour', and reducing society to 'a mass of faces in the High Street'[83]. This claim is sociologically simplistic, of course. In certain circumstances communities of residence *do* exhibit a high degree of cohesion in modern industrial cities. But they are communities of a distinctive type, self-consciously 'working-class' and unlike the older communities which had been based on a functional, albeit uneasy, integration of different classes. Organised religion, tending with an apparent inevitability in its denominational phase towards a middle class, professional leadership, has never been particularly welcome within them. Thus while the associational dimension of religious commitment can be effectively sustained only where a church or chapel congregation is linked with some viable community[84], the history of English religion from the late eighteenth century onwards has offered little evidence that religious associations can themselves provide the basis for fashioning communities out of an amorphous urban population, or of mobilising the particular kinds of communities which do emerge in urban contexts. Small sects may have succeeded in these tasks. But for large-scale religious movements, growth has depended on the capacity to exploit existing social structures rather than on the power to change or override them.

The ability to exploit early industrial social structures was one of the secrets of Methodist success. 'The very organisation that Wesley imposed on the Methodist Society', Elie Halévy wrote in 1906.

> seems to have been based upon the organisation of the industrial society at the time when Wesley went preaching from town to town. . . . In both schemes of organisation, the similar hierarchical orders corresponded to the half-urban, half-rural distribution of the population[85].

But what the young Methodist movement was able to achieve in a society in transition, the more mature Methodist organisations of the Victorian era failed to achieve in the sprawling industrial cities. 'The circuit system,' Hugh Price Hughes's *Methodist Times* observed in 1886, 'has, for the purpose of effective aggression, completely broken down in all the great cities'[86]. The enterprise of Methodism was flagging by 1886, but in any case Victorian cities were not open to the kinds of mobilisation which had succeeded in the 'half-urban, half-rural' populations of the previous century.

The early stages of industrialisation, in other words, had contributed to the breakdown of the parochial system without at the same time creating a cultural climate hostile to Nonconformity. Not only were parochial facilities generally meagre in the areas of major industrial development, but the new industrial settlements seldom coincided exactly with the prior deployment of what physical and human resources there were. Mining development, for obvious reasons, was no respecter of pre-industrial settlement patterns; and until the use of steam power became widespread after the Napoleonic Wars, most factories were built on the banks of streams, often well away from existing population centres[87]. But these settlements were at once small enough (if often virtually contiguous), and recent enough, for many of their often transient inhabitants to retain values inherited from rural community life, and perhaps even to retain a conscious demand for the satisfactions of religious associations[88].

William Cleaver, the non-resident Bishop of Chester and Master of Oxford's Brasenose College, recognised in 1799 that the demand for Nonconformity in his diocese was in many cases a simple response to a massive failure in the supply of parochial services. The Church had been swamped by the extremely rapid growth of the population in the north-west, he told his clergy, and the people flooding into Nonconformist chapels were motivated, not by preference for deviant doctrines or disciplines, but by 'that natural interest which the mind takes in religious services, to which though under a different mode it has been early habituated'[89].

This was a popular theory of Nonconformist growth among contemporary churchmen. Man was naturally religious, its proponents stated or implied, and if the Church failed to satisfy his religious needs then he would turn to Dissent[90]. True up to a point, the theory left several problems unsolved. It failed to accommodate the fact that many of those neglected by the Church did not become Nonconformists, even when presented with an opportunity for doing so; and it skirted the problem that people in the largest cities, who were the most neglected of all, displayed little of the 'natural interest' in religious services which led others into Dissent. The theory was applicable, for a generation or so, to people separated by migration from the associations and religious facilities of rural society, but not plunged directly into the areligious culture of some large city. It applied, in short, primarily to the industrial villages and outwork settlements of early industrial society: to the era and to the social structures of transition from pre-industrial to modern urban society.

As Bishop Cleaver argued, people turned to Dissent who, having been 'habituated' to conformist practice, were suddenly deprived of the facilities for it. But it was also true that the demand for an alternative to Anglicanism grew weaker as old habits were destroyed by time or by the pressures of an entirely new cultural environment. A later Bishop of Chester, John Bird Sumner, considered in 1832 that it already had become too late for church-building or clerical residence to remedy many of the gaps created in the parochial system by past neglect. A generation had grown up whose habits predisposed them to religious apathy, not religious practice, he said, 'and the present age is lamenting, when too late, and vainly endeavouring to repair, the culpable indifference of those who lived before them'[91]. For Nonconformist encroachment as much as for Anglican recovery, the receptiveness of neglected populations diminished as isolation from religious services became routinised by the passage of time. By the mid-1840s the populations to whom Methodists traditionally had 'access' had become much more difficult to mobilise than 'in the early days of Methodism', Wesleyan leaders admitted, noting that the problem affected their Connexion 'in common with other churches'[92].

The problem of 'Tillyard's thesis'

In the case of Methodism various studies have demonstrated clearly a high correlation between Anglican weakness and the growth of extra-Establishment religious practice. Using county data, Robert Currie has compared the regional distribution of Wesleyan membership with that of Anglican churches in 1781 and 1851, and has shown that 'the bulk of Wesleyan membership and the greatest sustained Wesleyan growth occurred in precisely the areas where the Church of England was weakest'[93]. Other studies of national and local data have confirmed this conclusion, and shown it to be applicable to the smaller Methodist bodies as well as to Wesleyanism[94].

But while the significance of spatial isolation from the Church of England has been carefully analysed in studies of Methodist growth, the growth of the Congregational and Baptist denominations has not been examined with the same precision, at least as a nationwide phenomenon. Indeed, the very inquiries which have confirmed the inverse relationship between Methodist and Anglican strength have suggested that a quite different relationship existed between the Church and the growth of the older Nonconformist bodies. In an article published in 1935 Tillyard calculated, on a county basis, the ratios of full-time ministers to total population for each of the major denominations. The analysis suggested that the distribution of Methodism *complemented* that of the Congregational and Baptist denominations: that Methodism tended to be strong where the other Nonconformist bodies were *weak* [95]. Similarly, the county data analysed by Currie indicated that while

> the older dissent generally grew strong where the Church of England was strong, deriving (at least historically) much of its membership directly from the Church of England, Methodism grew strong where the Church of England was weak, and recruited from those sections of the population that Anglicanism failed to reach [96].

These correlations between county indices of Congregational–Baptist, Anglican, and Methodist strength cannot be ignored. Whether the specific index used relates to ministers, churches, attendants, or church accommodation, the patterns suggest the same tendencies of Methodist strength to complement, and Congregational and Baptist strength to coincide with, the strength of the Established Church [97]. But the evidence does not necessarily imply that the older denominations grew for reasons quite different from those underlying Methodist expansion: that while Methodism exploited gaps in the parochial system, Congregational and Baptist recruiting prospered in direct competition with Anglicanism. What Gay has called 'Tillyard's thesis' does not, as he has suggested, provide evidence of the danger of treating Nonconformity as a homogeneous phenomenon of growth [98].

County patterns of denominational strength do contribute to the explication of Nonconformist growth processes, but they also obscure the existence of crucial local variations of religious adherence. The particular circumstances of individual parishes and groups of parishes were what determined the chances of Nonconformist success; and (as this chapter has argued) there were numerous deficiencies in the parochial system even in counties in which, overall, the Church appeared very strong. Pastoral neglect, outsized parishes, unamenable land tenure patterns, remote or recalcitrant extraparochial communities, market towns, and occupation groups sufficiently emancipated from the dependency system to engage in religious deviance, made the parochial system of southern, south Midland, and south-eastern counties vulnerable to Nonconformist encroachment on a considerable scale.

A recurrent theme in descriptions of areas which had proved receptive to Congregational and Baptist itinerancy in the late eighteenth and early nineteenth centuries was that the inhabitants had been previously 'neglected', that they had been 'destitute of the means of religious improvement', and that there had been 'no place of worship' available for them. The county associations and unions, and the itinerant and home missionary societies of the older denominations, were all constitutionally committed to concentrate their evangelistic efforts in towns and villages not being reached by other forms of organised religion. They were able to adopt this policy, moreover, despite the location of most of their operations in counties in which the Church was ostensibly strong. It is noteworthy that although the Congregational Society in London for Spreading the Gospel in England supported financially only those itinerants who were 'carrying the Gospel where it would not otherwise be heard', almost 90 per cent of the work it patronised in 1798 was being carried out in the south, the south Midlands, or southern East Anglia[99].

Table 5.3 Parish size and the relative strength of Anglicanism and Nonconformity in south-eastern England

Population of parish	Percentage of population accommodated by the Church	Anglican accommodation as a percentage of Nonconformist accommodation
Under 100	141.3	2,100.0
100–499	58.8	340.0
500–999	48.7	220.0
1,000–1,999	43.2	190.0
2,000–4,999	22.2	150.0
5,000–9,999	22.5	86.0

Note
The table is based on a sample of 832 parishes, most of them in Kent and Norfolk

Tables 5.3 and 5.4 provide statistical confirmation that in southern and northern England alike one feature of the typical context of Nonconformist growth was Anglican weakness. Apart from non-residence, parish population is perhaps the most obvious available index of Anglican weakness. Parochial church accommodation was rarely adequate for more than a few hundred participants, and pastoral effectiveness was in any case incompatible with high ratios of parishioners to clergy. Richard Yates noted in 1817 that a population of 640 people had traditionally been considered appropriate for an average parish, and while he conceded that the ideal might no longer be attainable he was aware that a single incumbent could not have responsibility for too many more parishioners without being unable to discharge his duties properly[100]. By the middle of the century the Ecclesiastical Commissioners, having come to terms with reality, were limiting their particular concerns to parishes with populations of 3,000 or over, and they had set 4,000 inhabitants as a maximum figure[101].

Table 5.4   Parish population and opposition to church rates

County or region	No. of parishes where church rate was opposed	Average population of all parishes	Average population of dissident parishes
Lancashire	25	8,350	22,000
London/Middlesex	16	7,150	19,150
Sussex	4	874	17,700
Warwickshire	9	1,640	16,550
Yorkshire	54	2,240	14,275
Northumberland	12	2,621	11,220
Cheshire	8	3,680	10,560
Staffordhire	17	2,895	10,360
Hampshire	14	997	8,850
Nottinghamshire	11	1,065	6,550
Westmorland	3	1,720	6,495
Kent	18	1,172	6,370
Surrey	9	3,450	6,200
Durham	10	3,340	5,990
Worcestershire	10	1,255	5,040
Essex	14	780	4,640
Devonshire	16	958	4,570
Northamptonshire	11	591	4,175
Bedfordshire	9	775	3,940
Cornwall	17	1,470	3,840
Derbyshire	10	1,705	3,780
Gloucestershire	13	1,140	3,750
Berkshire	5	945	2,790
Hertfordshire	4	1,076	2,660
Suffolk	8	582	2,660
Lincolnshire	19	502	2,500
Dorsetshire	8	595	2,430
Somersetshire	16	851	2,360
Wiltshire	7	800	2,300
Herefordshire	5	507	2,095
Leicestershire	8	929	1,965
Cambridgeshire	10	878	1,930
Cumberland	3	1,625	1,820
Buckinghamshire	13	730	1,530
Norfolk	24	534	1,465
Huntingdonshire	9	525	930
Shropshire	2	1,036	763
Oxfordshire	6	700	418
Rutland	—	389	—

Notes
1   Opposition included the rejection of a proposed rate by a Vestry

Notes to Table 5.4 — *continued*

       Meeting, or the refusal by individuals to pay a rate which had been levied.

2   Opposition does not include parishes in which no rate had been levied during the previous fifteen years, even though failure to initiate a levy often reflected the certainty of rejection. The *Protestant Dissenters' Almanack and Political Annual of the Year 1857* noted that of the 6,000—7,000 parishes from which returns had been made, two had had no rate levied for every one refusing a rate. The Almanack also pointed out that parishes where no rate had been levied were on average about six times the size of those in which a rate had been successful.

3   Returns were not received from more than 3,000 parishes. The figures on 'Average Population of all Parishes', however, are based on all the parishes in each county, irrespective of whether they made a return to the Parliamentary Committee.

Table 5.3 is based on a sample of 832 parishes extracted by Horace Mann from the 1851 Census returns. The bulk of these parishes were in Kent and Norfolk, and parishes of over 10,000 inhabitants were excluded by Mann on the grounds that most of them were in large towns, and so would 'introduce another question besides that of *size* into the question of comparative accommodation'. The sample, albeit somewhat unscientific, provides a cross-sectional view of the relationship between parish population and Nonconformist encroachment in the south-east before 1851. The evidence is unmistakable. The strength of Nonconformity varied inversely with the demographic size of parishes.

      Statistical evidence testing this relationship nationally is not readily available in either government or denominational sources. Indirectly, however, a Parliamentary Paper published in 1856, which dealt on a parochial basis with the refusal to levy or pay church rates, can be used to make deductions about the kinds of parishes in which Nonconformity was strong[102]. Five years earlier a Select Committee on Church Rates had reported that 'the non-conformist element' was 'the chief element in stimulating opposition to church rates'[103], and in the comments from individual parishes published in the 1856 Report this conclusion was fully substantiated. Table 5.4 is based on an analysis of returns from over 7,000 parishes, and relates the average population of parishes refusing a church rate to the average population of all parishes in each county of England. With the exception of Oxfordshire and Shropshire, where the samples were small, in every county parishes refusing a church rate were on average more populous, usually very much more populous, than was the normal parish within their county area.

      As Nonconformists were quick to point out on the publication of the Report, figures on refusals understated the degree of opposition to church rates. Failure to levy a rate more often reflected the weakness of the Church in a particular locality than the adequacy of parochial endowments without subsidy from ratepayers. A typical comment, from the parish of Seer Green, Buckinghamshire, explained bluntly: 'A church-rate has never been made, nor is ever likely to be, on account of the opposition of Dissenters'[104]. It is therefore significant that parishes not levying a rate (which outnumbered parishes refusing rates by more than two to one) were on average about six times the demographic size of those in which a rate had been levied[105]. Thus whether the refusal of a rate or the failure to levy one is the index, the same picture emerges of anti-church-rate sentiments—a fairly reliable sign of Nonconformist strength—being characteristic of parishes in which the Church of England faced the problems of overpopulation.

Granted that Nonconformist encroachment, whether in north or south, whether by Methodists, Congregationalists, or Baptists, was usually associated with some form of weakness in the parochial system, what is the significance of 'Tillyard's thesis'? The broad regional patterns of denominational strength *were* important in two respects. First, the concentration of the older denominations in the south, the south Midlands, and East Anglia was perhaps the main reason why, in England, they failed to grow as rapidly as Methodism during the late eighteenth and early nineteenth centuries.

Although the gaps in the parochial system became much more serious elsewhere than they were in these traditional strongholds of Baptist and Congregational influence, particularly as the industrial and demographic revolutions proceeded through the second half of the eighteenth century, the older Dissenting bodies were ill-equipped to achieve a radical redistribution of their geographical strength. The independent polity which they shared deprived them of the capacity to coordinate and sustain evangelistic efforts on the scale possible under the connexional polity of Methodism. It is worth emphasising that Congregationalists and Baptists *did* increase substantially in northern England during the pre-Victorian century[106], but because their centres of evangelist activity were extremely few at the beginning of the Evangelical Revival, the balance of their numerical strength (outside Wales) remained in the south and south-east. The principle of growth by encroachment into areas of Anglican weakness was shared by all the Nonconformist bodies, but in the major 'home mission fields' of the Congregational and Baptist churches the gaps were fewer and smaller. The overall rates of denominational growth consequently were somewhat slower.

The gaps being fewer and smaller had a second important consequence in addition to this effect on the relative growth rates of Methodism and New Dissent. It meant that relations between Church and Chapel tended to be far more strained in the south and the south-east than in those areas where the parochial system was weakest. The element of *conscious* dissent was not necessarily present in the huge destitute areas of the north-east, for example. There was often nothing to dissent from. But in that belt of counties stretching from Dorset and Wiltshire, through the south Midlands, into East Anglia, which the 1851 Religious Census would discover to have the highest overall rates of religious practice in England, the relatively close proximity of Church and Chapel strongholds produced competition, acrimony and sometimes considerable Establishment harassment of Nonconformists.

In this area of Anglican strength, unmatched elsewhere in

England, Nonconformity could be excluded from many parishes and villages, but not by any means from all. Partly because it was so strong, the Establishment tended increasingly to rely on manifest coercion rather than paternalistic influence; and by so doing—by resorting to legal and socio-economic sanctions to uphold the *status quo*—it enhanced the function of religious deviance as a symbolic expression of 'independence'. Thus while the gaps in the parochial system were fewer and smaller than elsewhere in England, the communities they contained had as a result a stronger political motive for embracing Nonconformity. This was the most 'religious' area in the country in 1851 primarily because the deployment of Anglican and Nonconformist forces in the early industrial period had made it the religious cockpit of England.

An insight into the kind of Church—Chapel relationships characteristic of areas where confrontation rather than isolation determined the development of the Establishment and Nonconformist religious cultures can be obtained in a report from a group of Lincolnshire clergy prepared in 1799. Appointed by the Bishop of Lincoln, a clerical commission received information from 100 Lincolnshire parishes before presenting a summary of conclusions and recommendations. Significantly, the final report stressed the success of 'itinerant enthusiasts' in a district in which the Church had an active ministerial presence[107]. If, as seems likely, the respondents interpreted a question about the average size of their congregations as referring to the number of attendants at their most numerously attended services, then religious conformity per head of population was *higher* in the seventy-nine parishes which made statistical returns than in any county in England or Wales on Census Sunday, 1851[108]. Significantly, in such an area of relative Anglican strength, where the clergy doubtless had shared in the rising economic and social standards of their profession during the previous forty years, Nonconformist growth was associated with strong anticlericalism and attacks on the ruling classes generally. The itinerants insinuated themselves into a local community, the clergy complained, by reviling the civil Establishment (possibly in the form of its local representatives), and by undermining 'esteem for, and confidence in . . . lawful ministers'[109].

The kind of direct competition described in the *Report from the Clergy of a District in the Diocese of Lincoln* was not typical of most Anglican or Nonconformist activity in early industrial England. Most people who became Nonconformists did so because the Establishment provided no adequate alternative: because for almost a century after 1740, while English society had expanded rapidly and undergone profound structural and cultural changes, the Church had failed to respond effectively. In the 1830s, on the eve of the Victorian era, Anglicanism was in danger of becoming a minority religious Establishment. Indeed, people already were arguing that Anglicans *were* a minority of those who practised their religion Sunday by Sunday. The reform of the Church of England could be delayed no longer, for reform had become a condition of survival.

Part three

Religion in Victorian England

6   The metamorphosis of the religious Establishment

By the early 1830s the feeling that the religious Establishment faced the alternatives of reform or 'complete destruction'[1] had built up sufficiently to break through the massive impediments to organisational innovation and pastoral renewal which had retarded for so long the Church's adjustment to the new society of early industrial England. The ranks of the reformers and the volume of their agitation had been swelling gradually since the opening decade of the nineteenth century, but in the 1820s the problems confronting the Establishment had begun to assume crisis proportions[2]. In 1828 the repeal of the Test and Corporation Acts and in 1829 the Roman Catholic Relief Act had symbolised dramatically the failure of the old monopolistic conception of the Establishment.

The repeal of the Test and Corporation Acts, which had long been the major political goal of Protestant Dissent, had the effect in 1828 of legitimating a *de facto* situation. In practice it altered the daily lives of Anglicans and Nonconformists very little. But the passage of the repeal legislation was evidence of the power of extra-Establishment forces within the society: forces which might reasonably be expected sooner or later to launch an offensive aimed at securing full religious equality. Because repeal had long been contested by the Church its coming was an index of the Church's vulnerability. The same was true of Catholic emancipation. In a speech which had become a virtual manifesto of the anti-emancipation position, the Duke of York had argued in 1825 that emancipation would destroy the unique position of the Church of England, and place it in certain respects 'upon a worse footing than any other church'[3]. Because many Englishmen shared these views emancipation helped set the stage for the early 1830s to become a turning-point in the affairs of the Church as well as in the history of the British State.

The ecclesiastical and political crises were closely connected. When on 8 October 1831 the House of Lords threw out the Reform Bill by 199 votes to 158, the wrath of the country, intense and prolonged, was directed at the privileged classes generally, but against none more savagely than the bishops of the Church of England. Two bishops had voted for the Bill and six had abstained. As the press and the reformers were quick to point out, if the twenty-one bishops who voted 'No' had voted differently Reform would have been carried. The Church was shocked and dismayed by the opprobrium and contempt of which it became the object[4]. 'Everyone was touched by panic and found it difficult to see clearly', Owen Chadwick has observed of the Reform Bill crisis. 'Churchmen were pardonably convinced that the country was near revolution, that the church faced disestablishment, that only drastic remedies could preserve it, that guillotines and temples of reason stood round the corner'[5]. The atmosphere of the period was recalled vividly by Sydney Smith in a letter to Bishop Blomfield in 1840. 'I believe', he wrote,

> that the old-fashioned, orthodox, hand-shaking,
> bowel-disturbing passion of fear had a good deal to do with
> the whole reform. . . . I remember the period when the
> Bishops never remained unpelted; they were pelted going,
> coming, riding, walking, consecrating, and carousing; the
> Archbishop of Canterbury, in the town of Canterbury, at the
> period of his visitation, was only saved from the mob by the
> dexterity of his coachman[6].

The period was one of general social unease, of economic depression (particularly in 1829 and 1832), agrarian unrest following a succession of poor harvests, and intense political agitation. This was the context in which the Church of England finally confronted the implications of the societal and ecclesiastical changes which in the previous century had been rendering the unreformed Establishment increasingly anachronistic. Some of these changes, it has been argued, had their origins as far back as the English Reformation, but the situation had become untenable only in the early industrial age. The reforms of the 1830s and 1840s may not, in retrospect, have gone far enough, but it is clear that as a whole they represented not merely a much needed modernisation and expansion of the Church's organisational structures, but also a profound metamorphosis of the Establishment religious culture itself.

Organisational renewal

The parochial system of the Church of England had been one of the most durable of the nation's institutions. A network of parishes, rural deaneries, archdeaconries, and dioceses, established at least as early as the *Taxatio Ecclesiastica* compiled under Edward I, had survived essentially unchanged for more than 500 years. Five new dioceses had been created and some urban parishes obliterated during the English Reformation, and under Queen Anne in the early eighteenth century there had been a certain amount of church building and subdivision of parishes. But in general the ancient parochial boundaries had remained more or less intact until the second quarter of the nineteenth century.

Queen Anne's efforts to improve the system had been neither far-reaching nor completely successful[7]. Moreover, they had failed to establish what might have been vital precedents for intervention in a system requiring constant modification in a changing and expanding society. Intervention in the financial arrangements of the parochial system would have mitigated the economic pressures which contributed to high rates of pluralism and absenteeism throughout the eighteenth and early nineteenth centuries. The possibility of intervention leading to the sub-division of existing parishes or the endowment of new ones would have meant that the Church had at its disposal machinery for adjusting its structures in accordance with changing demographic patterns.

The need for both kinds of intervention was immense. The wealth of the Church was more than adequate, but the inequity with which it was allocated was rightly regarded by reformers as a scandal. The Bishop of Durham received more than fourteen times the net income of the Bishop of Oxford in the unreformed Establishment; and while the ten wealthiest sees ranged in annual income from £5,435 per annum to £22,305, and had an average annual net income of £11,634, the remaining sixteen sees had an average net income of less than £2,800[8]. Economic inequalities among parochial clergy were even more pronounced, as well as being more deleterious in their effects upon the pastoral functions of the Church. While the Rector of Stanhope received a princely £4,843 per annum some of his colleagues had to survive on less than £12. The Rev W. N. Darnell, the incumbent of Stanhope, was inexcusably non-resident in 1833, paying two curates £270 between them to look after the parish[9]; but for thousands of other incumbents or curates dereliction of parochial duties resulted from genuine economic hardship. It was a situation which had been crying out for reform throughout the period of increasing Anglican weakness in early industrial society. Meanwhile, the need for creating new parishes and for subdividing unwieldly or over-populated existing parochial units had grown ever more urgent as the population had multiplied and settlement patterns had changed. But only an Act of Parlia-ment could effect such changes, and obtaining one involved the formidable task of manipulating tithe owners, patrons, and incumbents, each of whom had vested interests in preserving the *status quo*[10]. Like the problem of augmenting some benefices at the expense of others, the need for sub-dividing parishes (and consequently livings), and for financing new benefices, could not be resolved until a sufficient number of churchmen were either sufficiently dedicated or sufficiently frightened to accept large-scale reform, or until the wishes of the clergy were over-ridden by the State.

By the early 1830s the impetus towards ecclesiastical reform had assumed irresistible proportions within Church and State alike. The number of clergy dedicated to reform had risen; so had the number who, like Sydney Smith, felt sufficiently insecure to have given half their preferment to save the rest[11]. There had developed fairly generally a pragmatic acceptance of the principle which Henry Bathurst, the Whig Bishop of Norwich, enunciated in 1832. The greatest threat to the Church, Bathurst insisted, arose 'not so much from a restless spirit of *innovation* in some, as from as *obstinate adherence* to *antiquated abuses* in others'[12]. The Bishop was right. The *Zeitgeist* of 1832 was hostile to the abuse of privilege and intolerant of sinecures, ecclesiastical or secular. Utilitarian ideas were abroad even at Westminster, and Bentham, the prophet of Utilitarianism, had made quite explicit his evaluation of the unreformed Establishment. 'The Church of England system', he had written in 1818,

is ripe for dissolution. The *service* provided by it is of a bad sort: inefficient with respect to the ends or objects professed

> to be aimed at by it: efficient with respect to divers effects
> which, being pernicious, are too flagrantly so to be professed
> to be aimed at[13].

The almost clinical detachment which the Philosophical Radicals brought to their appraisal of the Establishment was never quite reproduced in the decision-making processes of the national government. But debate at Westminster often moved perilously close to thoroughgoing Utilitarianism. In a summary of the debate in the House of Commons over the controversial Irish Temporalities Bill of 1833[14], Bowen has drawn attention to Lord John Russell's argument that Church funds might properly be confiscated where there were more profitable ways of using them for moral and religious improvement, and to Sir John Graham's contention that the State had the right to redistribute Ecclesiastical endowments for any 'Protestant purposes'. During the same debate Sir Robert Peel expressed the opinion that the religious Establishment should be treated in the same way as any other great corporate interest[15]. The expression of such views by such men was the death-knell of the unreformed Establishment. 'No one now maintains the inviolability of corporate rights where a clear case of public necessity or expediency demands their sacrifice', Lord Henley wrote bluntly in 1832, advancing an influential plan for Church reform[16]. The generalisation may have been too emphatic, but the implication that the religious Establishment was subject to public scrutiny and State control was simply an echo of current public and political opinion in the early 1830s.

The initiative in the matter of Church reform thus passed to the State. The restructuring of the Establishment was something *imposed* on it by a Parliament which scarcely could afford to wait for some consensus about reform to emerge within the Church itself. Indeed, one of the most serious impediments to ecclesiastical reform during the early industrial age had been the prorogation of the Convocations of Canterbury and York during the entire period from 1717 to 1852[17]. There was simply no administrative machinery through which the Church might have formulated policies requiring merely the constitutional legitimation of a Parliamentary Act. Many churchmen welcomed the policies which the State imposed; others, notably High Church conservatives, and particularly the Tractarians, abhorred the Erastian implications of the State's ecclesiastical initiatives. But whatever the attitudes of contemporary churchmen, and irrespective of whether reform could have been effected in any other way, the fact remained that the Church of England was being reformed, not on its own terms, but according to the wisdom and the interests of a Parliament dominated by laymen not all of whom were even Anglicans by profession. The religious Establishment received a new lease of life in England, but only at the cost of a further secularisation of the Establishment ideal.

The Ecclesiastical Commission

In June 1832 the announcement of an Ecclesiastical Revenues Commission marked the beginning of a serious parliamentary commitment to Church reform, but for more than two and a half years little apparent progress was made. While the Commission went about its task of investigating and evaluating the entire financial structure of the Establishment, and the debate about reform intensified outside Parliament, at Westminster a succession of *ad hoc* measures designed to alter the organisation of the Church in one way or another were either defeated or allowed to lapse. The breakthrough came with the short Peel administration lasting from December 1834 to April 1835. Peel set up a new Commission to 'consider the State of the Established Church'[18]. The charter was deliberately vague, for even after the Ecclesiastical Revenues Commission of 1832 submitted its Report in June 1835 the dimensions of the problem remained partly conjectural. Under Lord Melbourne's Whig ministry in 1836 the new body was renamed and established on a permanent basis as the Ecclesiastical Commission. The Government appears to have envisaged for it an important but limited role in the improvement of diocesan and episcopal revenue structures; but partly because the ramifications of ecclesiastical finances implicated almost every aspect of Church organisation, and partly because the Commissioners, led by Bishop Charles James Blomfield, a skilled and tireless administrator, adopted the broadest possible interpretation of their duties, the Ecclesiastical Commission quickly became the main instrument of organisational improvement in the Church of England. In 1840 its crucial role in the reform movement was recognised when Parliament enlarged its membership from thirteen to forty-nine, officially recognised its wide-ranging responsibilities, and gave it increased powers to implement its policies. Its charter was a comprehensive one of 'making better provision for the cure of souls'[19].

The isolated or minimal efforts which had been made before 1836 to alter or expand the facilities of the parochial system, including substantial parliamentary grants for church building in 1818 and 1824, had been haphazard or misdirected. The only precedent for the rational bureaucratic procedures of the Ecclesiastical Commission had been the work of the Board which had administered Queen Anne's Bounty from its inception in 1704[20]. Not only was the capacity of the Bounty relatively limited, however[21], but it had been an *idée fixe* of the commissioners who had administered it 'that their augmentations should go to strengthen the church's stake in the land[22]. Meanwhile, in areas dominated by commerce and industry and in urban areas generally the parochial system had languished. But if the Bounty Board had been in league with the past, the Ecclesiastical Commissioners generally acted with a rational appreciation of what the Industrial Revolution had done to the settlement patterns of the Church of England's national constituency. And what was equally important, they brought not only rational planning but also mandatory power to the task of overhauling the machinery of Anglicanism.

The Commission devoted its energies primarily to the amelioration of spiritual destitution caused by the inadequacy of ecclesiastical facilities in overpopulated or outsized parishes. Its approach to the task was at once radical and realistic. It expropriated endowments considered excessive and used them to augment other livings which were inadequate, or to create new benefices in neglected areas. In the fifteen years after 1840, for example, 5,300 parishes were assisted in this way solely from economies effected as a result of the controversial abolition of cathedral offices[23]. New sees were founded at Manchester and Ripon on the suggestion of the Commission's first official Report, and radical readjustments were made to episcopal salaries. Following the passage of important enabling legislation in 1843, a straightforward procedure for parochial subdivision existed for the first time[24]. The old rural parish ideal, that 'each parish should consist of such a number of inhabitants only, as might conveniently and certainly be admitted into the Parish Church, and also fall under the restraining and corrective personal knowledge and superintendance of their Parish Ministers, and Parish Officers'[25], was beyond the resources of the religious Establishment by the early Victorian era. But the Commissioners worked with considerable success towards the more realistic goal of reducing large parishes by subdivision to a maximum population of 3,000–4,000.

This task involved the creation of numerous 'Peelite'[26] parishes in the decade after 1843, and produced a heavy demand for new churches and new clergy. Table 2.1 (p. 28) has summarised Anglican statistics on these aspects of Church life, and the rapid increases in the physical and manpower resources of the Church in the Victorian era which it records are significant indices of the impact of the organisational reforms of the 1830s and 1840s. In Table 6.1 more detailed figures on the building and renovation of Anglican churches confirm the importance of this turning-point in the organisational development of the Church of England. Not only was there a marked acceleration in church building in the first quinquennium of the Ecclesiastical Commission, but the subse-

Table 6.1 Anglican church building, 1801–75
Churches built, churches rebuilt, and total churches consecrated, quinquennially

Quinquennia	New churches	Churches rebuilt	Total churches consecrated
1801–1805	10	7	17
1806–1810	18	8	26
1811–1815	27	12	39
1816–1820	43	14	57
1821–1825	97	33	130
1826–1830	138	40	178
1831–1835	154	48	202
1836–1840	360	38	398
1841–1845	401	78	479
1846–1850	358	92	450
1851–1855	342	77	419
1856–1860	312	89	401
1861–1865	364	156	520
1866–1870	427	163	590
1871–1875	356	152	508

quent work of the Commissioners and the operation of other agencies of reform enabled the religious Establishment to maintain an impressive rate of expansion throughout the Victorian era.

The structure of the clerical profession

Churches were of very limited value without resident clergymen to serve in them. Probably the most important changes which raised the quality of pastoral care in the Victorian Church were changes in the attitudes and values governing the way in which incumbents discharged their parochial duties. But before turning to this religious-cultural dimension of the reform movement, it is important to recognise both the marked improvement in the organisational efficiency of the clerical profession during the 1830s and 1840s, and the sustained growth in the number of parochial clergy throughout the Victorian era. Table 2.1 has traced decennially increases in the number of Anglican clergy from 16,194 in 1851 to 23,670 at the beginning of the twentieth century, and although the figures covering the period 1811—48 are not strictly comparable with this later series it is clear that the number of clergymen active in English parishes more than doubled between 1835 and 1901.

Over the short term, however, a more important development associated with the ecclesiastical reforms of the 1830s and 1840s was the virtual eradication of the problems of pluralism and non-residence. Table 6.2 summarises trends of non-residence from 1810 to 1850. The percentage of beneficed clergy non-resident and not performing parish

Table 6.2   Resident and non-resident beneficed clergy, 1811—50

Year	All beneficed clergy	Non-resident clergy not doing duty	Non-residents not doing duty as a percentage of all clergy
1810	10,261	4,813	46.9
1827	10,533	3,581	34.0
1835	10,571	3,329	31.5
1841	10,987	2,677	24.4
1846	11,386	2,189	19.2
1850	11,728	1,815	15.5

Notes

1   Pluralists not resident in their parish but doing duty there have been regarded as resident.

2   Non-residents include holders of sinecures and dignities not requiring residence, sequestrations and suspensions, vacancies and recent institutions, and similar miscellaneous categories. The total number in this category remained fairly constant during the period covered, and consequently has disguised the actual percentile rate of decline of non-residence among parochial clergy. Only 9.5 per cent of beneficed clergy were non-resident in the normal sense by 1850.

duties fell slowly between 1810 and 1835 (when it stood at 31.5 per cent), then declined rapidly in the fifteen years before 1850. As a note to the table explains, only 9.5 per cent of all beneficed clergy were non-resident in the normal sense by 1850. Thus while the total number of clergymen was growing rapidly from the 1830s onwards the percentage of clergy neglectful of their parochial responsibilities was falling significantly. These trends combined to strengthen greatly the work of the Anglican ministry, and they were accompanied by another positive development: the increasing use being made by incumbents of assistant curates. The number of assistant curates engaged in parochial duties more than doubled between 1835 and 1841, when it stood at 2,032. Twelve years later it had risen to 3,437[27].

Religious-cultural change

In 1854, on his return from an absence of thirteen years in New Zealand, Bishop G. A. Selwyn told a congregation at Cambridge University that he had noticed 'a great and visible change' in the Church of England since 1841. 'It is now a very rare thing', he said, 'to see a careless clergyman, a neglected parish or a desecrated church'[28]. There was no simple explanation for the rapid improvement. The expansion and increased efficiency of the clerical profession and the marked and more or less immediate impact of the Ecclesiastical Commission's work in the 1840s were themselves related to other processes of change, less measurable but no less important. The speed with which structural and administrative reforms became effective was dependent partly on the mandatory powers vested in the Ecclesiastical Commission, while the Church Pluralities Act of 1838 and the Church Discipline Act of 1840 clearly contributed to the reduction of non-residence and the decline of other forms of clerical negligence. But legal or organisational innovations alone do not explain the emphatic changes reflected in Tables 2.1, 6.1, and 6.2, or the accompanying rapid growth in the use of assistant curates in English parishes. The metamorphosis of the religious Establishment around the beginning of the Victorian era implicated the essential nature of Anglican religious culture. It was based on vital changes in the role of the Church in English society.

A truly monopolistic religious Establishment does not, *ipso facto*, have to worry about growth: it has no competition. Ostrich-like, many sections of the eighteenth- and early nineteenth-century Church of England had either failed to recognise that Anglicanism had lost the virtual monopoly it once had enjoyed, or had failed to act on the recognition. But the gradual rise of reformist propaganda, culminating in the crisis of the early 1830s, had forced the Church as a whole to face realities. Coming to terms with the newly perceived situation required a fundamental change of values and goals. Indeed, the general alarm about the strength of irreligion and extra-Establishment religion in the 1830s amounted to a tacit admission that the Church was now operating in a pluralistic society in which religion was well on the way to becoming an entirely voluntary aspect of social behaviour.

Just as Methodism's early adjustment to voluntarist tendencies in English society had made it a dynamic sectarian movement within the conservative eighteenth-century Establishment, so when the Church as a whole came to terms with the reality of its ex-monopoly status energies were released which made it a formidable competitor for the allegiance of the wider society in Victorian England. But there were costs as well as benefits in this adjustment. The release of energies for specifically religious activities depended partly on the curtailment of the secular functions, the political power, and the material wealth previously enjoyed by the more fortunate Anglican clergy.

An improvement in the pastoral effectiveness of the clergy was accompanied both by a social devaluation of the status of the clerical profession and by a related change in the kind of social and religious role expected of a clergyman. Earlier the young William Lamb, later Viscount Melbourne, had chosen law rather than the Church because it had seemed the more honourable profession, although not the more lucrative[29]. In 1830 it was still possible for the son of a gentleman to look on holy orders as 'the most attractive of all professions', but those who did were doomed to disappointment. Thirty years later the notion would be extremely difficult to sustain. In the attraction of young men to the Anglican priesthood, Chadwick has written, 'The ideals became more prominent while the social incentives declined.' The number of Anglican ordinands increased rapidly in the early Victorian era, and continued to grow throughout the nineteenth century, but in 1862 there was only one Oxbridge graduate ordained for every two Oxbridge ordinands only twenty years earlier. Indeed, about one ordinand in three in 1862 was not a university graduate at all[30].

A related trend was the diminishing importance of the clergy on the County Bench. Because the position of magistrate was a life office, the number of clerical magistrates fell only slowly in response to a strong feeling in the 1830s, shared by Church and State alike, that clergymen should be appointed to the Bench only under very unusual circumstances. From a peak of 36.8 per cent at the end of the Napoleonic Wars, the clerical element in the Oxfordshire magistracy had fallen to 21.0 per cent by 1857[31]. Much more emphatic, however, had been the change in the amount of time devoted by the clerical magistrates to their juridical responsibilities. Up to the 1830s such magistrates had been much more active than their lay colleagues in the work of criminal prosecutions. A minority of the Bench, they had dealt with over 70 per cent of prosecutions. Around 1840, however, their share of this magisterial work fell suddenly to below 30 per cent[32]. In this change the Oxfordshire magistracy was following a national trend.

It was a trend which, like the diminishing status of the priesthood relative to other professions, was partly a reflection of a growing secularisation of English society. It had the effect, nevertheless, of reinforcing a new, positive emphasis on the more specifically religious aspects of the clerical role which both High Churchmen and Evangelicals, from their divergent ecclesiastical perspectives, were stressing with increasing success from the 1830s onwards. Where a clerical class loses 'social influence and privileges' which it has enjoyed previously, Bryan Wilson has argued plausibly, there is a tendency for its members to reinterpret the 'character and mission' of their institution in such a way as to emphasise 'the more traditional preoccupations of religious specialists—the narrow concerns of the priestly role, the administration of church affairs and the assertion of distinctive competances'[33]. Professional self-interest was not the only motive behind the notable resurgence of Victorian Anglicanism, of course. Yet it is clear that the growth of Anglican religious practice which resulted from increased clerical activity in evangelistic and pastoral work was related partly to the initial impact of precisely those secularising trends which ultimately would undermine practice itself. The Church was saved and made more efficient in the 1830s and 1840s by relinquishing or otherwise losing some of its social and secular administrative functions, and by a further surrender of autonomy to the State. Anglicanism became for a time a more ubiquitous religious-cultural phenomenon in English society, but, arguably, it did so only by becoming a less pervasive one.

In an analysis of the mid-Victorian conception of the Anglican ministry Brian Heeney has suggested that Joseph Baylee, the Evangelical who founded St Aidan's College, 'spoke for most clergy' when he wrote that a clergyman 'must be a man wholly given to his work, or he must be content to be looked upon in society as a careless shepherd of the Lord's Flock'[34]. This attitude, that while a man might be 'half a doctor, or half a lawyer', he could not, if he took holy orders, be 'half a minister of Christ'[35], became more or less normative in the Victorian Church. The hunting, shooting, fishing parson of the eighteenth century—the man whose specifically religious functions, however conscientiously they were discharged, rarely represented the dominant aspect of the role society ascribed to him—was gone. In his place was a man who was made to feel defensive about 'frivolous or boisterous' amusements, who would likely have to justify card-playing or the theatre to a society sceptical that such things were consistent with the clerical calling, and who would raise eyebrows if he danced. In the unreformed Establishment it had been regarded as acceptable, and even appropriate, for a clergyman to concentrate as much or more on the 'secular' responsibilities of his office as on his spiritual and priestly functions[36]. It was acceptable no longer in the Victorian Church. The religious dimension of the priestly office had become paramount.

The corollary of this increasing specificity of function—the marked improvement in the operation of the Church as an evangelistic and pastoral agency in English society—was evident right across the ecclesiastical spectrum, for the reorientation of the Church to the world of early Victorian England transcended differences between Tractarians, Evangelicals, and Broad Churchmen, at least to the extent that it left clergy and laity of each persuasion with a concept of the Establishment as a primarily religious institution with a spiritual mission to discharge. But granted the persistence of ecclesiastical divisions in the Victorian Church, and the often intense rivalry and disagreement between the various Church parties, the effect of the reform movement in promoting pastoral renewal and heightened parochial efficiency requires some elaboration.

The High Church 'party', a phenomenon characterised by religious-cultural, not organisational, homogeneity, had assumed a certain coherence in the late eighteenth and early nineteenth centuries. It had been in the vanguard of Anglicanism's reaction to the anti-Establishment animus of religious and political dissent from the 1790s onwards, a reaction which had been intensified by a typically conservative mistrust of ecclesiastical colleagues, especially Evangelicals, whose pastoral concerns had appeared to threaten the norms of the unreformed Establishment. But if High Churchmanship inhibited reformist tendencies within the Church before the 1830s, once reform was under way it played a curiously positive role in the metamorphosis of the Establishment.

The structural and administrative reforms of Blomfield and Peel not only horrified many High Churchmen, but (what was much more significant for the future of the Church of England) galvanised them into concerted actions which, however reactionary in inspiration, quickly exercised a marked salutary influence on the religious life of High Church parishes. This strand of the reform movement began with Tractarianism and can be traced more or less directly to the Ritualist clergy of the later Victorian era whose efforts contributed most to the modest achievements of the Church in urban working-class parishes[37]. There were important differences between the Ritualists of the later Victorian era and the original Oxford Movement. Notably, the exigences of ecclesiastical politics in which they were an unpopular and sometimes persecuted minority made Ritualists less enthusiastic than Tractarians had been about the authority of the episcopate. But there was continuity of commitment to a 'high' doctrine of Anglicanism, and the positive contributions of each movement to the pastoral work of the Church arose out of theological and ecclesiological values antithetical to the mainstream of Establishment religious culture.

In the famous Assize Sermon of 1833 which made him the herald of the Oxford Movement, John Keble described the secularising tendencies of the reform then being mooted as 'national apostasy'. But within a decade men influenced by the 'Oxford Apostles' were producing in the lower echelons of the Church precisely the kind of clerical leadership which had been too generally absent in the unreformed Establishment. Because the conservative reaction epitomised in the Oxford Movement took the form of a campaign by clerical intellectuals and lower clergy to save the Church which they felt to be endangered from above, its impact on the pastoral effectiveness of the parochial system had the effect of making Anglicanism, wherever Tractarian incumbents operated, the kind of aggressive, competitive religious culture which reformers like Blomfield, Howley, and Arnold, from their radically different theological and ecclesiological perspectives, also wanted it to become.

In his famous demand for Church reform in 1832 Thomas Arnold saw the greatest failure of the unreformed Establishment in terms of the breakdown of parochial relationships. Analysing the operation of a typical eighteenth- or early nineteenth-century parish, with its incumbent complacent and often non-resident, its parish clerk, churchwardens, overseers of the poor ('how little like the deacons of old'), its beadle, and its constable, Arnold exclaimed: 'What an organisation for a religious society! And how natural was it that men should form distinct societies for themselves, when that to which they nominally belonged performed none of the functions of a society'[38]. Effective ecclesiastical reform, Arnold argued, would depend on the Church's ability to capture the sense of mission characteristic of early industrial Nonconformity, and to achieve a comparable religious-cultural and social rapport with the constituents it sought to serve. Administrative and structural changes might facilitate this metamorphosis, but they could never effectively substitute for it[39].

Arnold was variously regarded as too radical, too latitudinarian, or too impractical in the 1830s to have much immediate impact on the reform of the Establishment[40]. But his ideas had a seminal influence on later generations of Churchmen. With S. T. Coleridge, he contributed significantly to the thought of J. C. Hare and F. D. Maurice, and through it to the nature of the Broad Church tradition within Victorian Anglicanism. In particular, his influence helped to ensure that the relatively liberal theological ethos of this tradition remained compatible with a missionary orientation to the wider society. 'I cannot understand', he wrote on one occasion, 'what is the good of a National Church if it be not to Christianise the nation'[41]. Echoed and re-emphasised by men like Maurice and Charles Kingsley, this conviction was transmitted to the Christian Socialist movement of the late Victorian and Edwardian eras, a movement embracing both Broad and High Church elements[42].

Evangelical Churchmen, who had long shared the ideological motivation underlying Nonconformist evangelism, but whose Establishment status had inhibited their use of the effective 'irregular' methods characteristic of Methodists and New Dissenters, enjoyed increasing freedom of action as the Church moved towards reform in the 1820s. They were quick to take advantage of the expansionist tendencies inherent in the reforms of the 1830s and 1840s. In 1836 the Church Pastoral Aid Society was founded under the aegis of Anglican evangelicalism for the purpose of financing the expansion of lay agencies and the employment of more curates in the pastoral and home mission work of evangelical parishes. Quickly arousing the hostility of non-Evangelicals who saw it as a partisan organisation, the Society prospered nevertheless. By the late 1850s its annual expenditure on parochial work was approaching £50,000[43].

The use of additional curates and the new willingness to rely on the talents of lay workers increased both the scope and the flexibility of the parochial ministry of the Church. Initiated sometimes at the diocesan level, sometimes more locally, visitation schemes involving laymen in pastoral, evangelistic, and social welfare work became popular from about 1830 onwards, and had an immediate and considerable effect on rates of Anglican religious practice in the areas they served. One such programme was instituted in Lancashire in the early 1830s under the leadership of John Bird Sumner, Bishop of Chester, and described by him in his Charge to the Clergy of the Diocese in 1832. The plan was for carefully selected laymen to visit families not contacted by the routine services of the parish, to provide them with religious literature, to aid them in periods of illness or special material need, to read the Bible and pray with them, and to encourage them to attend Church services and their children to attend Sunday School. In 1832 the newly formed Lancaster District Visiting Society dealt with 1,250 families, provided religious services for more than 200 persons unable to attend Church, and encouraged eighty-one adults to commence religious practice[44]. Similar programmes operated elsewhere under Evangelical leadership, and indeed became characteristic of Evangelical parishes. Outside the large towns the methods used were precisely those which in earlier generations had formed the basis of Evangelical Nonconformist expansion. In the period 1834–53, for example, Charles Jerram, the rector of Witney, succeeded in extending the influence of the Church in his parish through house-to-house visitation and cottage meetings which relied on considerable lay initiative[45]. Jerram's was a typical Evangelical parish. In the early Victorian age, as Chadwick has put it, 'evangelical religion seemed suddenly to be the most potent religious and moral force in England'[46].

As Chapter 1 has indicated, Wesley had insisted in the eighteenth century that the parochial system would remain ineffective until the clergy 'formed irregular societies and took in laymen to assist them'[46]. There had been a clear link between the expansion of Methodism and the inflexibility of the Establishment in this respect. But Victorian Anglicanism permitted, if it did not always exercise or encourage, a flexibility which, ironically, the heirs of Wesley came to envy. The change which had occurred was largely a matter of ecclesiastical norms and attitudes, but it did have certain legislative ramifications. In 1855 the Earl of Shaftesbury introduced into the House of Lords a successful Bill removing a legal restriction on the size of Anglican services not held within a church. The law had stated that such services could be held only if not more than twenty persons were present, and in lifting this restriction Shaftesbury's purpose was to facilitate Anglican evangelism in the open air and in unconsecrated buildings. The quest for greater flexibility was no hollow gesture. In 1866 Anglicanism was held up to Victorian Wesleyans as an exemplar of the qualities of spontaneous evangelism and lay initiative which had been characteristic of early Methodism. Noting that Methodists were increasingly intent on consolidating earlier growth while the Church of England was emphasising expansion, an anonymous Wesleyan minister pointed out that 'lay agents in large numbers' were being employed in parishes, and that new areas were being opened up by the use of hired rooms and temporary buildings. Comparing 'Church' and 'Chapel', past and present, he wrote:

> Churchmen can preach in the open air with only one short
> prayer before the sermon: some Nonconformists must have
> three prayers . . . vaulted roofs and steepled sanctuaries.
> Churchmen now think it is *good* to copy some of the old
> Nonconformists in their evangelistic efforts: Nonconformists
> think it is *grand* . . . to be a little like the old Church[48].

Even where such 'aggressive' methods were not employed the Victorian parochial system showed vast improvement on the eighteenth- and early nineteenth-century past. Urban parishes remained difficult to operate; certain types of communities remained unamenable to parochial organisation because of continuing cultural and social antipathy towards the Establishment; but the marked increase of clergy, churches, and parishes, coupled with improved standards of general clerical competence and a general reorientation of Anglican religious culture to the more specifically religious functions of organised Christianity, clearly reinvigorated the Church of England during the period from the 1830s to the First World War. The fact that a higher proportion of the English population practised Anglicanism in 1914 than in 1830 bears impressive testimony to the effectiveness of reforms in an Establishment which previously had been losing ground for centuries[49].

Paradoxically, however, a 'pessimistic' interpretation of the history of the Victorian Church remains tenable. For one thing it is evident that the Anglican resurgence was confined largely to a social constituency in which the working classes were grossly under-represented. 'I see very clearly', a Victorian Archbishop once wrote, 'that the Church of England must either come into closer contact with the working classes of the country, or else her national position will suffer, and her leading position perhaps be ultimately lost'[50]. K. S. Inglis has shown clearly how slightly Victorian concern for the religious welfare of these classes, a concern voiced almost *ad nauseam* by church leaders, religious periodicals, and ecclesiastical forums, was actually translated into improved rates of working class religious practice or reflected in a closer integration of the Church in working-class society[51]. Arguably, the strengthening of Anglican links with the Victorian middle classes, which improved the quantitative position of the Church within the whole society, was in overall perspective considerably less significant than the failure of the reformed Establishment successfully to woo the working classes. For while secularising tendencies, evident throughout the Victorian era, have continued to undermine the role of religion in middle-class culture, the twentieth century has seen working-class cultural values exercise an increasingly important influence on the life of a society dominated more and more by mass media and popular, as opposed to elitest, cultural mores.

But quite apart from the socially restricted nature of the Anglican resurgence of 1830–1914, the *significance* of the evident quantitative improvement in the position of the Church of England during this period remains open to question. For what took place in the Church in the 1830s and 1840s was not simply a revival. The Establishment was not simply made more efficient. It was metamorphosed, and the quantitative trends of the decades which followed arose out of an altered relationship between Anglican religion and English society. Only by examining the sociological implications of the metamorphosis can the consequences it entailed be evaluated adequately.

The denominationalisation of Anglicanism

Sociologists of religion have adduced many typologies of religious organisations since Weber and Troeltsch, early in the present century, introduced the important distinction between *church* type and *sect* type religious organisations[52]. Most of the subsequent work, however, has been concerned to elaborate rather than to challenge the original perception that religious bodies can usefully be classified in terms of their orientation to the wider society within which they exist. In one of the most sophisticated elaborations, J. Milton Yinger has postulated a continuum of organisational types ranging from the exclusive and intensely religious *cult* type, through the *sect, institutionalised sect, denomination,* and *ecclesia,* to the most inclusive and socially integrative of all organisational types, the *universal church* [53]. For the purposes of the present analysis the character of the typology need be adumbrated only in general terms, for only the central phenomena within the overall continuum—the *church* (the 'ecclesia' of Yinger's nomenclature), the *denomination,* and the *sect*—are specifically relevant to the argument.

The *universal church* type is highly inclusive, transcending national and social boundaries and comprehending within its membership virtually the total population of a multinational constituency; consequently it exercises important functions of social integration, legitimating and supporting the norms and values underlying the constituency's 'catholic' culture. It is a unique category in the sense that, while it survives, it embraces within it sectarian and cultic tendencies which in other circumstances would produce discrete organisational types. Thus it alone of all the organisational types can combine fairly effectively both the functions of social integration and the functions associated with personal religious satisfactions. For the student of post-Reformation society, however, the *universal church* type remains merely an historical paradigm useful for understanding the nature of newer organisational types. In the Church of England, and in its European counterparts, the Reformation produced a new phenomenon: the *ecclesia* type of church organisation.

The *ecclesia* type maintains the same inclusive and integrative goals as the *universal church,* but has less chance of success with respect to either. Precisely because it lacks the catholicity which enables the *universal church* to transcend social divisions within a particular society, the *ecclesia* type generally exercises socially integrative functions only in alliance with dominant social groups and at the expense of its functionality as a source of personal religious satisfactions. This point has been elaborated in Chapter 4 in the case of the unreformed Establishment of the Church of England. Its alliance with the squirearchy in the 'dependency system' of pre-industrial England made the unreformed Establishment an important integrative force in eighteenth century society, but at the same time reduced its capacity to combat the specifically religious and cultic functions of Methodism and New Dissent [54].

Thus while the unreformed Establishment in England clearly was a *church* type religious organisation, claiming the allegiance of the whole society, thoroughly integrated with the mainstream culture and social structure, and monopolistic in its attitude to religious rivals, it suffered the essential limitations distinguishing the *ecclesia* from the *universal church.* Specifically, it was structurally and religious-culturally unable to comprehend the sectarian tendencies within its constituency. As long as political sanctions against religious deviance were firmly upheld widespread support for sectarian bodies was not forthcoming, but from

1689 onwards English society moved gradually towards *de facto* religious voluntarism. The result was the rise of dynamic *sect* type religious organisations outside the Establishment, and the consequent erosion of its inclusive, monopolistic pretensions.

In its orientation to the wider society the *sect* type organisation represents a radical alternative to the *church*. The Evangelical Nonconformity of the early industrial age, for example, was a typically sectarian phenomenon, exclusive in attitude and social structure alike [55]. Far from exercising socially integrative functions on behalf of the dominant culture, its mediation of personal religious satisfactions was through a subcultural orientation which involved withdrawal from the 'world' and which was open only to individuals making a voluntary religious commitment which implicated them in a more or less totalitarian community. In contrast, the contemporary Church of England was an institution entry into which was virtually automatic and in which the means of grace had been formalised to the point where they could accommodate fairly minimal levels of commitment. The *church* type religious organisation, as Ernst Tröltsch wrote, 'is able to receive the masses, and to adjust itself to the world', but the *sect* type is 'a voluntary society, composed of strict and definite Christian believers bound to each other by the fact that all have experienced "the new birth"'[56].

If the original *church—sect* typology is useful in explicating the early eighteenth-century situation in English religion, the subsequent religious history of England indicates why the typology required modification before it could be applied in more recent societal contexts. Tröltsch's exhaustive dichotomy was appropriate enough for the historical contexts to which he applied it, specifically those preceding the Reformation or arising directly from it. But for the religious situation which was developing in early industrial England a more complex typology is necessary. England by the 1830s was well on the way to becoming a pluralistic society, a society containing not one monopolistic cultural system but a plurality of systems. As far as institutional religion was concerned, the trend had two related consequences. First, non-Anglican religious institutions, once forced to adopt the sectarian position of withdrawal from or rejection of the dominant culture, were able increasingly to choose the *denominational* alternative of accommodation to one of the cultural components of the pluralistic society. Secondly, the *church* type organisation was placed in an increasingly untenable position as the unitary culture fragmented. In the emerging pluralistic situation the socially integrative functions of the religious Establishment became progressively less capable of comprehending the whole of English society. Thus while the early nineteenth century saw previously *sect* type Nonconformist organisations evolving towards denominationalism (a process which will be examined in the next chapter), it also witnessed the religious Establishment being forced inexorably towards *de facto denominational* status. Mobility within the continuum of organisational types represented, in the English situation, a two-directional process of denominationalisation.

The *denominational* type of religious organisation represents, from the viewpoint of sectarian religion, a compromise with the 'world', for the denominational position involves no rejection of the wider society *per se*, but rather an orientation to a particular constituency within it. The *denomination* is less totalitarian than the *sect* in the kind of religious commitment which it demands, and thus more capable of performing socially integrative functions for particular social groups. And whereas both *church* type and *sect* type religious groups advance, at least in theory, monopolistic claims asserting their unique legitimacy, *denominations*, although they are inclusive in the sense of having relatively relaxed criteria of membership, claim only a pluralistic legitimacy[57]. The *denominational* type regards itself, not as the one true church, but as one of a plurality of legitimate institutional alternatives.

The process of religious-cultural and organisational evolution from *sect* to *denomination* is a much explored theme in the sociology of religion, but the corresponding process of evolution from *church* to *denomination* has received less attention, perhaps because it has had fewer historical exemplifications. Yet the latter tendency has been quite as important as the former in the history of modern English religion. In some respects, of course, even in the 1970s the Church of England retains some 'churchly' characteristics: it still possesses the rudiments of Establishment status, and in its theology, its rituals, and certain of the symbolic functions which it performs, continuity with the monopolistic and universalist Establishment of the past remains evident. But in practice both its claim to social exclusiveness and its assertion of unique legitimacy have been abandoned. It is one religious institution among many in an increasingly secular society, and (as its willingness to enter ecumenical conversations with certain extra-Establishment bodies indicates) it has come to terms with the *denominational* assumption of pluralistic legitimacy. Moreover, as far as the constitutional status of the Church of England as the National Church is concerned, William H. Mackintosh's description of the ecclesiastical reforms stretching from the 1830s to the end of the Victorian era as a process of 'gradual disestablishment'[58] seems entirely appropriate.

Kenneth A. Thompson, in a recent study entitled *Bureaucracy and Church Reform*, has noted the relevance of sociological typologies to his analysis, but has concluded (contrary to the argument of the above paragraph) that 'the Church of England appears to be closer to the *ecclesia* than to the denomination type'. Yet he has gone on to suggest that the process of metamorphosis has in fact proceeded far. 'It would be expected', he has explained plausibly,

> that any denomination which developed out of an *ecclesia*
> would show substantial traces of its origins. In the Church of
> England there remain substantial elements of its traditional
> inclusive aspirations and structure (for example, the territorial
> parish system). It also contains a relatively heterogeneous
> membership, and a more complex mixture of theological and
> ecclesiological principles than most denominations of the
> sect-originated type[59].

But this is virtually to concede that the Church of England has become a *denominational* phenomenon, albeit one retaining obvious residual characteristics of the *church* type.

142

And in the metamorphosis from *church* to *denomination* the reforms of the 1830s and 1840s represented a decisive turning point. Indeed, granted H. Richard Niebuhr's widely accepted definition of the denomination as a church which has accommodated itself to the reality of permanent competition with other 'churches' within its territory[60], it might be argued that as early as the beginning of the Victorian era Anglicanism had begun to function essentially as a *denominational* phenomenon. The ecclesiastical philosophy underlying government policy had ominous implications for the integrity of Anglicanism as *church* type religiosity. It was clear that while the State might intervene to support the Establishment, there certainly would be no political action to *restore* to the Church its constitutionally prescribed role as a monopolistic religion.

In his Assize Sermon of 1833 Keble rightly perceived that official ecclesiastical policy in the 1830s amounted to a tacit acknowledgement that the Church of England was 'henceforth only to stand, in the eye of the State, as one sect among many, depending for any pre-eminence she might still appear to retain, merely upon the accident of her having a strong party in the country'[61]. The policy was of course realistic. However much the Tractarians might lament the accommodation of the historic Establishment to the contingencies of secular politics, to the reality of Nonconformist competition, and to the evident increase of irreligion in the society, no alternative could have salvaged so much of the Anglican tradition.

Yet the fact remained that the effectiveness of the Victorian Church as a social institution, and the evident improvement of its quantitative position relative to other religious bodies, reflected a process more of metamorphosis than of revival. The survival of many residual monopolistic prerogatives (which were to disappear only with the extended process of 'gradual disestablishment'), together with the 'accident' of 'having a strong party in the country', obscured the extent to which the role of Anglicanism within the society had been altered and much diminished as a result of the ecclesiastical *realpolitik* of the 1830s and the 1840s. The religious Establishment, like the landed elite which had long dominated the political Establishment, was to fight a skilled rearguard action during the Victorian era, cutting its losses by compromise whenever the consequences of confrontation appeared likely to become intolerable[62]. But while the process may have been drawn out, the end had been more or less determined by structural and religious-cultural trends the essential features of which were emerging as early as 1840.

In 1840 leaders of extra-Establishment religious bodies rightly perceived that there was a long way to go before English society would have complete religious equality. William Baines, a Leicester Congregationalist, was in jail for refusing to pay a church rate, and his pastor, Edward Miall, was busy with plans for the publication of the *Nonconformist*, a trenchantly anti-Establishment newspaper which was to spearhead a new and prolonged campaign for genuine religious pluralism[63]. As the following chapters will argue, an important theme in the history of Victorian religion was a confrontation between Church and Chapel over the question of Anglicanism's Establishment status. Ironically, however, this new intensity of Church—Chapel rivalry was itself evidence of a closing rather than a widening of the functional differentiation between the two phenomena within the society. The history of Victorian religion took the form it did, in other words, partly because the Church of England, in the second quarter of the nineteenth century, had moved significantly towards a typically *denominational* solution to its intolerable situation as an ex-monopolistic institution in a pluralistic society. For whereas, in Berger's words, a *church* can behave 'as befits an institution exercising exclusive control over a population of retainers', a *denomination* must organise itself so as 'to woo a population of consumers, in competition with other groups having the same purpose'[64]. The sociology of nineteenth-century Anglicanism thus provides an important key to the understanding of Church—Chapel relations in Victorian society.

Church and Chapel in denominational relationship

The metamorphosis of the religious Establishment around the beginning of the Victorian era was bound to have profound effects on relationships between Church and Chapel in Victorian society. But Anglicanism was not the only form of organised religion undergoing fundamental religious-cultural and structural change during the second quarter of the nineteenth century, nor were developments within extra-Establishment organisations merely reflexive adjustments to the nature of the newly reformed Establishment. For quite apart from what was happening to the Church of England, important changes in the character of Evangelical Nonconformity and in the nature of the social constituency from which it drew its members, and an accelerating rate of Irish Catholic immigration to England after the Great Famine, were each in different ways fashioning a new scenario for the role of religion in English society.

Religion entered a denominational phase in the Victorian era. The old issues of Establishment privilege and Nonconformist protest were fought out in a new context. Anglican—Nonconformist rivalry was exacerbated as Nonconformists attempted to capitalise on the great improvement in their quantitative position achieved during the early industrial age, and as each party sought to recruit and retain members whose loyalty could be taken for granted no longer in a society progressively less subject to religious prescription. In an important extension of this competitive situation, Church—Chapel relations entered and frequently dominated the main arena of domestic politics in England. Yet in other respects the role of religion was a contracting one, for the major Protestant churches were forced increasingly to accommodate themselves to secularising social and intellectual processes within the wider society. And for Anglican and Nonconformist religious cultures alike, denominational competition and the challenge of secularisation was complicated by the continued massive growth of the Catholic subculture which, partly because it *was* a subculture, was at once much less conspicuous than either in the life of the society, and in the long run considerably less vulnerable to the dilemma of being the 'Church' in a 'world' where religion was becoming less pervasive if, at least temporarily, marginally more popular than in the past.

Such summary generalisations naturally require considerable elaboration, as do the various assumptions about Victorian religion and society on which they are based. First, however, there is a need to follow the examination of the Anglican resurgence of 1830—50 with a survey of the parallel transformation of Evangelical Nonconformity. For while *denominational* tendencies were emerging inside the Church of England there was a drift within Methodist, Congregational, and Baptist communities from the *sect* type religious culture of the early industrial age towards a new and patently *denominational* orientation to the wider society. Less obtrusively than in the case of the religious Establishment, but no less profoundly, trends coming to a head in the 1830s and 1840s effected basic changes in the character of extra-Establishment Protestantism in England.

The making of Victorian Nonconformity

As the statistical evidence examined in Chapter 2 indicates, the period around 1840 saw a significant change in both Anglican and Evangelical Nonconformist growth patterns. In the case of Nonconformity the problem to be explained is the beginning of a phase of decelerating growth and eventual decline. Previously, economic, demographic, and cultural conditions had combined to create a variety of societal contexts in early industrial England in which people had been highly receptive to Nonconformist recruitment. During the early industrial period, moreover, Evangelical Nonconformity had been ideally equipped to capitalise on this favourable combination of circumstances, for not only had it been an intensely conversionist religious culture, but in itinerancy, lay evangelism, and the Sunday School, it had possessed recruiting agencies at once flexible, effective, and relatively undemanding in overhead costs.

What then had begun to change around the beginning of the Victorian era? Three separate tendencies may be identified. First, the competition had become sterner with the resurgence of the Church of England from the 1830s onwards. Second, English society itself was changing in ways specifically unfavourable to Evangelical Nonconformity. And finally, Nonconformist religious culture was evolving new priorities and goals which directly effected its capacity for growth. The emergence of effective Anglican competition has been examined in the previous chapter, but it remains to look at the wider societal factors and the internal trends which were equally important in inhibiting the previously rapid rate of Evangelical Nonconformist expansion.

Social change and the Nonconformist constituency

If the rise of Evangelical Nonconformity had depended to a considerable extent upon the distinctive context of early industrialisation, the ending of the early industrial age was *prima facie* likely to demand basic readjustments within Nonconformist organisations. In that 'period of disturbed transition' between the initial disruptive impact of the Industrial Revolution and the subsequent emergence of new social and cultural systems apposite to a mature industrial society, religious deviance of the Evangelical Nonconformist kind had enjoyed unique opportunities. It had offered particular social groups not just other-worldly salvation, but also a welcome escape from anomie and a more or less legitimate means of affirming social emancipation from old deferential relationships. But both these latter functions were of maximum significance only during the late-eighteenth-, early-nineteenth-century hiatus between the destruction of one cultural system and its replacement by another. Neither could be expected to retain its original significance in the more settled society of Victorian England.

But the diminution of anomie and of the demand for associational symbols of 'independence' were not the only secular changes in the environment of Methodist, Congregational, and Baptist growth around 1840. During the 1830s and 1840s important social groups within the Evangelical Nonconformist constituency were not merely becoming less receptive to Nonconformist recruitment, they were becoming extinct. Irreversible socio-economic processes were at work before the middle of the nineteenth century in all industries which had depended on capitalist outwork for their early industrial expansion, and the disappearance of the traditional artisan—the craftsman outworker as distinct from the factory operative—meant the dissolution of a vital element in the social situation exploited by Nonconformity during its initial phase of rapid expansion. The loss affected recruiting in two ways. Factory workers in industrial cities were much more difficult to mobilise than craftsmen employed in domestic industry had been; and, equally important, they did not constitute a catchment area within which Nonconformity had any intrinsic advantage over the Established Church. Capitalist outworkers had been close enough, socially, to the old 'dependency system' for Anglicanism to have retained unwelcome associations with prescriptive social control; but for factory workers the emancipation generally was too complete for this factor to operate.

Artisans employed in domestic industry had been over-represented in early Evangelical Nonconformity in relation to most occupational groups. The association between Nonconformist religion and the textile trades, for example, had been primarily a reflection of the disproportionate number of handloom weavers in chapel communities; and in iron manufacturing areas like the Black Country, nail-makers, chain-makers, and other outworkers in iron had shown an unusual propensity for Nonconformist associations during the era of optimum Evangelical Nonconformist growth. These are merely the most obvious examples of a general trend. It is clear that Nonconformist recruiting was heaviest during the early industrial era partly because it depended to a considerable extent on the domestic sector of the industrial work force, a sector undergoing rapid expansion. But around the beginning of the Victorian era the transition from capitalist outwork to factory production was rapidly reversing this early industrial trend[1]. Table 7.1 illustrates very clearly the effect of industrialisation in first expanding and then destroying handloom weaving. The decline of the handloom weaver, extremely rapid from the mid-1830s, was typical of a crucial socio-economic change in the nature of the Nonconformist constituency.

On a scale less significant for Evangelical Nonconformity as a whole than the decline of capitalistic outwork, comparable economic changes undermined the basis of Nonconformist recruiting in many rural areas, and in the tin-mining districts of Cornwall. Discussing the decelera-

Table 7.1   Transition from capitalistic outwork to factory production
in the cotton industry, 1788—1862

	Handloom weavers	Factory workers		Handloom weavers	Factory workers
1788	108,000		1836	174,000	230,000
1801	164,000		1841	110,000	264,000
1806	184,000	90,000	1846	57,000	275,000
1811	204,000	102,000	1851	40,000	339,000
1816	224,000	117,000	1856	23,000	379,000
1821	240,000	129,000	1861	7,000	439,000
1826	240,000	175,000	1862	3,000	452,000
1831	240,000	187,000			

tion and eventual decline of Cornish Methodism, Probert has pointed out that during the second half of the nineteenth century the occupational groups from which Methodism traditionally had recruited most of its Cornish members were themselves declining. In the twentieth century, he has written, 'mining has almost ceased; fishing has suffered a severe decline, and so have the numbers employed in farming. Craftsmen are far less common in the age of mass produced goods. The advent of the chain store has diminished the number of shopkeepers'[2].

As in the case of the artisans losing their livelihood in the declining outwork industries of the second quarter of the nineteenth century, people forced out of these contracting occupations found employment elsewhere, although often only after migrating. Their receptiveness to Evangelical Nonconformity tended to diminish however, particularly if (as happened in many cases), they moved to the industrial cities, the foci of Victorian population growth. The 'degree of involvement in the work processes of modern industrial society correlates negatively with the degree of involvement in church-oriented religion', Thomas Luckmann has concluded recently, basing the claim on social survey evidence about the socio-occupational characteristics of churchgoing communities[3].

Receptiveness to religious recruitment, Luckmann has pointed out, has tended to survive longest amongst social groups involved only marginally in the industrial economy: farmers, rural labourers, some professional groups, white-collar workers, and 'those elements of the middle classes which are basically survivals of the traditional bourgeoisie and petite bourgeoisie'[4]. Certainly, in early industrial England, Evangelical Nonconformity was successful primarily among the artisan classes characterised by strong associations with pre-industrial economic patterns; and as these residual elements diminished within the industrial work force it lost much of its representation among the working classes. A rise in the social status of Nonconformist communities during the Victorian era, evident to most observers of Victorian religion[5], can be seen as something at least partly *imposed* on the movement by basic changes in the status and structure of social groups from which it traditionally had drawn the bulk of its members.

The same point can be made about the difficulties confronting rural Nonconformity during the Victorian era. Neither evangelistic strategy nor denominational social preferences could be blamed for the basic problem hindering the extension or maintenance of rural congregations. As the Baptist Union Council pointed out in 1893, social forces were at work with which no religious body could deal. In a perceptive sociological comment upon the growth of Nonconformity in rural areas, the Report said that whereas in the past smallhold farmers had been 'the backbone of religious Nonconformity', by the late Victorian era few of them remained. The trend towards a concentration of land in the hands of large land-owners had virtually eliminated a class once notable for its receptiveness to Nonconformist recruiting[6]. Without changes in land tenure arrangements which would 'create a class of small-holding proprietors', the cause of Nonconformity in the countryside would continue to decay[7].

The virtual disappearance of the traditional artisan classes of industrial society, and the traditional yeoman classes of rural society, left Victorian Nonconformity heavily dependent on those sections of its constituency least insulated socially from the influence of the religious Establishment. Artisans and smallholders had been among the social groups which most frequently had shown a positive preference for religious deviance even when not spatially isolated from the Church of England. And while the significance of spatial isolation as a source of receptivity diminished with the Anglican revival of the 1830s and 1840s, this distinctive socio-economic constituency, which had insulated earlier Nonconformity from the Establishment, was itself threatened in the second quarter of the nineteenth century.

In Victorian England the middle classes were the Protestant churchgoing classes, and both Anglican and Nonconformist communities depended on them for the bulk of their members. While in Victorian Wales class or socio-economic distinctions between 'Church' and 'Chapel' would remain obvious and significant, in England they had become blurred[8]; and an increasingly aggressive political posture in English Nonconformity emerged partly as a half-conscious attempt to define a political and ideo-logical basis for a coherent Nonconformist constituency at a time when the old distinctions, based on isolation and socio-economic differentiation, were losing significance. Thus the Congregational leader, Thomas Binney, in making his notorious claim that Anglicanism destroyed more souls than it saved, was reacting to an explicit Establishment challenge for the allegiance of the middle classes. The clergy were being encouraged to 'gain the people', he said, but 'the people, the mass of active, intelligent, and reflecting men, that compose the middle classes of the country, are those against whose enlightened opinion nothing in future can be expected to prevail; the reign of prescription has passed, or is passing'[9].

Whether by intuition or by reflection, Binney thus chose the tactics which many Nonconformists were to pursue, fairly consistently, until the eve of the First World War. By emphasising the wider political implications of the confrontation between Church and Chapel, by aligning Nonconformity with the general liberal and democratic forces which would continue throughout the nineteenth century to sap the prescriptive institutions of English society, it was possible to create a new kind of insulation against the influence of the Establishment. One cost of doing so, however, was to identify Nonconformist organisations with social forces and social groups at once too narrow and (in the long term) too impermanent to provide a constituency capable of supporting continued organisational growth.

This is not to imply that political involvements inhibited recruitment. Indeed, it is being argued that Nonconformists were led into such involvements partly as a means of countering Anglican 'aggression' in recruitment and proselytisation. Yet the fact remains that around 1840 one kind of orientation to the wider society was being replaced by another. Victorian Nonconformity became in many respects quite unlike the *sect* type conversionist movement of a generation or so earlier: the priorities and evangelistic methods effective in mobilising one kind of constituency were modified as Nonconformist organisations adapted themselves to their new middle-class constituency, and to the more settled societal context of the second half of the nineteenth century. But while the adaptation was partly imposed by the exigencies of social change and Anglican competition it was also partly a result of basic religious-cultural trends already apparent in Evangelical Nonconformity before the external pressures began to take effect. It is to these internal impulses for change that the discussion now turns.

The changing roles of ministers and laymen

The transition from *sect* to *denomination* involves processes of institutional change which Roland Robertson has explicated in terms of a distinction between 'movements' and 'organisations'. The point of the distinction is not that 'movements' are unorganised, although their organisation does tend to be of a fairly rudimentary kind. 'The major difference between the two', Robertson has written,

> is that a movement is geared to effecting a specific series of alterations in the condition of the wider society or at least in the environment of the collectivity, while a religious organisation exists to serve the needs and desires of members and clients[10].

A religious 'movement', understood in these terms, frequently represents the first stage in the evolution of a religious 'organisation'. Methodism provides an obvious example of such an evolutionary process. Wesley and his fellow-itinerants operated with a specific goal: 'to spread scriptural holiness over the land'. It was an expansionist goal, which dictated a preoccupation with growth. The *raison d'être* of early Wesleyanism was the mobilisation of the wider society on the basis of Methodist principles. 'You have nothing to do but to save souls,' Wesley told his preachers, 'therefore spend and be spent in this work'[11].

But by their very success in carrying out this injunction, Methodist itinerants created for themselves other kinds of work. The larger the Connexion became the more complex became the problems of administration, communication, and maintenance and deployment of resources which Wesley, without interruption to his evangelistic endeavours, had managed to supervise personally. Connexional leaders had to concern themselves increasingly with the superintendence of existing societies, with the task of retaining the loyalty of existing members, and with the problem of securing the commitment of members' children. Tensions between expansion and consolidation—between evangelism and pastoral care—obviously had existed as soon as the first Wesleyan society had been formed, but the 'movement' became an 'organisation', in Robertson's sense, when the exigencies of size and longevity relegated the initial conversionist goal to a secondary position in the priorities of Methodism. By 1848, for example, the Wesleyan Conference was ready to endorse a warning that the 'obvious benefits' of itinerancy and village preaching (the traditional instruments of Methodist recruiting) should not be permitted to disrupt the pastoral functions of the ministry[12]. The values implicit in such a warning were characteristic of a religious collectivity which had evolved from an initial phase of rapid expansion into one of organisational consolidation.

Earlier in the history of Methodism and New Dissent differences between ministers and laymen had been essentially minimal, reflecting simply the functional differentiation between full-time and part-time workers. Little attempt had been made to elaborate any theoretical or specifically theological basis for a differentiation of roles or competences. This had been evident, for example, in the recruitment of ministers. The Methodist Conference under Wesley, recognising that the work of expansion was being inhibited by a shortage of travelling preachers, had on one occasion noted the existence of many local preachers who possessed 'both gifts and graces equal to those of most itinerants'. The obvious question had been asked, 'Why then do they not travel?', and the answer had been that although willing and competent to become travelling preachers these lay workers were being hindered by genuine financial obligations[13]. It had been a significant answer, implying that entry into the ministry for such men would have been merely a matter of finding the economic resources to support them. No extra training would have been required; no skills which had not been exercised as laymen.

The same had been true of the process of ordination to the pastorate of an Independent or a Baptist congregation. When the Baptists at Whitchurch in Shropshire had invited John Himmers, a lay itinerant preacher from Shrewsbury, to become their pastor in 1815, he had already 'almost regularly dispensed to them the word of life' for about a year[14]. Ordination had simply enabled him to devote his energies full-time to the activities which previously he had combined with secular employment. His case had exemplified the ready acceptance of the 'priesthood of all believers' doctrine, the high level of lay participation in evangelism and pastoral affairs, and the access to ordination without formal training, which had been characteristic of Evangelical Nonconformity during its era of maximum growth. Rapid growth not only had depended on minimal role differentiation between ministry and laity, but also had reinforced it. In movements undergoing expansion as rapid as that achieved by

Methodist and New Dissenting bodies in early industrial society, formal ministerial training would have been impossible even if it had been more highly prized.

Nevertheless, the mere fact that the ministry was a full-time activity became *in time* a basis on which a specifically religious-cultural differentiation of roles could emerge, for full-time involvement as a rule entailed greater personal commitment to a collectivity than did part-time commitment. Power in a voluntary association is partly a reward for participation. It is the obverse of 'responsibility'. In a religious association full-time ministerial duties, which involve, almost by definition, the greatest participation and responsibility, provide an obvious basis for a coherent and enduring oligarchy; and there is an inevitable tendency for such oligarchies gradually to assume distinctive symbols of status, and to monopolise functions once exercised on a more democratic basis. This process of role differentiation has been documented frequently in studies of the organisational development of sectarian movements[15], and it was part of the movement away from the original sectarian orientation of Evangelical Nonconformity.

The process, not surprisingly, was evident first within Wesleyanism. The Wesleyan preachers, deriving corporate authority and a strong sense of group identity from the connexional principle, clearly were in a strong position to influence the development of the movement and the evolution of their own role within it. The trend was away from the conception of the ministerial role as one which a lay preacher might exercise simply by embarking on full-time itinerancy under the Conference Plan, and towards the definition of distinctive ministerial functions, the institution of formal ministerial training, and the employment of status symbols such as the title 'Reverend' (after 1818) and the laying on of hands at ordination (from 1836)[16].

This tendency towards professionalisation and institutional order gradually altered the essential character of the Wesleyan movement during the period between 1791, when John Wesley died, and the 1840s. Increased ministerial domination of connexional activities inevitably retarded the kinds of lay initiatives which had been characteristic of earlier Methodism. From the ministry, in short, came an impetus away from the original task of mobilising the wider society towards a new concern for consolidating the existing organisation. It is realistic, not cynical, to recognise that the ministerial profession was a livelihood as well as a vocation for the men attracted to it. The travelling preachers constituted a corporate interest within Wesleyan society, and the motives underlying the organisational strategies of this corporate interest certainly were not entirely disinterested. As Thomas O'Dea has pointed out, when a professional pastorate emerges within a religious movement,

> there comes into existence a body of men for whom the
> clerical life offers not simply the 'religious' satisfactions of the
> earlier charismatic period, but also prestige and respectability,
> power and influence, . . . and satisfactions derived from the
> use of personal talents in teaching, leadership, etc. Moreover,
> the *maintenance* of the situation in which these rewards are

forthcoming tends to become an element in the motivation of the group[17].

This is not to imply that the tendency towards organisational consolidation in Evangelical Nonconformity was confined to the ministerial element. As a movement grew larger activist elements among the laity tended to decline in relation to the total membership. Endogenous growth inevitably became more and more important as the passage of time produced an increasing body of potential members who had been born into Methodist or New Dissenting communities. And as the proportion of members who were the children of older members rose, each collectivity accumulated an internal constituency for whom socialisation, not adult conversion, had been the basis of the associational commitment. For such people the preservation of the association and the consolidation of its organisational structures, as distinct from the realisation of its original goals, easily became an end in itself.

Nevertheless, it was within the professional ministry that the original *sect* type religious culture received its earliest and most decisive challenge. As W. R. Ward has pointed out, to return to the Wesleyan example, both the real incomes and the social expectations of Wesleyan ministers had risen rapidly during the opening decades of the nineteenth century[18]. In an appeal for higher ministerial stipends the *Methodist Magazine* had argued in 1815 that 'a preacher (and especially in the present state of Methodism in this country) fills a respectable station in society; and he and his family are necessitated and expected to appear becoming in that station'[19]. This had been a relatively new idea. Under Wesley the travelling preachers had been 'helpers'. They had been in a quite literal sense the *servants* of the movement as it had been personified in Wesley. But after Wesley's death their role quickly had become *proprietorial*[20]. Except where Trust Deeds had not followed the prescribed pattern of vesting ultimate authority in the Conference, the resources of the movement had been very largely under ministerial control. And so, *ipso facto*, had been the problems of running an increasingly complex organisation. The rising costs of providing for themselves and their families at an economic level commensurate with what they perceived to be their social status, and the financial burdens of chapel mortgages, were powerful mundane pressures causing the interests and the evangelistic strategies of the ministerial oligarchy to diverge from those of the rank and file of Methodism. The problem was not simply that maintaining the ministry placed irksome, rising financial demands on members; it was that maintaining themselves, their families, and their homes, tended to divert preachers from the business of itinerant evangelism still expected of them by many laymen.

Granted their power to mould connexional policy, it is understandable that the Wesleyan preachers should have succumbed gradually to the temptation to make provision for their own comfort and status, even at the cost of fully maintaining the old itinerancy. Wesley had been well aware of the pressures to modify the system. Itinerancy committed a man to a life of more or less constant movement and uncertainty; to the repeated breaking of social ties; to the obligation of performing the duties

Table 7.2 Rate of membership growth per minister in Wesleyanism, 1791–1911

	Total ministers	Members	Decennial increase of membership per minister
1791	235	58,218	
1801	334	89,529	93.7
1811	648	145,614	86.6
1821	709	200,074	76.8
1831	846	249,119	58.0
1841	1,110	328,792	71.8
1850	1,217	358,277	24.2
1861	1,323	319,782	–
1871	1,649	347,090	16.6
1881	1,910	380,956	17.7
1891	2,018	424,220	21.4
1901	2,238	454,982	13.7
1911	2,478	485,535	12.6

Notes

1   'Ministers' relates to full ministers, probationers, and supernumeraries, all of whom were supported by the Connexion.

2   The figure for 1850 has been chosen in place of an 1851 figure to avoid the effects of the schism.

3   Because of the 1850s schism, no abstracted figure is provided for the decade.

4   The data relate to Great Britain.

of a minister in the most unprepossessing and sometimes uncomfortable conditions. 'I love a commodious room, a soft cushion, a handsome pulpit', he had admitted. But 'where is my zeal', he asked, 'if I do not trample all these under foot, in order to save one more soul?'[21]. Wesley's zeal had been abnormal. For his successors the lure of the 'commodious room' and the 'handsome pulpit' made recruitment an increasingly expensive operation, and one which had to compete with other activities for the time of ministers and the resources of the connexion. Table 7.2 which shows the decennial increase of membership per minister between 1791 and 1911, traces this gradual fall in the rate of recruitment per minister. Although the greatest decline occurred from the 1840s onwards, the table confirms that there was a significant rise in the cost of recruitment as early as the 1820s. Wesley's injunction, 'You have nothing to do but save souls', was becoming increasingly inappropriate during the second quarter of the nineteenth century. The temporal aspirations of ministers, their consequent growing dependence as a group on the wealthier elements of the Wesleyan laity, and the increasingly complex task of running a massive national association, were combining to produce organisational consolidation and concentration of effort in economically viable areas even before the resurgence of Anglicanism provided an external impetus in this direction.

The redirection of the Methodist movement under ministerial initiative imposed immense strains on it, and particularly on relations between ministers and laymen. The result was a prolonged period of conflict and schism, beginning with the New Connexion breakaway of 1797 and ending with the major disruptions and realignments of the years 1849—57. Their specifically professional interests placed ministers in the vanguard of those processes, inexorable in the long term, leading Methodism along the *denominational* road, and placed them in opposition to groups concerned to preserve the *sectarian* norms and values of the original 'movement'. The sectarian overtones of such names as 'Primitive Methodists', 'Bible Christians', 'Tent Methodists', and 'Wesleyan Reformers', were significant in the sense that they captured the element of protest against organisational consolidation and institutionalisation which underlay the fragmentation of the Methodist stream of Evangelical Nonconformity.

The Wesleyan ministry, for its part, developed an increasingly formal doctrinal legitimation of its authority within the Connexion. Excessive spontaneity—too much lay initiative—was construed as a threat to the integrity of Wesleyanism, and a theological basis for the definite differentiation of roles and functions between ministers and laymen was elaborated by leaders concerned to limit alternatives to ministerial leadership. Jabez Bunting, the dominant personality in the Conference for most of the first half of the nineteenth century, was, of course, the prime mover in this area; but under Buntingite leadership the preachers more or less consistently displayed a willingness to accept reduced recruitment and even schism as a price for organisational consolidation under minsterial leadership. The maintenance of existing norms and structures of status gradually gained *de facto* priority over the commitment to mobilise the wider society. In a carefully worded Resolution, passed against a background of mounting connexional unrest, the Wesleyan Conference of 1847 summarised what had emerged as ministerial policy towards unofficial evangelistic efforts. 'The Conference', said the Resolution,

> regret to perceive, not indeed generally, but yet in too many
> instances, a disposition to adopt (perhaps unawares) views and
> sentiments which, on the alleged ground of concern for special
> and extraordinary Revivals, have the effect of alienating in
> some degree the affections of our people from the
> well-accredited, long-tried, and officially-responsible Ministers
> and Pastors of our Churches, — of lessening them in public
> estimation, — of diminishing their legitimate and beneficial
> influence, — of substituting something new and irregular for
> the ordinary Ministry and standing Institutions of the Gospel,
> — and of leading some individuals, most injuriously to
> themselves, to undervalue the authority and eventual
> efficiency, under the promised blessing of the Holy Spirit, of
> the stated Preaching of the Word, and the other appointed
> means of grace[22].

There was a tightrope to be walked in this controversy. Leaning too far one way would mean disorganisation, and a devaluation (ideological and probably economic) of ministerial status; leaning too far the other would mean repudiating, rather too obviously, the traditional conversionist goals of Methodism.

The evolution of Methodism from 'movement' to 'organisation', the emergence of denominational characteristics in every aspect of Methodist life, involved much more manifest dissension than did the equivalent changes which affected Congregational and Baptist communities during the same period. In a connexional system there was a tendency for overt conflict to spread where it might have remained localised in an independent chapel society, and the greater individual and corporate power of the ministry under Methodist polity meant that changes sometimes were initiated without the kinds of ministerial—lay consensus which might have obviated the need for schism. But while the rise of 'offshoot' and 'secessionist' groups during the first half of the nineteenth century reflected opposition to the denominationalisation of the original Connexion, the growth and religious-cultural development of the breakaway bodies shows that they succeeded merely in slowing down the process, not in escaping from it.

Chapter 2 has argued that around 1840 growth rates began to slacken throughout Evangelical Nonconformity, and this turning-point presumably was partly a reflection of changing priorities as the demands of organisational consolidation consumed energies once devoted to the mobilisation of the wider society. The presumption certainly fits an interesting complexity evident in Methodist growth patterns in the quarter-century before 1840. For whereas the overall Methodist growth rate, like that of the Baptist and Congregational churches, slackened little, if at all, from the late eighteenth century to the Victorian era, the Wesleyan component of the combined Methodist series showed perceptible deceleration after the Napoleonic Wars. Thus Wesleyanism, the first branch of the movement affected by the trend towards organisational consolidation, was also the first to experience diminished growth; and the smaller bodies—precisely those elements of Methodism which defied the pressures towards institutionalisation and consolidation longest—continued to expand rapidly into the 1840s[23].

From the early Victorian era there was no differential growth rates within Methodism, however. Primitive Methodist, Bible Christian, New Connexion, and Free Methodist growth patterns began to follow more or less the same gradient as the Wesleyan pattern. An examination of the evolution of these smaller bodies shows that while the processes of organisational consolidation had been postponed by separation from the original Connexion, they had proved inexorable[24]. From as early as the mid-nineteenth century, Methodism was composed of a series of organisations which, for a combination of social, structural, and religious-cultural reasons, had reached a stage in their development at which much of the considerable energy they generated—the main application of the power available in their human and financial resources—was devoted to sustaining denominational life and satisfying the needs existing members and leadership groups. Recruitment from the wider society was still highly valued and much discussed, and it continued, at least sporadically, to be relatively heavy. But in terms of the practical priorities of Methodism it had been relegated to a position of secondary importance.

The same was true of the Baptist and Congregational religious cultures. The processes of organisational consolidation had not been as convulsive in the older denominations as they had in the Methodist movement, nor were the available statistical records precise enough to measure with much accuracy the impact of these processes upon the denominational growth patterns. One index of the change, however, had been the increasing diversion of resources into chapel building, an activity prompted not only by the threat of Anglican encroachment, but also by the aspirations of Nonconformist congregations and ministers. And in the older denominations, as in Methodism, the evolution from conversionist 'movement' to stable denominational life had been marked by the gradual differentiation of roles between ministers and laymen.

In 1814 probably the main complaint of Walter Wilson about his contemporaries in Dissent was their willingness, in the interests of growth, to call into the ministry 'nondescript persons': persons unlearned, untrained, and qualified primarily by their popular evangelistic appeal[25]. Wilson had looked back nostalgically to a time when Dissenting ministers had been separated from the laity they served by specific training and theological expertise. But he would have been pleased if he had been able to anticipate future trends. For, ironically, by the 1840s nostalgia in Nonconformist communities usually was evoked by memories of the simple evangelistic fervour which had actively united pastors and laymen in the late eighteenth and early nineteenth centuries. In February 1844, for example, 'An Aged Minister' precipitated a heated and lengthy debate in the *Congregational Magazine* when in a letter to the editor he attacked the 'wrong predilections' of the men recently entering the ministry[26].

The criticism involved three charges. The first was simply that the basis of qualification for the ministry had become too institutionalised. The old type of minister had been chosen because *as a layman* he had proved 'effective' in pastoral and evangelistic work[27]. He had not been required to pass through any formal ministerial training, and if he had done so, it had generally been at one of 'the little schools of emotional preaching which had satisfied Nonconformity at the beginning of the century'[28]. During the 1830s, however, while Wesleyanism had been establishing its first theological colleges, the Congregational Union had set up a committee to consider how best to raise the qualifications of ministerial candidates. Between 1840 and 1845 every Assembly of the Union discussed some aspect of the problem, and in 1842 it was noted that Independent colleges were 'increasing in number and respectability'[29]. In the middle of the 1840s, moreover, the Baptist Union organised its own special conferences on ministerial education[30]. The concern to raise and formalise standards was general. The ministry, in short, was becoming a profession for the professionally trained. Or, as the critics saw it, it was becoming the preserve of domineering 'young academicians'[31].

The second broad criticism of the changes occurring within the Congregational pastorate concerned the decline of ministerial involvement in evangelism and 'house-to-house visitation'[32]. The change (ministers themselves admitted) was partly a result of a proliferation of the formal and in some cases purely administrative duties attaching to the pastoral office; but it was also a consequence of religious-cultural developments within Nonconformist communities. The colleges were training, and the local churches were calling to the ministry, men whose aspirations and talents fitted them less for personal work and popular evangelism than for the maintenance of standards of preaching and worship acceptable to discriminating, theologically informed congregations. Nonconformity did not require *only* 'the studious, accomplished, and erudite' as candidates for the ministry, Binney conceded in 1848, but also 'the practical, popular, and persuasive'. But he added: 'The latter classes were furnished formerly in greatest numbers; the former are likely to predominate now.'[33]

Finally, the suspicions of traditionalists were aroused by the tendency of the ministers assuming office in early Victorian Nonconformity to claim prerogatives in church government which their predecessors had not claimed, and which were therefore easily construed as attempts to become 'lords over God's heritage'[34]. Two separate influences underlay the new emphasis on ministerial authority. One was the wider ecclesiastical climate, and particularly the belligerent claims to a monopoly of the pastoral office being made by the Tractarian clergy of the Church of England. The other was the internal ministerial aspiration to formalise denominational structures of order and status, the professional interest which had been evident in Wesleyanism for several decades. In a perceptive analysis, Edward Miall, editor of the *Nonconformist* and leader of the Anti-State Church Association, said in 1849 that each Nonconformist body had become dominated by

> a professional way of looking at things affecting the welfare of Christ's Church — a kind of corporate influence which works the subjugation of all individuality to a recognized pattern. . . . Hence, the ministerial order among all denominations is naturally conservative — the last class in the churches to apprehend and give way to the necessity of new spiritual enterprises[35].

A year earlier Binney, as Chairman of the Congregational Union, had made the same point somewhat differently. 'Most denominations', he had said, 'seem almost to have done their work—to have lived through their laborious manhood, and, as bodies, to be getting old'[36]. Maturity would have been a more appropriate biological analogy than old age—Evangelical Nonconformity was not decrepit—but Binney certainly had been correct in suggesting that the once dynamic movement had assumed a more sedate character by the early Victorian period. The emphasis was now on maintaining, consolidating, and capitalising upon the strong position achieved during the initial phase of mobilisation: the wider society had become distinctly less receptive, Anglican competition was now more fierce, and in any case there was now a huge internal constituency requiring pastoral care and demanding new varieties of religious-cultural satisfaction.

The emergence of the 'Philistine' culture

In *Culture and Anarchy* Matthew Arnold denigrated English Nonconformity for its 'provincialism', for the 'narrow and partial view of humanity' which inspired it, and for the endless round of 'disputes, tea-meetings, openings of chapels, sermons', and the like, which seemed to dominate its existence as a religious culture. It was a 'Philistine' element in English life, he claimed[37]. Whatever else *Culture and Anarchy* was, however, it was an expression of the chagrin of a once dominant cultural system confronted by a pretentious middle-class challenge to its ascendancy. Arnold attacked Nonconformity because by the time he wrote in the late 1860s it constituted a fundamental source of legitimation for that ascetic bourgeois value system which, from his perspective as one of the cultured 'Hellenes' of the old ruling classes, seemed likely to pervade and 'provincialise' the whole of Victorian society. His very attention to the phenomenon of Nonconformist culture, in short, was evidence of its emergence from the subcultural isolation of the early industrial age.

The impetus within the professional ministry of Nonconformist organisations towards role differentiation between ministers and laymen, and the consequent marked reduction in the scope for lay initiative in pastoral and evangelistic work, was successful, in the final resort, only because the laity acquiesced with the process. As the ordinary Nonconformist member emerged into the main theatre of social life, even if only to be called a 'Philistine' by actors already there, his religious attitudes and behaviour patterns inevitably changed. He tended to become less and less preoccupied with the prospect of sharing in the evangelistic, pastoral, or liturgical functions of the chapel community; his basic values and expectations altered in subtle but important ways, and far from resenting ministerial specialisation in religious matters, he welcomed it. There was a change, in short, in the character of his commitment, and it was reflected in a heightened regard for orderliness, taste, refinement, and for a minimum of old-fashioned 'enthusiasm'. Thus while a better educated laity often demanded a greater say in the affairs of denominational organisations (from 1877 onwards even Wesleyanism made provision for lay representation in Conference), the functions and concerns of the laymen so involved were essentially social and administrative. They rarely challenged specifically ministerial prerogatives. At the national level eminent laymen became guardians of the social, architectural, and cultural image which the denominations projected within the wider society; locally, they were diligent in their efforts to enhance the reputation and 'influence' of Nonconformity within the vicinity of their chapel.

The emergence among the ordinary lay members of chapel communities of these new religious-cultural traits which to people like Arnold made Victorian Nonconformity seem narrow, introverted and smug, cannot be accounted for solely in terms of external societal factors. Nor can it be attributed simply to the fact that the constituency from which Victorian Nonconformity drew its members tended to be of a higher social status than that which early industrial chapel communities had served. The impulse towards social and cultural 'improvement' was partly an internal one. For the history of English Nonconformity exemplifies 'Wesley's Law': the idea that ascetic Protestantism leads to economic and social improvement. Wesley had noted the phenomenon on many occasions, especially during the later stages of his ministry. While believing, perhaps wrongly, that there was an escape from the vicious circle, he had asked in a sermon on 'Causes of the Inefficacy of Christianity':

> Does it not seem . . . that Christianity, true scriptural Christianity, has a tendency, in process of time, to undermine and destroy itself? For whenever true Christianity spreads, it must cause diligence and frugality, which, in the natural course of things, must beget riches! And riches naturally beget pride, love of the world, and every temper that is destructive of Christianity. Now, if there be no way to prevent this, Christianity is inconsistent with itself . . . since, wherever it generally prevails, it saps its own foundation[38].

The only possibility of preventing this stultifying process, Wesley had insisted, was by Christians increasing their charity in proportion to any increase in their wealth. They had to avoid the ostentation, the luxury, the worldly pleasures which increased prosperity placed within their reach[39].

In examining the development of religious movements in contemporary mission situations, Donald McGavran has used the word 'lift' to describe the virtually inexorable processes which Wesley had detected and feared[40]. *Lift* is to be distinguished from upward social mobility, although the two are closely connected. It describes the social and cultural estrangement of members of a religious group from the social environment in which they were recruited. *Lift* does not necessarily inhibit growth. Indeed, the prospect of experiencing upward social mobility and *lift* can be a factor inducing commitment. But as McGavran has pointed out, 'men do not join churches where services are conducted in a language they do not understand, or where members have a noticeably higher degree of education, wear better clothes, and are obviously of a different sort'[41]. Horace Mann emphasised the same kind of point after the 1851 Religious Census in England and Wales[42]. Thus as *lift* creates *social distance* between the membership of a religious body and the wider social constituency which traditionally has provided its source of recruitment, there is an almost inevitable deceleration in the flow of recruits. In such a situation, unless it can draw on a socially more prestigious constituency appropriate to the new social circumstances of its members, the body becomes introverted, and its growth becomes increasingly dependent on the children of existing members.

Only when a religious body can recruit new members quickly enough to retain much of its original social character can *lift* be combined with continued recruitment from the original constituency. In Evangelical Nonconformity, for example, although, as Wesley recognised, *lift* was occurring well before the end of the eighteenth century, recruitment from the artisan, mining, and labouring sections of the population was continuing unchecked. It began to diminish significantly only in the late 1820s and the 1830s, when the vigorous itinerancy—lay as well as clerical, chapel-based as well as connexional—which had been the instrument of early Nonconformist recruiting, was either abandoned or adapted to other ends, notably to pastoral supervision rather than evangelism, and to the recruitment of children rather than adults. 'It is the Lord's work to convert sinners', a Baptist congregation decided in 1839 when statistical returns revealed that its own activity (or inactivity) was not producing growth[43]. Citing this example of introversion, a Congregational writer admitted that in Congregationalism, too, there was a general tendency for the earlier emphasis on agressive evangelism to be replaced by other goals. 'Pastors and churches', he said, were becoming content to

> live and labour for themselves, but make no aggressive
> movements upon the frontiers of darkness, . . . they pray for
> the *increase* of the kingdom of Christ, but their languid efforts
> and fruitless prayers scarcely maintain the numbers which
> years ago were enrolled among them[44].

From the 1830s onwards repeated exhortations by denominational leaders still particularly concerned about home missionary work *began* with the assumption that an earlier enthusiasm for evangelism, and old agencies for recruitment, had been largely abandoned. Allowance must be made for the hyperbolic nature of such prophetic utterances, but there is no doubt that they were prompted by a real and important change in Evangelical Nonconformist priorities. Ironically enough, some of the early Victorian advocates of aggressive evangelism provided evidence of the extent of the change partly by their naivety. In March 1849 Richard Knill, a minister sufficiently prominent to be addressing a county assembly of the Chester Congregational Union, announced, with evident pride in his innovative capacity, that he had begun to engage in village preaching in parishes surrounding his chapel. 'It has occurred to me', he said, 'that something of this kind might be adopted generally throughout the kingdom'[45]. Thus, incredibly, by the mid-nineteenth century a minister could advance as innovative precisely what had been normal a generation or so earlier.

The trend towards organisational consolidation was exemplified most obviously in chapel building. The acquisition of a permanent place of worship at once gave permanency to, and imposed limits on, the work of a religious organisation in a particular locality. But it also in many cases reflected the changing aspirations of denominations and congregations undergoing *lift*. Victorian chapels bore witness to what sociologists of religion have called the paradox of 'mixed motivation' underlying the behaviour of permanent religious associations[46]. It was possible to rationalise chapel building on the theory that a new chapel represented a new base for recruitment, and to an extent the rationalisation was justified. Suburban chapels, in particular, were foci for habitual church-goers migrating from city centres[47]. But the primary functions of the chapel had to do with the social requirements of an *existing* Nonconformist community. A chapel was a symbol of status, a focus for group identity, a centre of social as well as religious activity. It was 'the public equivalent of the parlour mantel-piece', John Betjeman has suggested in a passage emphasising the extent to which the erection of a chapel became an end in itself for many a Nonconformist community[48].

If, as their critics stated, there was a tendency by the 1840s for young Nonconformist ministers to 'go forth, not so much as labourers in the vineyard of Christ, as inquirers for an easy place, a good salary, and respectable society'[49], there was a parallel tendency for the Nonconformist rank and file to demand chapels in a 'style of building that did not suit the circumstances' of their fathers, sited 'in the most prominent and eligible positions' that their means could command, and constructed 'with a strict regard to the convenience and taste of the improving age'[50]. Neither tendency operated in isolation, of course, and described in isolation they are caricatures representing single aspects of the 'mixed motivation' underlying the behaviour of clergy and laity alike. But both tendencies reflected the effects of *lift* on the expectations which Nonconformists applied to the ordering of their communities, and both help to explain the link between the religious-cultural evolution of Evangelical Nonconformity and the change in its growth pattern around 1840.

Algernon Wells stated in 1849:

> God has not assigned to us the power or the duty of
> providing for the religious wants of the whole community. The
> influence of our testimony, example, and efforts is not always
> increased by extension; often it is so weakened, and would be
> augmented by concentration. We want the right men in the
> right places, well supported. A sufficient number of strong
> churches to assist their weaker sisters, but not so many weakly
> churches as to exceed the ability of the stronger to give them
> effectual aid[51].

This statement must be interpreted in the context of the kinds of priorities with which the 'stronger churches' were operating. Instead of the old readiness to subdivide in the interests of growth[52], ministers and congregations were becoming increasingly loath to diminish their own resources, human or financial, for the sake of supporting weak congregations or establishing new centres of denominational activity[53].

The improvement in taste evident in the kinds of meeting houses being built by Nonconformists in the 1840s was both 'unexpected' and 'agreeable', John Blackburn, a leading Congregational minister and editor of the *Congregational Magazine*, remarked to the Congregational Union in 1847[54]. His paper entitled, 'Remarks on ecclesiastical architecture as applied to Nonconformist chapels', was itself evidence of profound religious-cultural change in Nonconformity. It was not the kind of paper which had found either author or audience during the period of intense evangelisation a generation or so earlier in Nonconformist history. But in dealing with a subject which presupposed, not simply a strategy of consolidation but a preoccupation with the social and aesthetic satisfactions of established Nonconformist communities, Blackburn was introducing a theme which was to receive constant attention during the Victorian era[55].

'Most fervently do we hope that "the religion of barns" is

passing away from among us', Blackburn concluded. 'When money is to be spent for the service of God, we are bound to use it with taste and judgment, so as to attract, rather than repel persons of intelligence and respectability'[58]. Fifty years earlier Nonconformists had felt bound by other priorities. *Lift* had raised the expectations of Nonconformist members, diverting resources and energies from recruitment. Subscriptions instead of souls, the author of *Temporal Prosperity and Spiritual Decline* called the resulting emphasis[57]. But this was only part of the problem. The pretentiously middle-class ethos of the emerging Victorian Nonconformity, the preoccupation with order, respectability, and style, reinforced the external societal pressures cutting Methodist, Congregational, and Baptist communities adrift from the lower sections of the social constituency on which they had relied during the early industrial age. While Walter Wilson had complained early in the nineteenth century that 'large accessions in numbers' had been lowering the social 'quality' of Nonconformity[58], in 1849 Miall was worried about the 'preference of quality over numbers' characteristic of his contemporaries[59].

The Victorian confrontation between Church and Chapel

Chapter 6 dealt with the Church of England and the preceding section of this chapter has focused on Evangelical Nonconformity in an effort to account for the discontinuities evident in the development of each religious culture around the beginning of the Victorian era, discontinuities which help to explain the subsequent history of Victorian religion. Neither Church nor Chapel religiosity can be understood in isolation, however, for while the character of Victorian religion was moulded partly by separate internal developments within individual religious organisations, and partly by wider societal processes operating independently of any form of organised religion, it was also greatly influenced by *interactions* between these two phenomena. So important were the interactions, and so ubiquitous their effects on the general social and political life of the society, that from the late 1830s to the middle of the 1900s, in G. Kitson Clark's words, 'religion had received so political a shape, or politics so religious a shape, that it was for many people almost impossible to separate the two'. Victorian and early Edwardian England seemed to be 'obsessed' with the Church—Chapel confrontation, 'and referred everything back to it'[60].

Church, Chapel, and pressure-group politics

If one looks for political or, more precisely, for legislative evidence of progress towards religious equality in England, it is apparent that a profound change occurred during the second quarter of the nineteenth century. The period from 1789 to 1828 had been barren of concessions from the religious Establishment; indeed, in 1800 and 1811 Methodists and Dissenters had been hard-pressed to defend some of the most important religious liberties already possessed. But the Repeal of the

Test and Corporation Acts and the Roman Catholic Relief Act, passed in 1828 and 1829 respectively, were followed by a seventy-year period of intense, more or less continuous, and gradually successful political and ecclesiastical pressure against Establishment privilege. The following list of ecclesiastical legislation provides a rather skeletal view of what has been called the 'gradual disestablishment' of the Church of England, and emphasises the politicisation of Church—Chapel relationships during the Victorian era:

1836 Registration of Births, Deaths and Marriages Act
1836 Solemnization of Marriages Act
1854 Act for Reform of Oxford University
1854 Act for Extending Licences of Dissenting Places of Worship
1856 Act for Reform of Cambridge University
1860 Act for Opening Grammar Schools to Dissenters
1866 Act for Removing Religious Oaths for Public Offices
1868 Compulsory Church Rates Abolition Act
1869 Act for Removing Clerical Restrictions in Grammar Schools
1869 Irish Church Disestablishment and Disendowment Act
1871 Act for Abolition of Religious Tests at the Universities
1880 Burial Laws Amendment Act
1882 Act for Removing Clerical Restrictions in Oxford and Cambridge
1887 Act for the Restriction of Church of England Patronage
1891 Tithe Rent-Charge Recovery Act
1898 Nonconformist Marriages (Attendance of Registrars) Act

The list provides only a partial view of parliamentary involvement in the conflict between Nonconformists and Churchmen. In the first place, it includes only those pieces of legislation which were successful, yet in many cases a Bill became law only after much similar legislation had been rejected or shelved at Westminster. The Compulsory Church Rates Abolition Act of 1868, for example, came only as the culmination of a campaign lasting more than thirty years, and only after the House of Lords had thrown out several earlier Bills which had been passed by the Commons. Second, the list excludes education legislation which, while dealing with many non-ecclesiastical matters, raised some of the most serious and intense religious debates of the age. The Factory Education Bill of 1843, the Elementary Education Act of 1870, and the Balfour Education Act of 1902 aroused Church—Chapel animosities matched in intensity only by the peaks of anti-church rate and disestablishment agitation.

It is significant that 'gradual disestablishment' was implemented by a succession of governments all of which were composed very largely of Anglicans, landowners, and 'middle-class intruders' who 'blended into the aristocratic landscape—or wished to'[61]. Indeed, the mass of progressive legislation which emerged from Victorian Westminster, extending the foundations of modern British democracy, was to a large extent extorted from the ruling classes by pressure-group politics carried out by aspiring social classes and interests still on the peripheries of parliamentary power. This was as true of ecclesiastical legislation as it was of the repeal of the Corn Laws or the extension of the franchise. Consequently, the ecclesiastical battles of the age had to be fought and won at the popular level before the issues could be expected to win parliamentary approval. The result was a situation in which Churchmen and Nonconformists, through pamphlets and newspapers, public meetings and national organisations, sermons and petitions, sought to influence politicians, parties, and public opinion either for or against the residual and slowly vanishing privileges of the reformed Establishment. The heat of the controversy waxed and waned, but because it deeply implicated the rank and file of both religious cultures the confrontation exercised a decisive influence on the history and character of Victorian religion.

The religious division assumed added significance because both at the level of leadership and at the level of popular support it overlapped socially, and sometimes personally, with wider socio-political issues. The upsurge of Church–Chapel rivalry from the 1830s onwards was in fact part of a broad current of social change. The men who took over Vestry Meetings in the late 1830s were the same people who had gained access to municipal office as a result of the Municipal Corporations Act of 1835; and in many places the old municipal oligarchies consciously used their power to levy church rates as a weapon against the 'usurpers' of power in their municipalities[62]. The Anti-Corn Law League and its contemporary, the Anti-State Church Association of 1844, were generically related. Analysing religious alignments of the Corn Law issue, for example, Cobden explained:

> We have . . . the majority of every denomination with us – I mean the Dissenting denominations; we have them almost *en masse*, both ministers and laymen; and I believe the only body against us, as a body, are the members of the Church of England[63].

The Anti-State Church Association obviously attracted much less support than the Anti-Corn Law League. Its objectives were specifically ecclesiastical. But it did attract support from the same *range* of social groups as the larger movement: groups at odds with the Establishment, civil and religious. It also employed similar methods of organisation and agitation. And its successor, the Liberation Society, established in 1853, not only became 'the epitome of rational agitation' during the second half of the nineteenth century, but was 'connected with other radical and middle-class political and religious bodies by a system of interlocking directorates'[64]. It shared leaders as well as members, for example, with organisations such as the Reform Movement, the Ballot Society, and the Peace Society[65]. Its organs, *The Nonconformist*, under the editorship of Edward Miall, and *The Liberator*, were dedicated not only to disestablishment and the redress of Dissenting disabilities, but also to electoral reform, reform of the educational system and the armed services, and to the curtailment of the privileges of the landed interest.

Like any well-organised pressure-group, the Liberation Society combined continuous low key agitation with sporadic phases of intense campaigning. The latter naturally were timed to capitalise on critical situations, such as general elections, periods of parliamentary preoccupation with ecclesiastical legislation, or phases of public indignation aroused by notable episodes of religious discrimination. Thus the early 1840s, when Dissenters were jailed for refusing church rates; the period 1859—60, when the anti-church rate movement reached a peak of popular agitation; the early and mid-1870s, when opposition to aspects of the 1870 Education Act precipitated massive Disestablishment campaigning; and the period 1902—06, which saw actual civil disobedience provoked by the religious provisions of Balfour's Education Act, stood out as the high points of the Nonconformist confrontation with the religious Establishment[66]. During such periods, particularly from the 1850s onwards, there would swing into action a national network of local organisations, efficiently directed from the centre, supplied with polemical literature, linked in a coordinated strategy, and served by a staff of political experts and agents[67]. At the constituency level there was no better political machine in Victorian England. Through it Nonconformity exercised a powerful influence on the development of the wider society; but, obversely, the associations between local chapel communities and Liberationist activities, which became very close especially during the phases of intense anti-Establishment pressure, meant that popular loyalties to Nonconformity were tried to a significant degree to the exigencies of a political and ecclesiastical situation destined quickly to disappear as the twentieth century brought new issues and problems to the fore.

The political and social orientations of Victorian Nonconformity were not, of course, either exhaustively or exclusively those of the Liberation Society. The Society was merely the most conspicuous of a number of pressure-group organisations which implicated many Nonconformist individuals and communities in the multifaceted liberal and radical opposition to institutionalised privilege, inequality, or discrimination in Victorian society. Moreover, it had to compete for the political energies of Nonconformists with another pressure group which was neither liberal nor radical in its essential inspiration: the Temperance Movement. The 'Temperance Question' cut across party and denominational lines, although it evoked most sympathy in Parliament from the Liberals; and it created divisions within rather than between denominational organisations[68]. Insofar as it did succeed in effecting a profound change in English religious attitudes to alcohol, a change with important consequences for the social significance of religious commitment, the Temperance Movement played an important role in relationships between Victorian religion and society. But because it remained tangential to the fundamental ecclesiastical and political alignments of the age, it exercised an influence on the development of English religion less primary than that of the Liberation Society and kindred associations.

This was true despite the lack of consensus within Nonconformist communities about the appropriateness of pressure-group politics. It is clear from evidence about the denominational affiliations of leading Liberationists, and from the denominational breakdown of petitions sent to Westminster during controversies about education, Church Rates, or disestablishment, that Wesleyanism, even in the Victorian era, tended to be more apolitical, less radical, or at least less vocal than other forms of Nonconformity[69]. Many historians have seriously exaggerated the conservatism of Wesleyanism, however, and by so doing have exaggerated also differences of social and political orientation which certainly did exist within and between Nonconformist bodies. In the first place, there always had been an element of social and religious protest in Wesleyan commitment which, in a still prescriptive society, had carried obvious political implications[70]. The semblance of a conservative, apolitical consensus in early industrial Wesleyanism was an illusion based on the utterances and decisions of connexional leaders who were conspicuously unsuccessful in carrying the rank and file with them on precisely this issue. Second, even at the leadership level Wesleyan political alignments had begun to change decisively in a liberal direction around the beginning of the Victorian era. In 1843 an official Wesleyan campaign against the Education Act had been launched, and in the Annual Presidential Address to the Wesleyan Conference the leadership had conceded that an open anti-Establishment animus was abroad in Wesleyan communities[71]. Within the Nonconformist denominations of the mid-Victorian era, Frederick George Lee, an Anglican observer, wrote in 1868, only 'an uninfluential handful of Wesleyans' remained aloof from the Gladstonian Radical-Liberal coalition which seemed bent on destroying Establishment privilege. And by the close of the nineteenth century, when most of the major issues had been resolved, largely in favour of Nonconformity, and fresh doubts were beginning to emerge as to the appropriateness of Nonconformist involvements in politics, the 'religious' (as distinct from 'political') Dissenters were at least as strong within the Baptist denomination as they were in Wesleyanism.

The Church of England was not as dependent on the tactics of pressure-group politics as its opponents were, for it retained various channels of more direct access to decision-making processes within the society. But from quite early in the Victorian era Anglicans justifiably began to lose confidence in the will and ability of the reformed Parliament to uphold the religious Establishment against popular and interest group pressures. The result was the rise of Anglican agencies designed partly or wholly to counter the work of the Liberation society and similar bodies, and to strengthen the resolve of the predominantly Anglican Parliament on ecclesiastical questions. As early as 1848 local unions of churchmen were set up for 'defence against aggression' in many English towns particularly affected by anti-State Church propaganda[72]. Similarly, in the campaign to revive Convocation[73], which culminated in the Convocations of Canterbury and York becoming active again in 1851 and 1860 respectively, there was a strong element of defensive reaction against political Nonconformity[74].

A proliferation of local 'Church defence' committees and associations in the 1850s created a context from which two national Anglican organisations emerged during the period of intense Church–Chapel rivalry in 1859–60. One was the Church Defence Institution, a body defining itself as 'an Association of Clergy and Laity for Defensive and General Purposes'. It was established in 1859. The other was the

Church Congress, the original session of which was organised in 1861 by the Cambridge Church Defence Association. 'We are convinced', the local Association explained in proposing the Congress, 'that a zealous endeavour to stimulate the energies of the Church, and to apply correctives to acknowledged defects of the system from within are not less efficient measures of Church Defence than the defeat of destructive attacks from without'[75]. There were, in other words, two imperatives behind the rise of new forms of Anglican organisations: one being the need to counter 'attacks from without', the other the need to 'stimulate the energies of the Church' by internal changes.

The realisation of both objectives depended on the mobilisation of the Church of England laity. A recurrent theme in the Anglican press of the second half of the nineteenth century, and in forums such as the Church Congress, was the increasing inability of the old squire—parson alliance—the traditional alignment of the Church with the landed aristocracy—to guarantee the security of the religious Establishment. As political power and influence in English society passed gradually to the Victorian middle classes, enlisting the support of middle-class laymen and implicating them in Anglican affairs became an obvious and fundamental ecclesiastical strategy. As one clergyman put it in 1880: 'If we in the Church of England do not deal with the masses, the masses will deal with us. We depend, as far as our organisation goes at present, on the popular vote of the country'[76].

This kind of perception of the new Victorian relationship between the Church and the wider society led, within Anglicanism, to religious-cultural trends which were the reverse of those occurring in Victorian Nonconformity. For while the transition from *sect* to *denomination* involved the increasing professionalisation and functional dominance of the ministry, the trend towards denominationalism in a church type organisation like the Church of England made the organisation increasingly dependent on the active support of its lay members. In a denominational situation, where allegiance was voluntary and where alternative forms of religious commitment were available, the ex-monopolistic Church of England had to offer its laity new satisfactions and to find for laymen an expanded role in ecclesiastical affairs. The imperative was not simply that of membership retention. For as an evangelistic agency and as a pressure group confronting political Nonconformity, the Victorian Church could ill afford to rely on the combined efforts of the clergy and a handful of eminent lay patrons. The future of Anglicanism both as a religious denomination and as a religious Establishment had become too dependent on 'the popular vote of the country'.

The Church Defence Institution never achieved the organisational coherence of the Liberation Society, although it is evident that Henry Hoare, the prominent London banker, and his associates who launched the organisation in the 1850s, hoped that it would provide Anglicanism with an equivalent capability for national pressure-group politics[77]. It was not until the final decade of the century, when the effectiveness of the Liberation Society was beginning to wane, that the Institution had grown strong enough to match its Nonconformist opposition. Hoare's ambitious plans for a highly organised system of local, regional and national councils and associations devolved, in practice, into a fairly unwieldy system which was capable of effective action only during short periods of ecclesiastical crisis. When the Liberation Society, or the exigencies of national politics, thrust some major ecclesiastical issue into the forefront of national attention, local Church Defence Associations sprang to life, encouraged by the Anglican press and by the exhortations and strategies of individual Church leaders. At such times, like local Liberationist agencies, the Associations organised petitions, held public meetings, canvassed widely and lobbied local members of Parliament. Between crises, however, their organisational weaknesses prevented the kind of steady propagandist pressure which emanated from Nonconformist communities against the Establishment[78]. Thus in the political aspects of Church—Chapel conflict the Church of England was forced on to the defensive. It was capable of exerting fairly effective reactionary pressure, but political Nonconformity generally exercised the aggressor's prerogative of controlling the timing and the specific issues of the major confrontations.

Church, Chapel, and denominational competition

Besides being an aspect of the mounting social and political pressures in Victorian society against institutionalised privilege and inequality, the exacerbation of Church—Chapel relations from the 1830s onwards was also an inevitable consequence of the specifically religious processes of denominationalism which were transforming both the Church of England and the Nonconformist bodies. The anti-Establishment animus of Victorian Nonconformity, in other words, was partly a reaction against a Church which, as a Baptist editor conceded ruefully in 1859, had never before in its history displayed 'such signs of vigour, such evidence of awakening life'[79]. A denominational situation is a pluralistic situation in which commitment is voluntary. It is therefore a competitive situation. Hence as the Church of England began to assume a denominational type of orientation to the wider society in the 1830s and 1840s it placed a new pressure on all the Nonconformist bodies. If in the arena of pressure-group politics the Nonconformists had the initiative, in the matter of organisational growth the metamorphosis of the religious Establishment definitely threw chapel communities on to the defensive.

In 1859 the *Protestant Dissenters' Almanack* argued that the growth of Nonconformity determined its development in other respects, and explicitly linked the political aggression of Nonconformist bodies, and that measure of subcultural insularity which they still displayed, with the tendency for Nonconformists to react against social or ecclesiastical forces inhibiting the expansion of their communities. The political activities of Nonconformity, the *Almanack* claimed, were 'the incidental and contingent efforts *resulting from growth*'. They were the result of the movement's *'collision with the barriers that opposed that growth'*[80]. As a complete explanation this was simplistic. But the perception that the activities of the religious Establishment could be a 'barrier' restricting Nonconformist growth was significant. The awareness of Anglican competition, and in some cases the exaggerated awareness of such competition, suddenly had emerged as a major influence on the organisational strategy of Nonconformist leaders. In 1839 John Angell James explained to his Congregational brethren that:

> It seems to be the present policy of the Church of England to build us *down* and to build us *out*. Its members suppose that our congregations continue with us, only because there are no Episcopalian places to receive them; and acting upon this mistake, they are multiplying chapels and churches, many of which are erected in the immediate vicinity of ours, for the purpose of drawing into them the people *we* have gathered[81].

Granted the previous concentration of Nonconformist recruiting in areas where the parochial system was ineffective, this was an understandable response to improved parochial efficiency. There was, moreover, a strong element of *conscious* aggression in the Anglican resurgence, a commitment to reform with the specific objective of throwing back the Nonconformist advances of the previous century. Under the heading, 'What the Church needs; what the Church desires; and what the Church will have', *The Churchman* insisted in an 1843 editorial:

> She will have an adequate provision of churches, ministers, and schools for the population. She knows that voluntaryism cannot and will not provide for the spiritual wants of the population; and that it is just because the country has, during a century past, confided, most unwisely, the instruction of the masses to unauthorized and voluntary teachers, that therefore the people are now sunken in ignorance and left in thick darkness[82].

Despite the formation of the Evangelical Alliance in 1846, the early nineteenth century era of popular ecumenism, which occasionally had united Church and Chapel folk, had ended by the 1830s and 1840s. The Alliance, launched primarily as an anti-Catholic movement during the agitation surrounding the Maynooth Grant, and led (on the Nonconformist side) by men like John Angell James, and (on the Anglican side) by Evangelicals like Edward Bickersteth, had little apparent effect on relations between Church and Chapel at the local level. James's recognition of the conflict of interests between Nonconformist growth and Anglican expansion has been quoted above; and Bickersteth, from the opposite perspective, detected an anti-Church 'poison in the viens of dissent'[83].

It was probably inevitable that Nonconformist organisations would react strongly to the Anglican challenge, not just politically, but also in defence of the quantitative position they had attained in the religious life of the nation. Having described the expansionist policies of the Church in his 1839 speech, James insisted that to prevent the encroachment of the Establishment into areas of Nonconformist influence, Nonconformity would have to 'keep pace' in a race to claim territory by building permanent, respectable churches. The Church was consecrating an average of eight new or rebuilt churches per month in the early 1840s[84], and the leaders of Nonconformity were impressed and apprehensive. 'Enlargements, re-erections, and new erections must go on amongst us', James said, 'according to our ability, and with an energy in some measure resembling the Church of England.' In this work *extension* would have to give pride of place to *consolidation*. The implications of the policy were inescapable:

> Town Missions, etc., are all well in their place; but there wants something in addition, to gather up, consolidate and retain to ourselves, the effects which these means produce: and that something is the erection of places of worship. We must catch the building spirit of the age. We must *build, build, build,* . . . We cannot multiply our persons, unless we multiply our places[85].

The era of multiplying persons, whether in barns, cottages, or rented rooms, was being superseded by the era of church building. The recruitment of persons remained high in the professed objectives of Nonconformist organisations, but energies increasingly were being devoted to consolidation. While chapel building reflected many social and cultural pressures not connected with growth, Victorian Nonconformity made chapel building its basic strategy for the recruitment and retention of members. A chapel was regarded as the most effective magnet for holding a congregation together, and for drawing outsiders into a Nonconformist community. At a Wesleyan District Meeting in Norwich in 1850, the Conference President, advocating a hard line against recalcitrant 'reformers', argued that 'expulsion must be carried on through the land — to the extent if necessary of *every member*, and then . . . *we shall have* the chapels, and we can begin again, as Wesley did, and shall soon have Methodism more glorious than ever'[86]. The conception of growth under-lying this confident assertion was in fact far removed from that of Wesley, but it was, in somewhat extreme form, a conception typical of Victorian Nonconformity.

Because it depended on the availability of considerable financial resources, the effect of chapel building was to concentrate Nonconformist activities: it inhibited the kind of expansion characteristic of the early industrial 'religion of barns', and it threatened the survival of congregations too poor or too small to finance a chapel building pro-gramme. Two recurrent themes in the councils of Victorian Noncon-formity were the decline of Nonconformist representation in rural areas, and the failure of the movement to establish itself in the poorer districts of large cities. Both problems were compounded by the strategy of consolida-tion implicit in the emphasis on chapel building. The rural itinerancy of the eighteenth and early nineteenth centuries had been relatively un-demanding financially because it had relied considerably on lay agencies, and because the congregations produced had been content to use private or inexpensive accommodation for long periods. But its very success had bequeathed to Victorian Nonconformity a multiplicity of small rural congregations which quickly became insolvent in an era in which the policy was to *'build, build, build'*.

After the Bible Christians, the Primitive Methodist Connexion was the most rural of all Nonconformist bodies. In the period 1894—96, when they conducted a survey initiated by an awareness of growing organisational difficulties, Primitive Methodists discovered that 75 per cent of their chapels and most of their 'preaching places' were in villages. In the light of this fact, it was with justifiable alarm that the Conference noted 'that during the last twenty-five years we have abandoned 516 places, and only succeeded in opening up 236 new ones, thus showing a decline of 280 in our country societies'[87]. The previous twenty-five years had seen total Primitive Methodist membership increase by 21.5 per cent from 149,716 to 181,941. The process of retrenchment in rural areas, in other words, reflected the concentration of connexional resources, both human and material, in fewer, but large communities. This was a common phenomenon in later Victorian Nonconformity. 'In most of the rural parts of the country there is a decrease in church membership', a Baptist Home Mission report commented in 1884, noting that 'the increase is to be looked for in larger towns and in cities'[88]. The continuing conviction that in rural areas there was an unacceptable leakage of 'young men and women' to the Church of England because 'the chapels themselves are in many cases not very attractive'[89], meant that the defensive compulsion to build imposing places of worship continued to operate even where the strategy was not economically viable.

Denominational competition was only one element in the making of this impasse. Spurred on by the fear of Anglican proselytisation, by the assumption that the continuing allegiance of chapel members might in many cases depend on the provision of a satisfactory physical environment for worship, the preoccupation with chapel building was also a matter of changing tastes and priorities, of new expectations and satisfactions prevalent in chapel communities; and the serious financial pressures on rural Nonconformity in the final quarter of the nineteenth century were exacerbated by the prolonged agricultural depression which had begun in 1873. What is more, the Church of England was itself effected seriously by secular economic obstacles to the maintenance of adequate religious operations in many rural and working-class urban areas. The economic basis of the parochial system was still largely in landed property, and as the value of such property diminished, particularly after 1873, the endowments of rural livings inevitably suffered. By the first decade of the present century almost every second parish in England was obliged to augment its parochial endowment with a voluntary Easter offering, a practice which had been rare before the 1880s[90].

Nevertheless, in the economics of denominational rivalry the Church remained the more competitive religious system. Voluntary subscriptions, a source of additional income for the parochial clergy, were all that Nonconformist organisations had. The significance of this reliance on the beneficence of their laity was not so much to limit the total financial resources of Nonconformist organisations as to limit the objects of Nonconformist expenditure. There was an obvious tendency for wealthy congregations to be more forthcoming in support of local projects, from which their own immediate communities would benefit, than they were in support of denominational projects in poorer areas or on the 'home mission' field. One of the important victories achieved by the early Ecclesiastical Commissioners had been the establishment of the principle of *need* rather than the principle of *locality* as the basic criterion for dispensing financial assistance within the parochial system[91]. The principle was never established within Nonconformity, although the Wesleyan Yearly Collection, which had begun in the 1790s, like later Sustentation Funds in most other Nonconformist organisations, had been inspired by a recognition of the need to channel resources from rich districts to poorer ones.

In general, however, as the overhead costs of maintaining Nonconformist operations rose throughout the Victorian era, the tendency was for the denominations to flourish only where there was a clientele economically capable of supporting a minister and his family, and of acquiring a chapel sufficiently elegant to satisfy middle-class tastes and expectations. The same tendency was at work within the Church of England, but its impact was mitigated by the greater rationality of Anglican financial administration from the 1830s onwards, and by the resilience of parochial structures. The parochial system was not invulnerable, but a parochial ministry could not be discontinued in the way a rural Nonconformist ministry might. The social, legal, and historical ramifications of the system were too strong, too pervasive. It was therefore with some justification that Victorian Nonconformists often viewed the parochial basis of the Church with envy.

The Catholic subculture

While relationships between Church and Chapel dominated the public events of Victorian and Edwardian religion, and determined the essential role of religion within the society as a whole, an increasingly important ancillary process was the re-emergence of English Catholicism as a popular religious force. To that minority of the aristocracy and landed gentry which had sustained Catholicism throughout the grave difficulties of the century after 1689, Irish immigration, especially to the cities of the north-west, the west Midlands, and the Greater London area, added a constant flow of recruits which rapidly transformed the aristocratic minority religious culture into a movement capable of threatening the quantitative positions of Church and Chapel alike. Between 1851 and 1901 there were never fewer than 425,000 Irish-born residents in England, and this continuing inflow of migrants augmented the natural increase of a Catholic constituency of first and subsequent generations of Anglo-Irish[92].

Anti-Catholicism had deep roots in the consciousness of Protestant England, but its exacerbation during the Victorian era was a result both of the sheer growth of the Catholic population and of the association of this growth process with the vexed and complex question of Anglo—Irish relations. The process of Catholic expansion, in short, was not made less alarming by the fact that it was almost entirely exogenous. Very few English Catholics were recruited from the natural constituencies of either Anglicanism or Nonconformity; and although the rhetoric of Catholic leaders sometimes was ill-advisedly aggressive, there was not between Protestants and Catholics the kind of denominational competition characteristic of relations between Church and Chapel. Yet for English Protestantism generally the rise of this new kind of English Catholicism inspired an apprehension which transcended denominational rivalries.

The Evangelical Alliance of 1846 was an example of anti-Catholicism uniting Churchmen and Nonconformists even during a period of considerable conflict between them over almost every other political or ecclesiastical issue. The formation of the Alliance occurred during the aftermath of the Maynooth controversy[93], and while the shock of John Henry Newman's defection to Rome remained to stir the fears of those who saw Tractarianism as a form of Catholic subversion[94]. A comparable explosion of anti-Catholic feeling occurred five years later when the papal Rescript of 1850 reconstituted a Catholic hierarchy in England, and when statements issued by Nicholas Wiseman, the new Cardinal, and by Pius IX, seemed to be inaugurating a phase of concerted 'Papal Aggression'[95]. But between such high points of Protestant reaction an underlying anti-Catholicism remained an important ingredient of English religious culture. Itinerant lecturers made careers out of exploiting anti-Irish and anti-Catholic themes during preaching tours which spread legacies of violence and bitterness across the nation[96]. In so doing, however, these extremists were merely echoing prejudices already well nourished by popular polemics and by the attitudes and example of a multitude of Protestant ministers and clergymen.

It is an index of the seriousness of Protestant apprehension about the re-emergence of a strong Catholic element in English society that William Gladstone, a statesman identified with the rights of extra-Establishment religious bodies, could while Prime Minister associate himself with a major attack on the Catholic Church. Prompted by the promulgation of the Vatican Decrees, Gladstone in 1874 detected 'foreign arrogance' in Catholic claims, and questioned the loyalty of the Catholic Church as an English institution by arguing that its authority-structures made it potentially subversive of national loyalties[97]. But to these traditional ingredients of the anti-Catholic ideology he added a specifically ecclesiastical factor: the continuing insistence of the Catholic Church on its exclusive legitimacy in a societal context attuned increasingly to the denominational assumption of pluralistic legitimacy. 'All other Christian bodies', he pointed out, were 'content with freedom in their own religious domain'.

From a sociological point of view this principle of exclusive legitimacy reinforced the religious-cultural orientation imposed on English Catholicism by the ethnic distinctiveness of its major constituency and by the generalised antipathy which it had inherited from its sixteenth- and seventeenth-century past. For within the English religious context the *churchly* assertion of exclusive legitimacy amounted, for all practical purposes, to the adoption of a characteristically *sectarian* position. Victorian Catholicism was a subcultural phenomenon. Upper-class converts found themselves ostracised, and sometimes debarred legally from exercising spiritual care over their heirs. Lady Herbert of Lea, who was converted to Catholicism in 1865, found herself powerless to bring up her five children, including the heir to the earldom of Pembroke, according to her newfound faith. As a biographer put it, 'the engines of the Law separated mother from children and they were carefully brought up in the Church of England as wards in Chancery'[98]. Such overt discrimination against the aristocratic Catholic minority was merely an adjunct to less obvious but more pervasive social pressures. Herbert Vaughan, a future Cardinal, complained about the Catholic aristocracy and gentry in 1867, remarking 'that if they wish to act upon Society they must love *public duty*'[99]. But it was not lack of initiative, it was social and religious-cultural marginality within the society which underlay the evident incapacity of upper-class Catholics to play a very prominent role in the social changes of the Victorian era. And at the other extreme of English Catholicism's polarised social spectrum, working-class Catholics from the Anglo-Irish subculture were separated just as emphatically from the mainstream of English life.

Thus while English Nonconformity emerged from the religious-cultural isolation of its sectarian phase to challenge the Anglican ascendancy in Victorian and Edwardian society, English Catholicism stood aloof from the ensuing Church—Chapel confrontation. Its quantitative position greatly improved, but only because of its appeal to socially marginal constituents. In the denominational competition for the Victorian middle-class constituency, which involved the competitors in the main arena of British politics, the Catholic Church was not implicated deeply[100]. Benjamin Disraeli once remarked that only if grocers began to embrace Catholicism would he begin to worry about a Catholic reconversion of England. But while in saying this Disraeli showed a clear perception of the subcultural nature of the Catholic resurgence, he at the same time betrayed a midunderstanding of the general direction of religious change in England. For English society was moving rapidly towards an era of complete religious pluralism, when each religious culture would be able to appeal effectively only to subgroups within the wider society; and it was changing less rapidly, but no less definitely, in a secular direction. Religion *per se* would in the long run become a subcultural phenomenon. Therefore the subcultural orientation of Victorian Catholicism, while it kept Catholics on the periphery of the major social and political issues of Victorian society, at the same time helped to render the Catholic Church more impervious than other religious bodies to the secularising tendencies of the late nineteenth and twentieth centuries[101].

Ecclesiastical history sometimes appears to be neither more nor less than the history of the religious intelligentsia, and the temptation to tolerate so partial a view is particularly strong in the case of Victorian religion. The age was marked by controversies bitter and prolonged, precipitated by such things as the intellectual polemics of the Tractarians, Darwin's *Origin of Species* (1859), the provocative theological symposium *Essays and Reviews* (1860) and its milder successor *Lux Mundi* (1889), and the publication of the Vatican Decrees in 1870. The *Zeitgeist* of Victorian society was fascinated by the impact on traditional verities of new worlds of thought emanating from scientific and social theorists, secular philosophers, students of comparative religion, and iconoclastic German theologians. Poets and novelists portrayed the trauma of the loss of faith in individuals[1], and the editors of newspapers and serious journals provided forums for a religious elite which grappled publicly with questions of doubt and disbelief. Pessimistic about the future of religion, articulate Victorians were preoccupied by it almost to the point of morbidity.

But those Victorians articulate still, in the second half of the nineteenth century, obviously did not constitute a cross-section of their society. They were the talented, the well-educated, the fortuitous, the kinds of people whose beliefs and values are recorded for posterity either by themselves or by others, the kinds of people whose private papers find preservation in archives. It is no easy task to generalise from what they wrote, and what was written about them, to the attitudes of the whole society. 'I falter where I firmly trod', wrote Tennyson in his famous *In Memoriam*,

> And falling with my world of cares
> Upon the world's great altar stairs
> That lead thro' darkness up to God
>
> I stretch lame hands of faith, and grope
> And gather dust and chaff, and call
> To what I feel is Lord of all,
> And faintly trust the larger hope[2].

Evocative of a spirit of profound doubt and uncertainty which pervades the whole poem, these words are adduced by some observers as characteristic of the Victorian age. *In Memoriam* has been called the 'representative' poem of mid-nineteenth century England[3]. But *was* Tennyson's 'crisis of faith' part of a new phenomenon of ideological secularisation which set the Victorian age apart from early periods of English religious history[4]? And if it was, *can* the decline of religion in the twentieth century be attributed at least partly to a gradual erosion of religious practice by this tide of doubt and disbelief which began to rise within the minds of Victorian believers?

The Victorian crisis of faith

In arguing, as this chapter will seek to argue, that the intellectual ferment of the Victorian years differed from that of earlier periods in important aspects of tone and substance, and in the extent to which it implicated the ordinary churchgoing population as well as the religious intelligentsia, notice must also be taken of the historical continuities in the situation. For the growing institutional stability of the mid-nineteenth century was accompanied by a reappearance of the problem of theological radicalism and counterreligious thought which had plagued the early Hanoverian Church, but which had been largely submerged by other issues in early industrial society. Indeed, in many respects the pessimism of Victorians beset by doubts or surrounded by doubters echoed laments about the future of religion which had become commonplace during the controversies over Deism and Rationalism in the early eighteenth century.

The early Hanoverians had of course greatly overemphasised the extent to which doubt and disbelief in their own society had subverted the influence of religion. One of the most famous of them, Joseph Butler, had prefaced his *Analogy of Religion*, published in 1736, with the remark that for many of his contemporaries Christianity had ceased even to be a subject of serious inquiry. He had observed that 'all people of discernment' were dismissing religious belief as 'fictitious', and that it remained in vogue simply as 'a principal subject of mirth and ridicule'[5]. But Butler had been wrong, and his pessimism is a standing warning against the uncritical acceptance of contemporary observations about the beliefs and values of a society. There was irony in the fact that within a few years of writing these words he had felt obliged, as Bishop of Bristol, to upbraid the young John Wesley for precipitating excessive religious enthusiasm in English society; and Wesley, for his part, had begun to demonstrate how slightly the intellectual fads of the upper classes reflected the religiosity of the whole society.

A question of obvious importance is whether the Victorian 'crisis of faith' was similarly limited in its impact. Kitson Clark, to cite perhaps the most eminent authority to have addressed the issue, has gone as far as to suggest that

> viewed from, so to speak, more nearly the ground level of the
> ordinary not very intelligent, not very erudite, human being
> the scene changes, the intellectual issues raised — the problems
> propounded by biblical criticism or the question of the

whereabouts of authority in religion or even the challenge of
evolution — fade into the background and other equally
important problems take their place[6].

But while a preoccupation with ideological aspects of a religious system
does in many instances obscure the attitudes, concerns, and activities of
the ordinary churchgoer, there is evidence that in the Victorian Churches
the very problems identified by Kitson Clark did loom large in the popular
mind. This was a crucial difference between the intellectual crises of the
early eighteenth and mid-nineteenth centuries. The Victorians certainly
faced other equally important problems, but the fact remains that doubt
and theological uncertainty percolated downwards into the ranks of
ordinary believers to an extent unprecedented.

This popularisation of radical and potentially subversive ideas
in Victorian society added a new dimension to the relationship between
the Churches and the wider intellectual world. Victorian laymen, judged
by the diet served them in popular religious newspapers, periodicals, and
sermons, were capable of considerable theological subtlety, but even those
who were unsubtle could be caught up in the crises of Darwinism or
biblical criticism. Following the appearance of a new English version of
D. F. Strauss's *Das Leben Jesu* in the 1860s, for example, people 'who had
never heard of the name of Strauss or the title of his book, were repeating
the rumour that a German scholar had proved Christianity a fraud'[7].
More commonly, however, the popularisation of controversy involved
many of the rank and file of Church and Chapel communities in earnest
debate and soul-searching. Indeed, it was the involvement of the 'general
public' in Victorian religious controversies, as much as the controversies
themselves, which contemporaries often found noteworthy[8]. W. H.
Mallock, a novelist and frequent commentator on religion, wrote in 1877
of 'Sunday luncheon-tables' at which people who had just arrived home
from church could be heard 'avowing their disbelief in eternal punishment,
and discussing their several theories of a future life'. He was worried about
'the more and more popular form' of theological speculation, and by the
fact that newspapers and periodicals 'addressed avowedly to a lay
audience' were encouraging this trend[9].

What was novel about the situation Mallock described was the
emergence of popular theological speculation within the Churches. Popular
infidelity was not new, but in the past its very hostility to the Christian
tradition had militated against its chances of subverting the faith of the
churchgoing population. Its most famous articulation, in Thomas Paine's
Age of Reason of 1794, was worlds apart from the reverent uncertainties
which troubled Victorian believers. Paine had set out to lay an axe to the
roots of popular religiosity, and he had reached a wide audience. As City
Mission workers discovered unhappily among later generations of the
London working classes, a strong undercurrent of proletarian secularism,
Paineite in the bold invective and blunt ribaldry with which it was expressed, flowed on throughout the nineteenth century[10], augmenting
the more urbane secularism of people like Charles Bradlaugh, George
Jacob Holyoake, and Annie Besant[11]. But as far as the Churches were
concerned, and indeed, in relation to the mainstream of English culture

generally, these were countercultural phenomenon: fear and defensiveness they sometimes provoked, but very seldom the kind of dialogue which might have undermined religious belief. The irreligious might have been reassured or amused, but with few exceptions the faithful usually met counterreligious propaganda with closed minds.

But the Victorian 'crisis of faith' was not precipitated by such counterreligious propaganda. Not secularists, but devout Christians were its most effective proponents. The controversial *Essays and Reviews* of 1860, for example, was the work of six Anglican clergymen and a devout laymen, including a future Archbishop of Canterbury. *Septum Contra Christum* they were called, but the enormous impact of their questioning of traditional approaches to historical theology and Biblical exegesis was inevitable precisely because they were the very opposite. There could be no automatic rejection of ideas couched in reverent language and propagated by theologians professing profound sympathy for the Christian tradition. All the denominations shared this kind of dilemma. As Currie has pointed out, Methodists were bewildered in the second half of the nineteenth century by the fact that their own theological leaders were instigating the challenge to traditional assumptions[12]. As the *Methodist Monthly* put it in 1892:

> They are God-fearing men, they are scholars deeply versed in the letter of the Word of God; they are men whose amiable 'charity' it was an offence to call in question; nay, they are recognized and influential ministers of religion who are the foremost to add to or take from the oracles of God: some questioning the very possibility of inspiration[13].

There was profound misgiving in all the Churches, and like the authors of *Essays and Reviews* within the Anglican community, those in the vanguard of Nonconformist moves to come to terms with wider intellectual tendencies were anathema to some of their brethren. The most famous Victorian Baptist, C. H. Spurgeon, whose periodical, *The Sword and Trowel*, brought tensions among Baptists to a head in 1887 by publishing a series of articles accusing the radicals of the denomination of virtual apostasy, felt that a 'serious question' existed as to 'how far those who abide by the faith once delivered to the saints should fraternise with those who have turned aside to another gospel'[14]. This 'Down Grade' controversy, as it was called, threatened for several years the fairly fragile unity among Baptists which the Baptist Union symbolised and nurtured. Similar internal crises had arisen in Wesleyanism in the early 1880s, when the Rev W. H. Dallinger had been prevented from delivering a Fernley lecture advancing a synthesis of Methodist theology and evolutionary theory[15]; and also among Congregationalists as a result of the airing of advanced theological opinions during a meeting associated with the autumnal session of the Congregational Union held at Leicester in October 1877.

But granted the popularisation of these issues, and the obvious fascination they held for denominational editors, preachers, and pamphleteers, the existence of tension and controversy within the

Churches was less significant than the absence of permanent divisions. And not only was the 'crisis of faith' contained, it also produced very little actual loss of faith. For while there were notable cases of apostasy, doubt generally led not to disbelief but to theological revision of one kind or another. Indeed, it is fundamental to any attempt to explain the decline of religious adherence in modern English society to recognise that the process of decline never has been caused by the *loss* of existing members. Membership retention has not been a major problem.

From as early as 1834, when various churches associated with the Baptist Union began compiling statistics on components of annual membership turnover, a growing number of English religious organisations have collected and collated data on aspects of recruitment and loss. A similar picture emerges in every case[16]. While they have been growing rapidly the religious organisations have had very high turnovers of membership: losses by expulsion, lapsing, and leakage[17] have been high by later standards, but extremely rapid recruitment has more than offset such losses. But as their growth rates have declined, so have their membership turnovers. Losses have actually diminished during the era of serious organisational decline, and the overall decline has taken place simply because recruitment has diminished even more rapidly. In Wesleyanism, for example, annual losses fell from 14.1 per cent of total membership in the previous year in 1881 to only 6.8 per cent in 1932, but the denomination was nevertheless in severe institutional difficulties. For whereas in 1881 it had attracted enough new members to offset the 14.1 per cent loss, fifty years later recruitment had slumped to the point where even greatly reduced losses meant overall decline. Recruitment, not loss, was thus the crucial variable in the process of decline.

But before turning to possible links between the Victorian 'crisis of faith' and this growing inability of the Churches to draw new members from the wider society, it is instructive to inquire why the crisis failed to produce any significant rate of defection among existing adherents, and why controversies like the 'Down Grade' and the Leicester Conference were surmounted without producing the kinds of lasting divisions which the Socinian controversy had created in early eighteenth-century Dissent. The answer is not that, on closer scrutiny, the intellectual issues fade into the background of Victorian religious history; it is that Victorian Christians were impelled by strong social and cultural pressures towards similar ideological compromises. The heat was gradually taken out of the crisis by an almost irresistible imperative towards accommodation with the wider intellectual world, an imperative as much social as intellectual. Indeed, the crisis was precipitated as well as resolved by a distinctively modern religious-cultural preoccupation with making the Christian faith relevant to a society dominated no longer by a pervasive religious belief.

It was a preoccupation which stemmed inevitably from the basic reorientation of religion and society which previous chapters have described as a process of denominationalisation. The quest for 'relevance' is characteristic neither of *church* type religion, for which relevance is assured by societal dominance, nor of *sect* type religion, which involves an acceptance of subcultural marginality. But in a *denominational* situation it is a prerequisite of survival, for denominations depend on the voluntary allegiance of members who adhere in general to the prevalent ideas and intellectual fashions of their age. Without resort to sociological categories, the Victorians themselves recognised the significance of this new denominational dilemma. In the kind of society which was emerging believers could achieve neither 'the fierce intensity found in a minority under persecution, nor the placid confidence that belongs to an overwhelming majority', Mallock observed in 1878.

> They can neither hate the unbelievers [he continued], for they daily live in amity with them; nor despise altogether their judgment, for the most eminent thinkers of the day belong to them. The believers are forced into a sort of compromise, which is a new feature in their history. They see that the age is against them; and yet they are obliged to make excuses for their enemy. . . . By such conditions as these, even the strongest faith cannot fail to be affected. It may not lose its firmness, but it must lose something of its fervour; and it is a significant fact that men who most devoutly believe in God would smile at the simplicity of any one who should presume, in a mixed company, that His existence should be taken as an axiom[18].

This was an acute observation, particularly in its perception of the compulsion underlying the efforts of Victorian Christianity to come to terms with biological and geological science, social science, archaeology, comparative religion, historical scholarship, and philosophical theology. The alternatives were the achievement of some kind of ideological accommodation or (in the absence of such accommodation) the increasing marginality and cultural isolation of organised religion within English society. The 'crisis of faith' was part of a broader process of secularisation.

Unlike sects, denominations have a segmental rather than a totalitarian hold over their members. Membership does not exclude other commitments, and for most of those caught up in it denominational life is only one of a variety of associational activities. The denomination must compete for the energies and the time of individuals with other associations, recreational, social, cultural, and vocational. Thus while on the one hand the transition from sect to denomination means that an organisation can no longer expect or demand from its members levels of participation once regarded as normal, on the other hand the transition creates a membership whose beliefs and values are moulded as much by 'worldly' associations as by 'religious' ones. The significance of this kind of change naturally was more evident within the Nonconformist bodies than within the Church of England. Anglicanism had long had the capacity to accommodate people willing to worship in church but unwilling to tolerate too intense or too disciplined a religious life. 'A national church', as A. G. Dickens has observed, 'cannot become a club for religious athletes'[19]. But in certain respects Nonconformity during its sectarian phase had approached a normative structure demanding considerable spiritual athleticism.

There is no way of measuring precisely the tendency for Nonconformists, while retaining membership, to reduce gradually the level of their commitment. But it is clear both that the level of commitment *did* decline, and that the process of decline set in before the middle of the nineteenth century. In 1847 Samuel Jackson and Robert Newton, as President and Secretary respectively of the Wesleyan Conference, spoke with concern of 'the comparative lukewarmness of our own, as well as of other sections of the Christian church'; and there were already before 1850 many spokesmen throughout Nonconformist communities echoing the added observation that 'attendance on week-day services—preaching, prayer-meetings, and class meetings—becomes more rare just when most needed'[20]. There had begun a process which was to continue throughout the Victorian era.

The first twentieth-century Wesleyan President told the Methodist laity: 'You are in the world, brethren, steeped in its affairs, conversant with its ideas, and affected by its fashions and maxims to a degree that would have shocked your fathers'[21]. Such statements of course recur almost ritualistically in the exhortations of religious leaders at almost every stage in the evolution of a religious movement. But in many ways this observation by Thomas Allen in 1900 was literally and objectively true. During the previous sixty-five years Nonconformists had for the first time assumed municipal office on a large scale, had entered the worlds of Parliament and Cabinet, had studied and taken degrees at the ancient universities, and had won public recognition as 'the backbone of British Liberalism'[22]. Their leaders had enjoyed close personal relations with Gladstone and other leading members of the Liberal Party[23], and in 1874 and 1880 particularly their votes had been credited (not without reason) with a decisive influence on the results of general elections. Such changes were an inevitable part of the gradual emergence of Nonconformity from the subcultural insularity typical of early Methodist, Congregational, and Baptist communities. The very success of the struggle for religious equality provided Nonconformists with increased access to the social, educational, and political rewards of the wider society; and the higher levels of social status and material comfort typical of denominations experiencing *lift* brought with it new opportunities for 'worldliness'.

Part of the reason for declining attendance at weekday prayer, preaching, and class meetings, the Wesleyan Conference of 1847 had noted during the critical analysis initiated by Jackson and Newton, was that Wesleyans who were more 'respectable' than the average member had been in the past, and more involved in secular activities, were also more interested in 'the pleasures of life'[24]. There were already by the middle of the nineteenth century greater opportunities than there had been previously for recreational satisfactions outside the chapel community, as well as for wider social and political involvements. And by the close of the Victorian era denominational leaders often felt that, as one of them put it, the 'Means of Grace' were fighting a losing battle to rival 'the social party, the secular concert, or the tennis club' as a claimant for the time and energy of members[25]. The problem was not the complete withdrawal of allegiance, but the tendency for participation in denominational affairs to be both more passive and less frequent.

The role of the class meeting (an institution apposite to a sectarian rather than a denominational phase of religious development) troubled Wesleyans throughout the Victorian era[26]. The Report of a Committee set up to consider the relationship between the class meeting and Wesleyan membership, adopted by the Conference of 1889, confirmed the early diagnosis of the 1847 Annual Address. Explaining why attendance at classes had become 'very lightly estimated', the Report said:

> The claims of secular business are both more numerous and more urgent than ever. Social life is more restless, and makes greater demands upon the time of our people, especially in the evening. . . . Perhaps, too, an increase of self-consciousness, and the growth of a fastidious spirit arising from the influences of modern culture, may, in some cases, have fostered a distaste to speaking freely of the deepest thoughts and feelings[27].

The Wesleyan laity, in short, had accepted the values of *denominational* religion. Conversionist zeal and active participation in recruiting were no longer normal. Worship and fellowship belonged to the province of religion; the spiritual experience of the individual had become a private matter. The ethos of denominational life discouraged the devotional intensity and religious enthusiasm which, as the 1889 Report put it, had 'shaped and tempered' Methodism's 'finest evangelical instruments' in the past[28].

This was a general phenomenon in Nonconformity. 'There are large numbers of professors whose only outward sign of a religious character is an attendance at the Sunday morning service, with possibly a certain amount of contribution to the funds of the Church', a correspondent wrote in the *Congregationalist* in 1885. 'Week evening services have almost passed into disuse', he added[29]. As in Methodism, the danger inherent in this decline was *not* that loss of denominational membership would result. Charles Booth in the 1890s and R. Mudie-Smith in 1902—03 observed that in London the social and recreational activities of Nonconformist communities often flourished and expanded while the services catering for the 'essentially spiritual' interests of the laity virtually disappeared[30]. In a host of ways, from the establishment of denominational sporting clubs, music societies, debating groups, excursion and holiday associations, and similar ventures, to an increasing emphasis on entertainment in specifically religious services, the tendency was for the Churches to cater for the new expectations of their members by attempting to compete with the burgeoning entertainment industries of the wider society. Currie has pointed out that the advocates of novel evangelistic aids like the 'magic lantern', a fad of the late Victorians and Edwardians, in fact relied on 'the criteria of entertainment rather than evangelism'[31].

There were notable exceptions to this general diminution in the intensity of religious commitment. The sporadic periods of heightened commitment during Victorian religious 'revivals' will be examined later in this chapter, but there were in addition elements within each denomination which persistently met the secularisation of the wider society with a response, not of accommodation, but of intensified pietism. Fundamentalist and anti-intellectual, such responses emphasised the experiential aspects of evangelicalism to the point where expressions of faith bordered on one hand on mysticism and on the other on pentacostalism. The best known institutional expression of this reaction was the Keswick movement, a fairly incohate religious-cultural phenomenon, cutting across denominational boundaries, which took its name from conventions held in the Lake District, annually from 1875 onwards. During convention time Keswick became a Mecca for the uncompromising sections of Church and Chapel communities confronted with the dilemma of secularisation. But if they escaped the Scylla of creeping 'worldliness', the Keswick folk courted the Charybdis of alienation both from the wider culture and from the great majority of their Victorian and Edwardian brethren who opted for *rapprochement* with the changing time spirit. Accommodation, not reaction, was the norm.

Thus while it is true that outside the working classes the ethos of English society remained distinctly religious as late as 1914, the character of its religiosity had changed; and although the transformation had been most evident in the once sectarian Nonconformist religious cultures it was a general phenomenon. A public conscience which was intolerant of moral turpitude in high places and hostile towards public professions of atheism remained powerful, as did social conventions which reinforced the individual commitments underlying church attendance. In most Churches, moreover, credal formulations of orthodoxy had not changed greatly during the previous three-quarters of a century: the tendency had been to interpret them more flexibly rather than to abandon them. The accommodation of the Churches to the 'world', in short had been as subtle as it was pervasive. Although Spurgeon was inaccurate in his 1887 claim that as a result of new theological tendencies the Atonement was 'scouted', the doctrine of biblical inspiration 'derided', the Holy Spirit metamorphosed into 'an influence', and eternal punishment into a 'fiction', he was not mistaken in feeling that (from his stern viewpoint) there had been an insidious softening of emphasis, an elimination of elements considered too harsh for the more fastidious patrons of Victorian chapels[32]. Changes of emphasis had in some cases become so pronounced that they seemed to foreshadow changes in the essence of old theological verities. Hugh Price Hughes, the most famous Methodist of his generation, said as much in 1898 when he spoke of 'an unhealthy softening of the fibres of faith' in Methodism, and observed that 'men do not believe so heartily and emphatically as they once did'[33]. Similarly the Congregationalist, R. W. Dale, spoke of the less palatable aspects of evangelicalism being 'silently relegated, with or without very serious consideration, to that province of the intellect which is the house of beliefs which have not been rejected, but which we are willing to forget'[34]. And whereas in 1853 the eminent Anglican theologian, F. D. Maurice, had lost his professorial chair at King's College, London, 'for throwing a cloudiness about the meaning of the word "eternal" and for suggesting a possibility of mercy for the wicked hereafter'[35], half a century later neither his fellow churchmen nor society at large would have been moved to censure such views[36].

The Victorian 'crisis of faith' was essentially a matter of the

Churches coming to terms ideologically with secularising tendencies within the wider culture, but the *rapprochement* was only partially successful. Partly by an expurgation of elements considered too demanding or too implausible for popular consumption, and partly because of the gradual de-emphasis of such elements and the acceptance of new hermeneutic principles and scientific theories, each of the major religious cultures was successful in retaining the support of adherents increasingly exposed to potentially subversive beliefs and values. But if defections of existing members did not become a serious problem, effective communication with the wider society did. For what was a 'crisis of faith' for believers was for outsiders a 'crisis of plausibility', and the failure of the Churches to deal effectively with the latter crisis clearly inhibited their capacity to maintain an adequate rate of recruitment from the 'world'.

The crisis of plausibility

Far more important for the future of English religion than the specific challenges of Darwinism or biblical criticism, or the internal adjustments which these challenges demanded of the Churches, was the gradual divergence, increasingly evident during the Victorian era, between religious and secular modes of interpreting reality. Previously there had been something approaching a consensus between believers and unbelievers about the *plausibility* of a religious world view. Religious definitions of reality had been credible even to those who had rejected or ignored them. There had been for English Christianity no fundamental problem of communication, for religious issues, and the premises of religious arguments, had seemed relevant and authentic within the dominant cultural milieux of pre-industrial and early industrial society.

The same is not true of the milieu of modern industrial England. For the contemporary religious organisation the initial barrier to making converts and members out of the wider society is not a matter of truth and falsity but of relevance and *a priori* plausibility. The significance of this profound change in the context of religious activity is of course not confined to English society. The crisis of plausibility is the fundamental problem confronting religion in the secular milieu of modern industrial societies generally. Dietrich Bonhoeffer, for example, faced the problem squarely in his famous prison correspondence of 1944. Nineteen-hundred years of Christian preaching and theology had been 'based upon the religious *a priori* of men', he observed, but at last the *a priori* plausibility was ceasing to exist. During 'the last hundred years or so', Bonhoeffer wrote, modern man had developed a consciousness of 'autonomy' which had tended to destroy the traditional predisposition towards religious understandings of reality[37].

'It can hardly be disputed', Horton Davies has written confidently, 'that the prevailing culture of England since the 1850s has been scientific humanism'[38]. The judgment may be somewhat prochronistic, but there is good evidence for the view that by the middle of the Victorian era English religious organisations were confronted by a society which to a significant degree was no longer predisposed to a religious worldview. Perceptive commentators were insisting well before 1900 that the most serious threat to English religion was not the incompatibility, real or imagined, between specific aspects of science and religion. It was the growing tendency for people without much knowledge of theology or interest in it to become alienated from the modes of thought and definitions of reality which made religiosity explicable and relevant. Two powerful forces were operating within the society to produce this fundamental secularisation of the values and beliefs of the population outside the Churches.

One was the popularisation of what was often called 'the scientific spirit'. Already before 1850 science had begun to exercise a normative influence on most aspects of English thought[39], and as the century proceeded it increasingly dominated popular definitions of reality. The scientific ethos as a popular philosophy tended to stultify all forms of metaphysical speculation, including what Bonhoeffer was to call 'the religious *a priori* of men'. It was subversive of 'even the mere notion of a supernatural power', and although the human facility for tolerating contradictory elements within a single worldview might for a time effectively shield traditional religious dispositions, the popularisation of science threatened in the long run to pervade and secularise the wider culture generally[40]. 'It is truly said that ideas "are in the air"', W. S. Lilly wrote in the *Quarterly Review* of 1893.

> Ambient, invisible, irresistible, they enter into our moral life and we know it not. . . . One cannot take up a newspaper or a magazine, in Europe or in America, without finding evidence how widely these doctrines have been diffused, and how largely they have been received[41].

In some of these magazines, moreover, the effect of the 'scientific spirit' in destroying the *a priori* plausibility of faith was explicitly and sympathetically examined. Thus the eminent jurist, Sir James Stephen, told readers of the *Nineteenth Century* in 1884 that,

> If human life is in the course of being fully described by science, I do not see what materials there are for any religion, or, indeed, what would be the use of one, or why it is wanted. We can get on very well without one, for though the view of life which science is opening to us gives us nothing to worship, it gives us an infinite number of things to enjoy. . . . The world seems to me a very good world, if it would only last. It is full of pleasant people and curious things, and I think that most men find no great difficulty in turning their minds away from its transient character[42].

However naive or optimistic such sentiments appear almost a century later, they typified a strain of ideological secularisation in Victorian culture.

But the passage is also significant because in it Stephen articulated the second kind of societal pressure threatening the traditional credibility of religious belief within the wider society. It was the pressure of an emerging popular materialism which undermined the religious *a priori*, not in any direct ideological sense, but by deadening what once had been a strong metaphysical element of popular consciousness. There was an obvious and important link between the Industrial Revolution and this basic secularising trend. For the consequences of industrialisation, as various historians have pointed out, amounted to a watershed in human experience with which only the prehistorical Neolithic Revolution is comparable. Poverty, scarcity, and disease—life lived on the margins of subsistence and privation—had been the common lot of all but a fortunate few in pre-industrial societies[43]. But in nineteenth-century England, for the first time in history, the material wealth of a whole society began steadily and persistently to improve. By the Victorian era the self-sustaining economic growth of a maturing industrial economy was already undermining attitudes and values which had taken shape amidst the poverty and relentless economic insecurity of generations before the Industrial Revolution.

If one accepts the Weberian premise that man is at his most religious in situations in which the powerlessness, contingency, and material insecurity of human existence are most acutely apparent, then it is reasonable to assume that the relative affluence of an industrial economy, and the increased capability of an advanced society to manipulate and control its environment, would tend to depress popular religious impulses. Logically, the technological and scientific developments of the past 200 years may have no implications whatever for the truth or falsity, relevance or irrelevance, of religious faith. But in practice the breaking-points in human existence, the crises, real or anticipated, of powerlessness, contingency or insecurity, simply occur less frequently or less acutely in the more controlled environment of a modern industrial society. For individuals and for particular social subgroups the generalisation breaks down, of course, and for every member of such a society the ultimate breaking-point of death remains to nurture the weakened religious *a priori*; overall, however, the rationality and comparative material security of the society as a whole offers sufficient insulation from these transcendental issues to produce a popular consciousness for which religious beliefs and values retain little of their traditional authenticity. The fundamental cause of secularisation, according to Peter Berger, is 'the process of rationalisation that is the prerequisite for *any* industrial society of the modern type'[44].

The crisis of plausibility produced by the emergence of industrial society in England was beginning to make its presence felt early in the Victorian era. Howard R. Murphy has analysed changing attitudes towards religion during this period in terms of a distinction between 'meliorism' and 'salvationism'. From a previous situation in which people had taken for granted that the world was 'a vale of tears that must be passed through on the way to eternal bliss or eternal damnation', there was beginning to emerge 'the idea that the world was susceptible to systemative improvement through a sustained application of human effort and intelligence'[45]. The new meliorism was an obvious ideological concomitant of successful industrialisation, and in its most popular form it amounted to little more than a fairly unthinking and essentially optimistic materialism. As De Laveleye put it in 1888:

> The modern man fixes his affections on the things of this world, and desperately pursues the good things therein attainable, as if this were his last dwelling-place and there were nothing beyond. In this cold and dry atmosphere religion grows daily weaker and tends to be swept away[46].

There was truth in these words despite the fact that they were uttered at a time when rates of religious practice in England were actually rising as a result of the Anglican growth of the period 1885 to 1913[47]. The Churches were not suffering serious losses, certainly by past standards; but they were losing touch both with large sections of the wider society and with a slowly secularising wider culture. This widening gap between the Churches and the 'world' can be detected most clearly by examining the modes and patterns of membership recruitment in Victorian and Edwardian religious organisations; for, ironically, both the notable revivalism of this period and the increased efficiency of Victorian Sunday Schools as recruiting agencies, although in one sense expressions of the life that continued in the Churches, were at the same time early manifestations of growth processes which in the twentieth century would lead to serious organisational decline.

Revivalism and Church growth

The most sensitive available index of short-term growth in a religious organisation is obtained by focusing, not on the kinds of total membership figures examined in Chapter 2, but on net changes in membership from year to year. A *growth rate* series, abstracted by expressing annual gain or loss of membership as a percentage of total membership in the previous year, identifies annual variations within a broad pattern of organisational development. In the case of pre-1914 English religion growth rate analysis inevitably is complicated by the incompleteness of the statistical data. But by using growth rates abstracted from the virtually complete Methodist membership series, and examining the less complete records of other Churches in the context of Methodist trends, it is possible to construct a fairly accurate picture of the short-term development of all the major Protestant bodies, at least during the Victorian and Edwardian eras.

In Table 8.1 and Fig. 8.1 growth rate series on the major Methodist organisations in England between 1845 and 1914 have been juxtaposed for the purpose of comparing connexional trends of short-term growth[48]. There is considerable evidence to support the use of the common Methodist pattern evident in these connexional series as a basis for generalising about the growth of other religious organisations. Between 1834 and 1878, for example, a majority of Baptist congregations in

Table 8.1 Methodist growth rates, 1845–1914

Annual net turnover of membership as a percentage of total membership in the previous year

Year	Wesleyan	New Connexion	Primitive Methodist	Bible Christian	W.M.A./ U.M.F.C., and U.M.C.
1845	1.1	−2.7	−1.1	−3.3	−3.8
1846	0.5	1.5	−1.0	−1.5	−3.2
1847	−0.2	−2.4	−0.7	−4.7	−1.4
1848	−0.2	2.1	2.9	3.4	4.5
1849	2.8	3.6	6.8	7.1	4.0
1850	2.9	9.5	9.6	7.0	3.2
1851	−15.8	−3.9	3.7	−3.1	−3.0
1852	−7.0	−2.5	0.7	5.8	−4.9
1853	−3.7	−2.8	−1.0	−6.1	−6.5
1854	−2.8	−0.4	−1.5	−1.9	−4.1
1855	−1.3	5.4	−2.3	−4.8	−0.5
1856	1.3	9.0	2.4	12.6	4.1
1857	2.5	4.7	1.7	0.6	
1858	2.8	5.7	4.6	9.2	6.9
1859	5.6	4.9	6.7	13.6	10.0
1860	4.9	3.2	5.7	−0.9	11.4
1861	3.0	3.2	2.3	−2.3	4.3
1862	2.0	9.0	3.9	8.9	7.5
1863	1.6	−1.1	3.4	1.4	4.9
1864	0.0	−1.6	1.4	−0.1	1.2
1865	0.4	1.2	1.2	0.5	0.6
1866	0.1	−0.9	0.1	0.3	−0.7
1867	1.7	0.3	2.0	0.0	3.6
1868	1.8	2.6	2.1	2.6	0.8
1869	1.5	−2.5	1.6	−2.0	−0.2
1870	0.5	−2.5	0.3	−3.5	−0.1
1871	−0.4	−2.8	−0.7	−0.7	−1.5
1872	−0.1	−3.6	0.0	2.2	−0.9
1873	0.6	0.5	−0.6	−2.1	−1.1
1874	0.9	−0.9	2.4	−0.9	1.0
1875	1.9	0.8	2.8	2.4	1.8
1876	4.2	4.2	3.4	7.3	3.8
1877	2.5	4.4	2.8	6.4	2.1
1878	−0.4	2.5	0.7	−1.4	−0.8
1879	−0.9	1.6	−0.3	−2.8	−0.7
1880	−0.4	0.7	0.0	3.1	−0.7
1881	1.3	2.2	2.1	2.6	0.6
1882	3.6	3.0	2.5	9.6	1.9
1883	3.4	2.4	2.2	1.8	1.9
1884	0.6	0.0	1.1	−0.8	−0.7

Table 8.1 — *Continued*

Year	Wesleyan	New Connexion	Primitive Methodist	Bible Christian	W.M.A./ U.M.F.C., and U.M.C.
1885	0.5	−0.2	0.9	−0.5	0.3
1886	−0.1	2.0	−0.3	1.3	−0.5
1887	−0.1	0.6	−0.5	3.2	−0.5
1888	0.9	1.6	0.4	0.8	0.4
1889	1.2	1.1	0.7	2.2	0.6
1890	0.4	0.0	−0.4	0.4	0.4
1891	0.0	0.4	0.2	2.2	−0.5
1892	0.1	0.9	−0.8	−1.7	0.7
1893	0.6	1.2	1.2	2.1	0.4
1894	1.2	0.9	0.6	1.8	0.1
1895	0.9	0.4	−0.7	1.2	1.3
1896	−0.8	0.6	0.1	−1.3	0.9
1897	0.8	1.2	0.6	2.9	1.6
1898	0.8	1.9	0.7	0.8	0.8
1899	1.1	1.9	0.7	1.3	1.1
1900	1.3	1.1	0.2	−0.2	0.2
1901	0.5	1.7	1.2	2.7	0.7
1902	1.8	3.6	1.6	0.5	3.3
1903	1.0	1.7	1.3	2.6	1.8
1904	1.3	2.5	1.2	2.6	1.1
1905	2.3	2.6	2.1	7.1	1.7
1906	2.8	3.3	1.9	0.8	2.4
1907[2]	−0.4	0.0	0.6	−0.4	−0.5
1908	−0.9		0.2		−0.5
1909	−0.3		−0.2		−0.1
1910	−0.5		−0.3		−0.9
1911	−0.6		−0.5		−1.2
1912	−0.6		−0.2		−1.3
1913	−0.1		−0.5		0.0
1914	−0.2		0.4		0.1

Notes

1   The 1845−56 Wesleyan Methodist Association series ceases in 1857 when the Association entered the United Methodist Free Churches.

2   In 1907 the latter body merged with the New Connexion and the Bible Christians to form the United Methodist Church.

England made statistical returns to the Baptist Union from which it is possible to construct a series measuring annual net increase in membership per congregation. This series, presented in Table 8.2 and included in Fig. 8.1, provides a picture of Baptist growth from year to year which is comparable with Methodist growth rate data.

Table 8.2   Baptist growth rates, 1834—77
Net increase in membership per church per annum

1834	4.6	1856	4.2
1835	3.7	1857	5.8
1836	4.4	1858	6.3
1837	4.5	1859	12.6
1838	4.7	1860	11.0
1839	7.9	1861	4.0
1840	8.8	1862	4.6
1841	13.1	1863	1.6
1842	9.8	1864	1.2
1843	7.1	1865	1.7
1844	6.3	1866	2.2
1845	3.7	1867	5.2
1846	2.9	1868	4.8
1847	1.7	1869	3.3
1848	3.1	1870	2.0
1849	2.9	1871	3.2
1850	13.0	1872	1.3
1851	1.9	1873	2.1
1852	1.6	1874	4.3
1853	1.3	1875	5.3
1854	2.3	1876	7.9
1855	2.2	1877	5.4

Notes

1   Relating net annual increase of membership to the number of churches submitting statistical returns is the only way of abstracting from Baptist Associational records a series comparable to a Methodist *growth rate* series. This is because the number of churches upon which annual denominational totals were based varied significantly from year to year.

2   The figures relate to calendar years.

Examining Fig. 8.1, it is clear that each growth pattern consisted of a succession of short-term cycles, and that the peaks and troughs of these cycles occurred at intervals of between five and ten years. There were five peaks between 1845 and 1885, and even a cursory examination of the various graphs indicates that these peaks coincided from one pattern to another. There were obvious anomalies, such as the attenuated nature

Fig. 8.1   Selected Nonconformist growth rates, 1845—85. *Sources: Tables 3.1 and 3.2*

* Note: Reformed Methodism includes:

1   Wesleyan Methodist Association

2   Wesleyan Reformers

3   United Methodist Free Churches.

† Baptist data covers new members per church per annum.

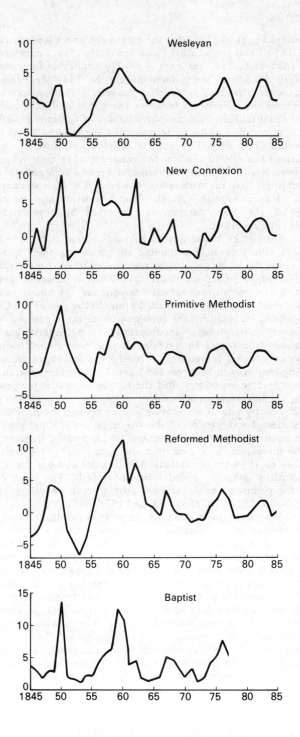

of the Wesleyan peak of 1848–50, the extremely severe Wesleyan losses of the early 1850s, and the unusual character of the New Connexion cycles between 1855 and 1862, but each is readily explicable in terms of the serious Wesleyan schism precipitated during the 1849 Wesleyan Conference. Thus when allowance is made for the effects of idiosyncratic factors such as schism the correlation between these five Methodist and Baptist patterns is unmistakable. And the phenomenon of common growth trends certainly was not limited to these particular organisations and this particular period. The virtually complete religious statistics of the major denominations since 1900 confirm the existence of an underlying cyclical pattern characteristic of both Anglican and Free Church growth[49], and the presumption that the correlation had existed at least since the emergence of denominational Church–Chapel relationships around the beginning of the Victorian era is supported by considerable non-quantifiable evidence[50].

During the Victorian and Edwardian eras, then, the success of the English Churches in maintaining or improving their quantitative position within the wider society was due, not to consistent recruitment at levels sufficient to offset inevitable losses, but to sporadic periods of extremely heavy recruitment which compensated for longer intervening phases of virtual stagnation or actual decline. In the case of the Church of England, which, certainly by the final quarter of the nineteenth century, was definitely outgrowing Nonconformity, these intervening periods appear in most instances to have involved slower growth rather than stagnation or decline; moreover, explaining the prolonged phase of improved Anglican growth between 1885 and 1914 involves the analysis of factors best treated separately. But the fact remains that the problem of explaining the long-term trends evident in the total membership series of Chapter 2 is partly one of accounting for the timing, the periodicity, and the amplitudes of a succession of short-term cycles of rapid growth. And while the word 'revival' has connotations which perhaps threaten to complicate the discussion, it is clear that the high *growth rate* cycles of the period 1840 to 1914 are the statistical reflections of what the Victorians and Edwardians generally called religious revivals. The most emphatic peaks in the common cycle, the phases of general 'revival', occurred in 1849, 1859–60, 1874–76, 1881–83, and 1904–06.

Before seeking to interpret these revivals within the context of Victorian religion it is illuminating to compare them with the type of short-term growth pattern which had been characteristic of the pre-1840 period, at least as far as Evangelical Nonconformity had been concerned. Wesleyan growth rates from 1767 onwards and growth rate series relating to other Methodist bodies from early in the nineteenth century had exemplified a situation in which the relationship between the Churches and the 'world' had been dominated on the one hand by high receptiveness and on the other by intense conversionist zeal. The minimum growth rates experienced during this period of very rapid growth had not differed greatly from those of the Victorian and Edwardian years, but in the amplitude of cycles of high growth rates and in the duration of high and low growth cycles the contrast had been very pronounced. For what was an outstanding growth rate in 1905–06 (2.8 per cent in the case of

Wesleyanism), would not even have been an average advance in the 1790s, when Wesleyan growth had exceeded 3 per cent per annum on seven occasions and had reached 14.4 per cent in 1793–94. Wesleyan growth rates of 4 per cent or over were achieved only three times in the three-quarters of a century after 1840; yet this was a level of expansion which had been reached eleven times in twenty-six years up to 1793, eighteen times between 1794 and 1816, and six times in the twenty-three years before 1840. Similarly, the Primitive Methodists, after achieving growth rates of at least 4 per cent thirteen times in the fifteen years after 1829, did so on only five further occasions between 1844 and 1914.

Thus the Victorian religious revivals, and that of 1904–06, far from reflecting a new dynamism in English religion, represented sporadic and shortlived resumptions of the kind of growth which had been normal during the earlier phase of mobilisation in Evangelical Nonconformity. Not only did the amplitudes of the peaks diminish as the nineteenth century wore on, but the peaks became more isolated. Where previously cycles of high growth rates had resembled plateaux divided by abrupt chasms, during the period 1840 to 1914 they resembled mountains separated by wide valleys. These revivals were notable, the pattern suggests, not because of their absolute magnitude but because they were in sharp contrast with the normal level of Victorian growth. Earlier peaks had been higher but less conspicuous.

Whatever else they are, religious revivals are social phenomena with social antecedents. Early Evangelical Nonconformists, and especially Methodists, whose accurate statistics gave them an unusual awareness of short-term fluctuations in recruitment, had been in no doubt about the connexion between high growth rates and the operation of external societal influences. Periods during which Nonconformity's artisan- and working-class constituencies had been preoccupied with political issues or troubled by economic recession had been relatively unfavourable for growth, for at such times the attention both of members and outsiders had been diverted from the kinds of interests and concerns likely to have intensified or induced commitment[51]. Jabez Bunting's famous aphorism that Methodism hated democracy as it hated sin was appropriate at least in the context of *early* Methodist growth.

This negative correlation obviously demands some explana-tion, both because there had been an element of protest, a quasipolitical assertion of 'independence', in early Methodist commitment[52], and because by the Victorian and Edwardian eras the correlation had under-gone a complete reversal, and a situation had emerged in which revival consistently *coincided* with political agitation. Despite the conservatism of the Wesleyan Conference, early industrial Methodism generally had capitalised on many of the social aspirations which had sustained popular radical politics during the unsettled years between 1792 and 1821. Why then had periods of extreme political excitement produced slower growth? The answer is that all the Evangelical Nonconformist bodies had suffered at such times from the perennial problem of adopting a moderate stance in an extremist situation. Able to exploit, in normal circumstances, the wide-spread social and political dissatisfactions of lower- and lower-middle-class constituents, they had suffered setbacks when this muted radicalism had errupted into violence or been channelled into overtly political organisations.

In contrast, however, the period from around the beginning of the Victorian era to the First World War saw phases of political agitation and instances of religious revival actually coinciding. The more or less revolutionary character of political crises in early industrial society, the kinds of extreme radicalism which had inhibited religious recruitment, were absent in Victorian society. In their place was well-organised, essentially moderate middle-class agitation which, on every occasion when it coincided with high growth rates, was concerned with specifically religious issues. Explicating the link between the two phenomena is one of the best ways to understand the social causes and effects of Victorian revivalism.

A revival, according to the Chartist Methodist, Thomas Cooper, began among the existing membership of a religious group with an increased 'striving for holiness' which attracted the attention and evoked the commitment of non-members[53]. The interaction between the wider social climate and the atmosphere within the religious organisation was what precipitated unusually high recruitment. Special agencies for bridging the gap between the 'Church' and the 'world', heightened lay commitment, and novel circumstances which brought religious issues to public notice: these were the concomitants of revival in the Victorian and Edwardian Churches. And one of the most important catalysts producing them was political agitation associated with religious controversies. The class and socio-economic radicalism of early nineteenth-century society had distracted people from matters religious; but when religion and politics became inseparable in Victorian society so, too, did the tasks of canvassing political support and securing religious commitments.

This was true particularly of the periods 1859—60, 1873—76, and 1902—06, when the politics of church rates and education mobilised both Church and Chapel communities into resolute action. It was no accident, for example, that what Orr has called the 'Second Evangelical Awakening', which reached its peak in 1859—60, coincided with the most intense phase of popular agitation during the prolonged campaign against church rates. During the second half of 1859 the Liberation Society launched a concerted nationwide drive to harness popular support for a Church Rates Abolition Bill soon to proceed to the House of Lords. By petitioning, by initiating massive public protests across the country, and by forcing the church rates issue into the centre of national attention, the aim was to coerce the Lords into accepting the bill. Signatures were wanted for anti-church rate petitions on the Nonconformist side, and on the Anglican side for a hastily organised but powerful counterpetitioning movement.

In both cases the confrontation produced precisely the kinds of organisational strategies successful in a revival. House-to-house visitation by lay volunteers, pamphlet distribution, public meetings, and large-scale advertising campaigns advocating (or denying) the social and spiritual benefits of voluntarism in religion, were carried on in most areas, either by Liberation Society branches and Church Defence Associations, or in the absence of such formal agencies by *ad hoc* groups drawn from local Anglican or Nonconformist communities. By early April 1860 5,274 petitions opposing church rates had been received at Westminster, representing more than 580,000 petitioners. This compared with only 20,000 signatures on the one previous occasion, in June 1858, on which a Bill for the abolition of church rates had been presented to the Lords. On the Establishment side there were more petitions, 5,317 in all, but slightly less than one-third as many signatures[54]. The entire organisation and atmosphere of the contending campaigns had been as much religious as political, and while the crisis cannot be adduced as a complete explanation of the accompanying religious revival, it evidently contributed to it in two ways. On the one hand, it clearly produced a polarisation of Church–Chapel support which tended both to increase the active participation of existing members and to induce adherents on the periphery of membership to make a full commitment; and on the other hand it effected an unusual, and temporary, bridging of the gap between the Victorian Churches and their external constituencies.

Similar conjunctions of political and religious developments occurred in the mid-1870s, when Nonconformist opposition to the 1870 Education Act, having contributed to the Liberal defeat in the 1874 general election, split over into a massive popular disestablishment campaign in 1875–76; and again in the aftermath of Balfour's Education Act of 1902. The first of these phases of intense politico-religious agitation, by coming to an abrupt end as news of the Bulgarian Massacres began to grip public attention in the second half of 1876, illustrated the specific nature of the link between religious and political trends. As the country became bogged down in 'a mudpool of foreign politics'[55], the high growth rates of the mid-1870s revival subsided. Political excitement *per se*, in other words, was not conducive to Church growth, and even the 'Eastern Question', with its element of high moral fervour and religious persecution, and with Gladstone at its head, did not have an effect on organised religion comparable with a crisis over church rates, disestablishment, or religious education. Politics abetted growth only when specifically religious issues were raised: when a national agitation was able to involve the rank and file of Anglican and Nonconformist communities in active support of religious objectives. R. W. Dale, one of the leaders of the 1875–76 disestablishment campaign, wrote in October 1875: 'I have not much faith in popular movements which are not sustained by religious intensity'[56]. Under such leadership peak periods in the Church–Chapel confrontation of the Victorian era led naturally to high points of evangelistic and pastoral activity.

In the period 1902–06 this confrontation produced its final crisis, and arguably its most bitter. The Balfour Education Act of 1902 provided for the maintenance of voluntary denominational schools on the rates, a provision which clearly favoured the Church of England, and abolished the Cowper–Temple compromise of 1870 which had prohibited specifically denominational teaching in board schools. As a result of these provisions 'practically the whole of Nonconformity was in revolt' for more than three years, and a 'fighting alliance' was formed between organised Nonconformity and the Liberal Party, with which relations had been strained since the Irish Home Rule crisis of 1886[57]. Within a year Nonconformists were suffering distraint of goods for refusing to pay full rates; by March 1904 'passive resistance' (as this form of protest was called) was spreading rapidly, and two Nonconformist ministers were among those in gaol; by October 1905 more than 230 people had been imprisoned, and thousands fined[58]. Meanwhile the Free Church Council, an interdenominational body formed in the 1890s, was providing a powerful network of local and regional opposition groups intent on arousing grass roots support for the Nonconformist campaign against the Act, and at the same time the Liberation Society was mounting its last major assault on what remained of Establishment privilege.

This final Church—Chapel drama coincided with the last of the great religious revivals, and in Wales, where the conflict was most intense, the revivalist fervour was also greatest. It is difficult to avoid the conclusion that the phenomena were causally connected. 'It required a sophisticated audience indeed to distinguish between the nonconformist minister as revivalist and as sectarian politician', K. O. Morgan has written of the situation in Wales. 'It was noted in the press how frequently meetings directed against the Balfour Education Act would be transformed with a religious passion: *Marchog Iesu yn llwyddiannus*, the battle hymn of the revival, rang out from many a Liberal platform'[59]. And in its report on the Free Church Council meeting held in Manchester in the spring of 1905 the *Liberator* noted that the atmosphere had been at once 'intensely political and intensely evangelistic'. The speeches and resolutions of the Council had been 'frankly and resolutely hostile' to the Conservative Government of the day, and the campaign against the Balfour Act had been a major preoccupation. But at the same time the Council had succeeded in initiating unprecedented evangelical activity. 'Bands of devoted Christian men', the Liberator reported,

> many of whom had suffered imprisonment, or the spoiling of their goods, in their sturdy resistance to a law forced through Parliament by clerics without any mandate from the country, went out in procession through Manchester at night, and gathered in a vast congregation from the streets and public houses to a midnight service, at which hundreds were converted. This is the work of political Dissenters which their persecutors cannot contemplate without a deep feeling of uneasiness[60].

But if there was in the 1902—06 period a clear link between sectarian politics and energetic revivalism among Evangelical Nonconformists, the progress of Anglicanism was less straightforward. Plotting Anglican growth in the mid-Edwardian years is complicated by a discontinuity in the Easter Day communicant series due to a change in 1905 in the form of inquiry eliciting data from parochial clergy. Furthermore, the Balfour Act controversy produced widespread popular agitation in the Church of England on only two occasions: briefly in 1902 while the legislation was under parliamentary consideration, and in the spring and summer of 1906, when the recently triumphant Liberals attempted to secure the passage of a new Education Bill more favourable to Nonconformist interests. During this period an estimated 1,400 Anglican protest meetings were organised, and more than 750,000 signatures were collected on petitions against altering the 1902 legislation[61]. While the Lords destroyed the Liberal-Nonconformist Bill in Committee, the number of Anglicans participating in Easter-Day Communion rose by almost 50,000 in 1906, the largest annual increase since 1902.

This fairly extended discussion of links between the major political crises of the Church–Chapel confrontation and the outbreak of religious revivals has not sought to offer a complete explanation for the religious phenomenon, but rather to draw attention to the fact that during the denominational years of the Victorian and Edwardian eras high growth rates depended on some abnormal conjunction of external societal and internal organisational factors. With the lower levels of commitment tolerable in denominational religious cultures, and the increasing emphasis on organisational consolidation rather than expansion, novel or unusual social, political, or religious stimuli were required to produce the kinds of conversionist agencies and methods, and the kind of lay enthusiasm and activity which had been characteristic of dynamic religious organisations in early industrial society. Political agitation was only one of many possible stimuli.

The social and psychological impact of cholera had a comparable effect in 1832, 1849, and (in some localities) in 1866, intensifying the commitment of Church and Chapel members and increasing temporarily the receptiveness of the wider society. In all the Churches the epidemic was regarded as a 'visitation of God'. Before it broke out special evangelistic campaigns had been planned specifically in preparation for its arrival, and while it endured religious activity and recruitment reached levels unsurpassed in the nineteenth century[62]. 'A fountain has been opened, and refreshing streams flow from it in all directions', the *Congregational Magazine* was told in 1832 in a report from an area afflicted by the cholera morbus[63]. All denominational periodicals published similar reports about the special agencies and heightened commitment associated with the epidemic, but in every case the fountain of the 'cholera revival' disappeared rapidly once the epidemic withdrew[64]. Like the peak of an anti-church rate or disestablishment campaign, the impact of the epidemic was essentially impermanent and the relationship between the Churches and their wider constituencies which it produced was essentially abnormal.

Indeed, it was the transitory nature of revivalism which made it tolerable within the ordered and respectable life of the Victorian Churches. It is significant that during the peak growth rates of 1849, 1859–60, 1874–75, and 1881–83 the leading personalities of English revivalism were outsiders, usually Americans, whose involvement in the religious life of the society was manifestly temporary. Not only were Americans like Charles Grandison Finney, James Caughey, Dwight L. Moody, and Ira Sankey influential partly because they were exotic, they were more acceptable to English religious leaders for precisely the same reason. They were neither invited nor expected to remain in the country. Indeed, even Edward Miall, who had little admiration for the 'professional spirit' abroad in the Victorian Churches, suggested that the agencies employed during the 'special time of seed-sowing' were legitimate because they were 'for temporary ends only'[65]. For the same reason the order-loving Wesleyan Conference was willing to support and emulate the 'combined and well-organised efforts' of revivalists. Not intended to endure, the aggressive, lay-oriented initiatives characteristic of a revival could be reconciled with denominational order; and because of their novelty they were able to evoke a breadth of support which the routine activities of the churches could not hope to sustain.

Endogenous growth and organisational decline

The 'most remarkable feature' of the revival of 1859–60, according to a report in the *Wesleyan-Methodist Magazine*, was that 'its power was chiefly felt, and its greatest results achieved, within the enclosures of the church, rather than upon the world without'. An intensification of commitment among existing members was characteristic of communities affected by the revival, and 'of those who repented and believed for the first time, by far the larger proportion consisted of persons trained up in association with our own or some other Christian congregations'[66]. Similar observations were made within all the Churches, and it is apparent that although the impact of organised religion on the 'world' was greatest during periods of revival, the bulk of those persuaded to seek membership already had some connexion with a Church or Chapel community[67]. Indeed, the express objective of much revivalistic activity was, in the words of an Anglican reporter in 1860, a 'large increase of true conversions, especially in the families of believers'[68].

But if a concentration of evangelistic activity among people already on the peripheries of organised religion was apparent during revivals, it was even more pronounced at normal times. It is useful in this context to distinguish between the *external* and the *internal* constituencies from which religious organisations obtain new members, the former category referring to sections of the wider society without previous associations with the organisation concerned, and the internal constituency comprising non-members already more or less implicated in its affairs. In the latter category would be the children of existing members, and a mass of 'adherents' ranging from regular churchgoers who are not full members to nominal supporters whose participation is limited to such non-recurrent rites as marriages and funerals. There was a definite trend during the period from around the beginning of the Victorian era to the First World War, as the crisis of plausibility weakened the religious *a priori* of the wider society, for the effective evangelistic activities of the Churches to be confined increasingly to internal constituencies. This shift to endogenous growth both reflected and accentuated the widening cultural gap between the Churches and the 'world'.

> All the Christian Churches of England to-day have to deal with
> the question of their relation to numbers of people who join
> them in public worship, subscribe to their funds, live
> honourable lives, but decline to take the definite

responsibilities of Church membership [a Wesleyan preacher observed in 1907]. If they are Anglicans they are not ready to be confirmed, if they are Baptists they are not willing to be baptised, if they are Congregationalists they will not face an interview with the minister or deacons, and if they are Methodists they will not go to the Class Meeting[69].

This class of adherents who were not full members was not new, but as recruitment from the wider society diminished it had taken on a new significance. In Nonconformist organisations, certainly, there is evidence that a gradual but definite liberalising of membership standards was before the end of the nineteenth century producing a form of lateral growth at the cost of reducing steadily the once considerable reservoirs of partially committed adherents. In 1819 Congregational churches had reported that full members were a fairly small minority of those attending their services[70], but by 1903, in London at least, total Sunday morning congregations in the denomination were actually smaller than total membership, and Sunday evening congregations only marginally larger[71]. In Primitive Methodism, while membership rose from 165,535 in 1880 to 195,448 in 1932, the number of 'hearers' fell from 520,241 to 460,675[72]. In Wesleyanism attendants had outnumbered members by about three to one in 1851, but a century later total attendance tended to be smaller than total membership[73]. There is no reason to doubt that this type of endogenous membership growth, with its effect of obscuring the full extent of religion's institutional difficulties, was characteristic of Anglicanism as well as Nonconformity.

For the Church of England, of course, a growing concern for secure effective agencies for channelling members of an internal constituency into full Anglican membership represented, not a shift away from exogenous growth processes, but simply a practical adjustment to de facto denominationalism. While the Victorian Church often was more aggressively evangelistic than its Nonconformist rivals, its priorities were not essentially different. Having operated previously on the premise that to be English was to be Anglican, from the 1830s onwards the Establishment sought increasingly to attract and preserve the allegiance especially of those sections of the society which it could influence most readily. Concern for an external constituency was not absent; indeed, Victorian churchmen discussed no subject more earnestly than the problem of reaching the unchurched masses. But if the priorities of the Church are ranked in terms of the actual expenditure of resources and energy it is clear that the maintenance and extension of established Anglican congregations, and the recruitment of juveniles through day school and Sunday School work, were paramount. Especially after the initial period of reform and augmentation, the Ecclesiastical Commissioners encouraged this tendency by their grant allocations[74]. The reformed Establishment was concerned about growth, and as time went on it gradually devoted its energies more and more to activities which promised the most predictable and regular flow of confirmees and communicants. The trouble with such a policy, of course, was that it left the external constituency less and less subject to consistent religious influence.

The Visiting Societies, recreational and sporting associations, and welfare agencies which flourished in the Victorian Church on a parochial, district, diocesan, or national basis were among the most effective institutional preservers of an internal Anglican constituency. A penumbra of adherents especially open to effective pastoral or evangelistic work, people associated with these agencies were also particularly likely to permit or encourage their children to assume full church membership. And, increasingly, this juvenile constituency assumed major importance. Between 1818 and 1887, according to statistics presented to Parliament, the proportion of the total population attending Sunday Schools in England and Wales rose from below 5 to about 20 per cent[75]. The Church of England, which had followed Nonconformity in adopting Sunday School work, had 2,222,000 scholars enrolled by 1887, a number exceeding the combined totals of Wesleyan, Congregational, and Baptist Schools[76]; and in keeping with the primary function of the Victorian Sunday School as a recruiting agency for active Church membership, catechising had become an integral part of Anglican Sunday School operations from the mid-Victorian era onwards.

A growing dependence on the recruitment of juveniles explains the bitterness with which Church and Chapel interests clashed over national education policies in the 1870s and again in the period 1902–06. As the gap between the Churches and their external constituencies in the wider society widened, the preservation of the internal constituencies afforded by Sunday and denominational day schools became more vital. The relationship between the education controversies and the recruitment policies of the Churches was often recognised explicitly. A. A. Markham, Vicar of a Liverpool parish, wrote in an Anglican newspaper in 1902:

> When I see that many of my day children are attached to
> Dissenters' Sunday-schools, I argue that it is a fortunate thing
> that I can teach them for five days out of seven. I know, too,
> that the teaching will not be lost. I shall find it after many
> days, when many of these same children leave their sect and
> seek confirmation[77].

If justified, this Anglican expectation of eroding a crucial section of the internal constituency of Nonconformity certainly represented a serious threat to the continued expansion of Chapel religiosity in England.

For by the beginning of the twentieth century Nonconformity had become even more dependent on endogenous growth than the Church was. A shift from the exogenous processes which had allowed Evangelical Nonconformist movements to recruit heavily from the wider society of early industrial England had occurred gradually from the second quarter of the nineteenth century onwards. It had been evident particularly in the functional evolution of the Nonconformist Sunday School. During the phase of optimum expansion Sunday Schools had been auxiliary agencies[78]. A natural progression of older scholars from the Sunday School to the adult membership of a chapel community had been neither the object nor the effect of these early Sunday Schools. Itinerant preaching and village prayer meetings appealing primarily to adults had been the main instruments of recruitment, and between about 1780 and 1830 the most talented and enthusiastic lay workers in a chapel community had been drawn naturally into lay preaching. When a Sunday School teacher had impressed chapel leaders as a promising speaker he was more than likely to have been withdrawn from the School and 'sent out into the villages to preach'[79].

This order of priorities had been reversed in the 1830s and 1840s. Sunday Schools, previously either undenominational or without any strong denominational element in their aims or their teaching, had been transformed into nurseries for denominational membership. The process had begun first in Wesleyanism. The Conference of 1819 had insisted on the nature of the Sunday School as a specifically and exclusively 'religious institution', and the 1820 Conference had recognised a need to make it a more clearly denominational agency[80]. In 1826 the Wesleyan Conference Minutes had included for the first time a Sunday School Report, and the Conference had set up a Committee to recommend ways of regulating Sunday School work[81]. In 1827 this Committee had submitted its report, stressing the need for greater ministerial control over Sunday Schools, more denominational teaching, and closer liaison between Sunday Schools and particular local Methodist societies. 'We regard the rising generation who are under instruction in Sunday-schools, as catechumens', John Stephens, President for the year, had told the Conference. It had to become the prime purpose of Sunday Schools, he had continued, 'that the children may be habituated to a regular and devout attendance upon the public worship of Almighty God, and the ministry of his word'[82]. By the late 1820s, in other words, Wesleyanism had begun to pay increasing attention to the prospect of recruitment by the socialisation of juveniles into its communities. In practice, the change of emphasis had not occurred immediately. The need for the more effective exploitation of the Sunday School as a catchment area for Wesleyan membership had been stressed throughout the 1830s with a regularity which suggested that the Connexion had been responding to the advice rather less quickly than Conference might have wished. But by the mid-1840s the 'systematic and efficient' pastoral care of the young clearly had become a major Wesleyan preoccupation, and, already, an important means of growth. Wesleyan leaders were talking about the prospect of drawing 8,000 to 10,000 new members per annum from the previously neglected juvenile constituency 'within the skirts of Methodism'. It had seemed a panacea for the declining growth rates already beginning to concern early Victorian Nonconformity. 'If we do but cultivate this interesting field of Christian toil', a Wesleyan preacher told the 1849 Conference, 'we shall be an increasing people, while the sun and the moon endure'[83].

Other Nonconformist organisations had turned in the same direction around the middle of the nineteenth century. At the 1848 Assembly of the Congregational Union the need to transform the functions of the Sunday School had been discussed explicitly in the context of diminishing recruitment from the wider society[84]. Introducing a paper dealing with methods of recruiting Sunday School scholars for full denominational membership, J. L. Poore, a minister in Salford, had explained:

> The churches have hitherto regarded Sunday schools only as
> institutions for teaching poor children to read the Scriptures,
> and for keeping them out of harm's way during certain
> portions of the Sabbath. . . . Very different schools do we
> expect and hope to see. They are yet, generally, in a
> rudimental state . . . we cherish a *new idea*. . . . Our Sunday
> schools . . . will become the most fruitful nurseries of our
> churches, and the finest bulwark of our Protestant
> communities and Sabbatic enjoyments [85].

These sentiments had been representative of an emerging
Nonconformist consensus [86]. 'With the growing importance of the school
as a *religious* force,' Dale wrote in the 1880s, 'it has gradually drawn to
itself nearly the whole evangelistic zeal of the Churches.' He saw a clear
connexion between the new emphasis and the decline of lay preaching and
village evangelism, recognising that Nonconformists had become less and
less concerned about the wider society as a source of converts. In a
significant contrast he concluded that 'It would probably have been almost
as difficult in 1820 to find a Congregational Church without a body of lay
preachers as it would be now to find a Congregational Church without a
Sunday School' [87].

The lay preacher as employed in the Independent churches
had been an agent of aggressive evangelism *par excellence*: when successful
he had contributed to growth by the recruitment of adults from the wider
society. The successful Sunday School teacher recruited juveniles. He
operated in a constituency already associated with the chapel, and his
function was to a large extent pastoral.

The flow of recruits from denominational Sunday Schools
never fulfilled expectations. Comparisons of the size of Sunday School
membership with the growth of adult chapel membership indicate that low
returns from Sunday School evangelism were general [88]. Recruitment by
socialisation probably was quite effective, for the influence of the Sunday
School reinforced that of the home. But the statistics confirm the conclusion of Henry Pelling that, for the children of outsiders, as a general rule,
'Sunday School teaching, if absorbed at all, was forgotten when the
children grew up' [89]. From the middle of the Edwardian era, moreover,
this internal constituency, like that of adult adherents, began to contract.
Wesleyan Sunday School enrolment, which had risen from 543,067 in
1866 to more than a million in 1906, fell to 759,968 by 1931 [90]. During
the period 1906–31 the number of Congregational Sunday scholars
declined from 532,547 to 375,497, and a further loss of more than
200,000 occurred in the next thirty years [91]. Baptist Sunday School
enrolments followed precisely the same pattern [92]. Churches which had
lost touch with their external constituencies now faced the problem of
rapidly declining internal constituencies.

It took the illusion-destroying experience of the Great War to bring home
to the Churches the full extent of their estrangement from the 'world' of

modern English society. Chaplains confronted with battalions which the *Church Times* called 'a microcosm of the nation'[93] were forced to face the reality of how little the religious cultures of either Church or Chapel pervaded the wider secular culture. Victorian fears about the total alienation of the working classes from organised religion were seen to have been amply justified, and it was equally apparent that for the middle and upper classes religion was becoming an increasingly epiphenomenal cultural influence. The pessimists of the 1914—18 period were to be vindicated in the decades ahead as these religious-cultural deficiencies found expression in accelerating organisational decline, but it is clear that the roots of both the cultural and the institutional secularisation of the society were embedded in an earlier age. The denominational compromises of the Victorian Churches, like the crisis of plausibility which had undermined their influence on the wider society and encouraged a defensive shift to endogenous growth, were the ultimately unavoidable adjustments of organised religion to the emergence in England of a society pluralistic, urbanised, and relatively affluent, whose rhythm of life was dominated by the artificial rationality of an industrialised economy.

Conclusion

While in the long term the Industrial Revolution was instrumental in diminishing the cultural and institutional role of religion in English society, the early industrial era saw the emergence of a situation in which the interests of Church and Chapel became deeply implicated in the crucial social and political processes of adjustment from a pre-industrial to a mature industrial society. The rise of a popular extra-Establishment Protestantism rivalling the quantitative strength of the Church of England left the Victorians with a legacy of religious conflict to reinforce and symbolise the fundamental division between the traditional landed ruling classes and the newer social and economic interests associated with industry and commerce. Ecclesiastical struggles for religious equality and disestablishment consequently merged in Victorian politics with the ongoing movement of the society away from the prescriptive, hereditary, and unrepresentative political and social structures of the past, and towards liberalism and democracy. And as a result of this historic conjunction of political, social and religious developments, the social significance of Victorian religion was immense despite the gradual emergence of external societal and internal religious-cultural and organisational conditions essentially antithetical to the Churches.

These themes have been the subject of the foregoing chapters, which have sought to recognise and to explain the centrality of religious issues and religious institutions in English life almost to the eve of the First World War, while at the same time arguing that the processes underlying the decline of religion in the twentieth century had begun to effect the development of the society as early as the mid-nineteenth century. The Church–Chapel confrontation, in short, succeeded in delaying for more than half a century the most obvious manifestations of secularisation. It ensured for Victorian religion an undiminished public role and social significance throughout a period in which all the Churches were experiencing mounting difficulties in the task of mobilising the wider society for religious ends. One index of its importance was the rapidity with which Nonconformity, in particular, declined once the process of 'gradual disestablishment' drew to a close.

Between the passage of the First Reform Act and the Irish Home Rule crisis of the mid-1880s, Nonconformity was one of that fairly heterogeneous amalgam of aspiring interests which eventually came together in the uneasy alliance which was Gladstonian Liberalism. Like the alliance as a whole, Nonconformity as a political force suffered significantly from the Home Rule split; but also like other liberal and progressive interests, it suffered even more from the kind of institutional irrelevance which was the price, not of failure, but of success. For by 1885 the struggle for religious equality—the process of 'gradual disestablishment'— was virtually complete, and the fresh outbreak of sectarian conflict in the period 1902—06 represented merely a temporary revival of the kinds of politico-religious alignments typical of the pre-1885 era. In a most perceptive observation in 1897 the eminent Congregationalist theologian, A. Martin Fairbairn, remarked:

> It is perhaps harder to be a Nonconformist today than it has ever been in the history of England. The very decay of the disabilities from which our fathers suffered has made it harder for us than it was for them to dissent[1].

With the exception of the years between 1902 and 1906 Nonconformist density indices, which had remained more or less stable during the first half-century of Victoria's reign, declined significantly after 1885. The Church of England, on the other hand, experienced increases in communicant participation between 1885 and 1914 which were more rapid than population growth in the society as a whole. But these trends, which have been examined in Chapter 2, did not reflect changes in the organisational strategies or goals of either Anglicanism or Nonconformity. Rather, they were the inevitable consequences of basic changes in the mood of the wider society and in the role of religion within it. In very general terms, these were years in which nationalist and imperialist sentiments tended to replace the previous preoccupations with internal issues at the centre of national attention; and religious deviance, often more functional than commitment to an Established Church in a context of social protest and sectional competition, obviously was less functional than late Victorian Anglicanism as a symbol of national identity. However passionately the Nonconformist orator might associate his religious commitment with imperial patriotism or even jingoism, the Church of England clearly was in a much better position than its rivals to capitalise on the exuberant patriotism of the late Victorians. Furthermore, the kinds of sectional alignments which did gain in importance and coherence during the period after 1885, notably those associated with the rise of organised labour, tended to disrupt rather than to reinforce the social basis of the old Church—Chapel confrontation. The traditional resonance between religion and politics gradually disappeared, and its brief reappearance after 1902 served merely to illustrate how much it had been responsible for the prominence of the Churches in Victorian life.

Indeed, in a curious sense it is precisely the increasingly epiphenomenal nature of religious influences within the society which has given the Church of England an advantage over the various Nonconformist denominations of modern industrial England. Nonconformity, by definition, represents a positive commitment to one religious system rather than another; and for this reason it is much less likely than Anglicanism to survive as a residual loyalty in a secular society. In contemporary England, Martin has observed, 'many people are grateful for the existence of the church so long as they are not brought close enough to share in its confusions'[2]. Anglicanism, as a cultural expression of national identity, as an obvious if merely nominal concomitant of being English, has stood to gain from such minimal religiosity. For in denominational competition with the Church, Nonconformist organisations were likely to succeed most during phases of strong, specific religious commitment, when the 'confusions' of religion were either regarded as being intrinsically important or were able to symbolise and legitimate conflict situations within the wider society.

Thus the Industrial Revolution, by accelerating the disintegration of the old prescriptive order and abetting the rise of a pluralistic society in England, produced a basic religious division between Church and Chapel to mirror the emerging complexities of the industrialising nation. But denominational religion was a midwife of the new, urbanised industrial society, not an offspring. For the long term concomitant of industrialisation was secularisation, and modern English society is a context in which significant religious commitment is a subcultural phenomenon.

Bibliographical note

References and sources to tables listed separately in the final Reference section, provide a reasonable indication of the primary and secondary materials on which the text has been based. This note attempts merely to summarise the kinds of sources which are available for the social history of English religion between 1740 and 1914, and to draw attention to some of the more important secondary material.

From the perspective of the social historian many aspects of English religion remain unexplored; and much of what has been written, being located in monographs, local histories, or studies concerned mainly with subjects other than religion, is not easily assimilable. For a general background to the religious history of the period 1740–1914 one can turn to such works as R. T. Jones, *Congregationalism in England 1662–1962*, Independent Press, 1962; J. R. H. Moorman, *A History of the Church in England*, A. & C. Black, 1963; W. J. Townsend, H. B. Workman, and G. Eayrs, *A New History of Methodism*, 2 vols, Epworth, 1909; A. C. Underwood, *A History of the English Baptists*, Kingsgate Press, 1947; and E. I. Watkin, *Roman Catholicism in England from the Reformation to 1950*, Oxford University Press, 1957. Specifically on the eighteenth century, C. J. Abbey and J. H. Overton, *The English Church in the Eighteenth Century*, London, 1886; S. C. Carpenter, *Eighteenth Century Church and People*, Murray, 1959; M. Edwards, *John Wesley and the Eighteenth Century*, Epworth, 1955; N. Sykes, *Church and State in England in the Eighteenth Century*, Cambridge University Press, 1934; and B. Willey, *The Eighteenth Century Background*, Penguin Books (Peregrine), 1962, are useful; although none matches the profound and comprehensive treatment which O. Chadwick has brought to a later period in *The Victorian Church*, 2 vols, A. & C. Black, 1966 and 1970. Bridging the gap between the end of the eighteenth century and the Victorian era is a recent detailed and penetrating study by W. R. Ward, *Religion and Society in England 1790–1850*, Batsford, 1972. F. W. Cornish, *History of the English Church in the Nineteenth Century*, 2 vols, Macmillan, 1910; and H. S. Skeats and C. S. Miall, *History of the Free Churches of England, 1688–1891*, London, n.d., are divergent and fairly contemporary interpretations; and H. Davies, *Worship and Theology in England* (vol. iii, *From Watts and Wesley to Maurice, 1690–1850*, Princeton University Press, 1961; and vol. iv, *From Newman to Martineau, 1850–1900*, Princeton University Press, 1962), although essentially a theological and liturgical study, contains a wealth of valuable insights into social aspects of English religion.

Specifically religious historians have not, however, been in the vanguard of the developing study of religion as a social phenomenon. Most major problems in the social history of English religion have been identified and explored initially by historians concerned primarily with secular issues and institutions. E. Halévy, *A History of the English People in the Nineteenth Century*, 6 vols, Benn, 1961; and *The Birth of Methodism in England*, trans. B. Semmel, University of Chicago Press, 1971, are likely to remain compulsory reading for the social study of English religion; as also are E. P. Thompson's, *The Making of the English Working Class*, 2nd edn, Penguin Books (Pelican), 1968, and the related studies of E. J. Hobsbawm. Similarly, the discussions of religion in G. Kitson Clark, *The Making of Victorian England*, Methuen, 1965; H. Perkin, *The Origins of Modern English Society, 1780–1880*, Routledge, 1969; and G. M. Young, *Victorian England: Portrait of an Age*, 2nd edn, Oxford University Press, 1960, remain among the most penetrating available. And local historians like Alan Everitt (for example, in his 'Nonconformity in country parishes', *Agricultural History Review Supplement*, xviii, February 1970), and political historians such as John Vincent and H. Pelling, have in recent years drawn attention to new ways of looking at the social reality of English religion.

Partly in response to the issues raised by such authors, the past decade or so has seen the appearance of a number of important monographs and unpublished theses on aspects of the social history of religion, and a new appreciation of older works such as E. R. Bebb's *Nonconformity and Social and Economic Life, 1600–1800*, Epworth, 1935. The following publications are of primary importance, although the list is not offered as an exhaustive one:

G. F. A. Best, *Temporal Pillars: Queen Anne's Bounty, the Ecclesiastical Commissioners, and the Church of England*, Cambridge University Press, 1964.

J. C. G. Binfield, 'Nonconformity in the Eastern Counties, 1840–1885, with reference to its social background', Cambridge Ph.D. thesis, 1965.

R. Currie, *Methodism Divided: a study in the sociology of ecumenicalism*, Faber, 1968.

B. Greaves, 'An analysis of the spread of Methodism in Yorkshire during the eighteenth and early nineteenth centuries (1740–1831), with special reference to the environment of this movement', Leeds M.A. thesis, 1961.

B. Greaves, 'Methodism in Yorkshire 1740–1851', Liverpool Ph.D. thesis, 1968.

B. Harrison, *Drink and the Victorians: the temperance question in England 1815–1872*, Faber, 1971.

K. S. Inglis, *Churches and the Working Classes in Victorian England*, Routledge, 1963.

P. d'A. Jones, *The Christian Socialist Revival 1877–1914: religion, class, and social conscience in late-Victorian England*, Princeton University Press, 1968.

S. Mayor, *The Churches and the Labour Movement*, Independent Press, 1967.

D. McClatchey, *Oxfordshire Clergy 1777–1869: a study of the Established Church and of the role of its clergy in local society*, Oxford University Press, 1960.

W. H. Mackintosh, *Disestablishment and Liberation: the movement for the separation of the Anglican Church from State control*, Epworth, 1972.

E. P. Stigant, 'Methodism and the working class, 1760–1821: a study in social and political conflict', University of Keele M.A. thesis, 1968.

D. M. Thompson, 'The Churches and society in Leicestershire, 1851–1881', Cambridge Ph.D. thesis, 1969.

E. R. Wickham, *Church and Society in an Industrial City*, Lutterworth, 1957.

This list might have been extended greatly to include a mounting number of academic articles from a wide variety of journals. Articles like K. S. Inglis's pioneering study of the 1851 Census of Religious Worship, 'Patterns of religious worship in 1851', *Journal of Ecclesiastical History*, ii, No. 1, 1960; and W. R. Ward's 'The tithe question in England in the early nineteenth century', *Journal of Ecclesiastical History*, xvi, No. 1, April 1965, advanced the social study of English religion as much as many books. But details of such publications are readily available in bibliographical and reference sections of most of the secondary sources listed above.

The future development of the social history of religion will depend on the exploitation of methods of inquiry and types of evidence which in many cases still offer historians fields little-explored but apparently fertile. There is much fresh work to be done on *Visitation Returns* and other diocesan records which, as Greaves and McClatchey have shown, offer a unique view of the Established Church at the parochial level. Some of these returns have been edited and published; for example, H. A. Lloyd Jukes, ed., 'Articles of inquiry addressed to the clergy of the Diocese of Oxford at the Primary Visitation of Dr Thomas Secker, 1738', *Oxfordshire Record Society*, xxxviii, 1957; S. L. Ollard and P. C. Walker, eds, 'Archbishop Herring's Visitation Returns, 1743', *Yorkshire Archaeological Society Record Series*, vols lxxi, lxxii, lxxv, lxxvii, and lxxix, 1929–31; and E. P. Baker, ed., 'Bishop Wilberforce's Visitation Returns for the Archdeaconry of Oxford in the year 1854', *Oxfordshire Record Society*, xxxv, 1954. Most of the material, however, remains in manuscript form, and it is located in many cases in provincial archives.

Tables 3.1 and 3.2 (pp. 63 and 67) in this book illustrate the value of *non-parochial records* as evidence about the socio-occupational structure of Nonconformist communities in early industrial society. These records, of which the Public Records Office has a substantial collection, doubtless will reward further research. The same is true of the wealth of material located, and often hidden, in *Parliamentary Papers*. All these *Papers* have, of course, been used extensively; but it is evident that methodological ingenuity, and specifically the use of quantification and sampling, can make many of them the sources of new insights into nineteenth-century religion.

Little need be said of the value of the traditional published and archival sources. The official minutes and reports of religious assemblies, conferences, and congresses; the semi-official and unofficial denominational newspapers and periodicals which the late eighteenth and nineteenth centuries produced in profusion; and the various manuscript collections on religious leaders and organisations contained in denominational and other archives, must remain the basic materials for any historical study of English religion during this period. The recent work of W. R. Ward and E. P. Stigant, referred to earlier in this note, has indicated something of the extent and value of the little-used manuscript resources of the Methodist Archives; and despite the valuable work of Vincent and Mackintosh (referred to above), and I. G. Jones, 'The Liberation Society and Welsh Politics, 1844–1868', *Welsh History Review*, i, No. 2, 1961, the records of the Liberation Society and kindred bodies promise to reward further exploration.

Finally, the present study, and the thesis on which parts of it have been based (A. D. Gilbert, 'The growth and decline of Nonconformity in England and Wales, with special reference to the period before 1850: an historical interpretation of statistics of religious practice', Oxford DPhil thesis, 1973) have followed the example of Robert Currie's *Methodism Divided* in using extensively the official statistics of eighteenth- and nineteenth-century religious organisations. Such material, which offers a range and comprehensiveness not available in government data on religion, or indeed in any comparable body of social statistics on the period before 1900, seems likely to occupy social historians and sociologists for many years. A detailed compendium of British and Irish religious statistics, and a preliminary analysis of basic trends in British church growth, is at present being prepared by R. Currie, A. D. Gilbert, and L. H. Horsley, and will be published in due course. It is hoped that the ready availability of such evidence will encourage the development in the social history of English religion of a use of quantitative methods without which many important hypotheses seem likely to defy further analysis.

Abbreviations used in the notes

Ag. Hist. Rev.	*Agricultural History Review*
Am. Hist. Rev.	*American Historical Review*
Bapt. Ann. Reg.	*Baptist Annual Register*
Bapt. Hbk	*Baptist Handbook*
Bapt. Mag.	*Baptist Magazine*
Best, *Temporal Pillars*	G. F. A. Best, *Temporal Pillars: Queen Anne's Bounty, the Ecclesiastical Commissioners, and the Church of England*, Cambridge University Press, 1964.
Bogue and Bennett, *Dissenters*	David Bogue and James Bennett, *History of Dissenters from the Revolution in 1688 to the year 1808*, 4 vols, London, 1812.
Brit. J. Sociol.	*British Journal of Sociology*
C. of E.	Church of England
CSP (D)	Calendar of State Papers (Domestic)
Cong. Mag.	*Congregational Magazine*
Cong. Ybk	*Congregational Yearbook*
Cont. Rev.	*Contemporary Review*
Ev. Mag.	*Evangelical Magazine*
J. Eccles. Hist.	*Journal of Ecclesiastical History*
J. Presbyt. Soc.	*Journal of the Presbyterian Society*
Mitchell and Deane, *Abstract*	B. R. Mitchell and P. Deane, *Abstract of British Historical Statistics*, Cambridge University Press, 1962
PP	*Parliamentary Papers*
P.R.O.	Public Record Office
R.S.	Record Society
Prim. Meth. Mag.	*Primitive Methodist Magazine*
Proc. Wes. Hist. Soc.	*Proceedings of the Wesleyan Historical Society*
Sociol. Rev.	*Sociological Review*
Trans. Bapt. Hist. Soc.	*Transactions of the Baptist Historical Society*
Trans. Cong. Hist. Soc.	*Transactions of the Congregational Historical Society*

Wesley, *Journal*   *The Journal of the Rev. John Wesley, M.A.*, edited by Nehemiah Curnock, 8 vols, Epworth Press, London, 1938.

Wesley, *Letters*   *The Letters of the Rev. John Wesley, M.A.*, edited by John Telford, 8 vols, Epworth Press, London, 1931.

Wesley, *Sermons*   *Sermons on Several Occasions*, 3 vols, London, 1876.

Wesley, *Works*   *The Works of the Rev. John Wesley, M.A.*, 6 vols, Wesleyan Methodist Book Room, London, 1810.

Wes. Conf. Min.   *Wesleyan Conference Minutes*
Wes. Meth. Mag.   *Wesleyan Methodist Magazine*

Notes and references

Chapter 1 *Religion and society in 1740*

1   *Whitefield's Journals*, ed. W. Wale, London, 1905, p. 209.
2   Christopher Hill, *Economic Problems of the Church from Arch-bishop Whitgift to the Long Parliament*, Oxford U.P., 1956, p. 14 and *passim*.
3   Members of the higher clergy owned about one-fifth of these impropriations.
4   Hill, *Economic Problems of the Church*, p. 151.
5   D. McClatchey, *Oxfordshire Clergy 1777–1869: a study of the Established Church and of the role of its clergy in local society*, Oxford U.P., 1960, p. 13; [Anon], *The Necessity of the Abolition of Pluralities and Non-Residence with the Employment of Substitutes by the Beneficed Clergy . . .*, London, 1802, pp. 271–4.
6   R. A. Marchant, *The Church and the Law: justice, administration and discipline in the Diocese of York 1560–1640*, Cambridge U.P., 1969, pp. 205–27.
7   *Lincoln R.S.*, xxiii (1926), p. lviii.
8   Cf., C. Hill, *Society and Puritanism in Pre-Revolutionary England* (Secker & Warburg, 1964), n.e. Panther, 1969, pp. 457–9; K. V. Thomas, *Religion and the Decline of Magic*, Weidenfeld & Nicolson, 1971, pp. 159–61; and R. G. Usher, *The Reconstruction of the English Church*, London, 1910, i, 279.
9   S. R. Gardiner, *History of England, 1603–42*, London, 1884, viii, 133.
10 S. Patrick, *A Treatise on the Necessity of Frequency of receiving the Holy Communion*, 4th edn, London, 1696, p. 1.
11 W. Roberts, *Memoirs of the Life of Mrs Hannah More*, London, 1834, i, 451.
12 Some non-resident clergy lived close enough to their parishes to discharge their parochial responsibilities.
13 *PP*, 1812, x, 157, 159.
14 The legislation was summarised in the Act repealing it, passed in 1865 long after it had ceased to be implemented. See *PP*, 1865, i, 127–8.
15 CSP (D), 1693, King William's Chest 14:89, p. 449.
16 *Ibid*.
17 E. M. Thompson, ed., *Letters of Humphrey Prideaux to John Ellis, 1674–1722*, Camden Society, n.s., 1875, xv, p. 154.

18 *Ibid.*
19 H. A. Lloyd Jukes, ed., 'Articles of inquiry addressed to the clergy of the Diocese of Oxford at the Primary Visitation of Dr Thomas Secker, 1738', *Oxfordshire R.S.*, no. 38, 1957, *passim*.
20 'A Representation of the present State of Religion . . .', *The Harleian Miscellany*, London, 1809, ii, 22.
21 The so-called Bangorian Controversy, prompted by Bishop Hoadly's ultra-Erastian sermon of 31 March 1717.
22 'Oxford Diocesan Visitation, 1738', Lloyd Jukes, *loc. cit.*, p. 18.
23 Figures on numbers of households and communicants were required from each parish. The percentage of communicants to households was 36.6.
24 S. L. Ollard and P. C. Walker, 'Archbishop Herring's Visitation Returns, 1743', *Yorkshire Archaeological Society Record Series*, lxxi, lxxii, lxxv, lxxvii, and lxxix, 1929–31.
25 P. Laslett, *The World We Have Lost*, Methuen, 1965, p. 73.
26 Cf. C. J. Abbey and J. H. Overton, *The English Church in the Eighteenth Century*, London, 1878, pp. 453–4; and G. V. Bennett, 'Conflict in the Church', in G. A. Holmes, ed., *Britain After the Glorious Revolution 1689–1714*, Macmillan, 1969, pp. 162–3, and 'The Convocation of 1710', in G. J. Cuming and D. Baker, eds, *Studies in Church History VII: Councils and Assemblies*, Cambridge U.P., 1971, pp. 311–19.
27 S. Webb and B. Webb, *English Local Government from the Revolution to the Municipal Corporations Act: The Parish and the County*, London, 1906, pp. 104–45, 152–63.
28 The phrase employed by Harold Perkin in *The Origins of Modern English Society 1780–1880*, Routledge, 1969.
29 Cf. G. F. A. Best, *Temporal Pillars: Queen Anne's Bounty, the Ecclesiastical Commissioners, and the Church of England*, Cambridge U.P., 1964, pp. 59–60.
30 *Ibid.*, p. 61.
31 See Chapter 4.
32 E. I. Watkin, *Roman Catholicism in England from the Reformation to 1950*, Oxford U.P. (Home University Library), 1957, p. 101.
33 R. H. Tawney, *Religion and the Rise of Capitalism*, Murray 1926, repr., 1961, p. 234.
34 Cf. G. E. Swanson, *Religion and Regime: a sociological account of the Reformation*, Univ. of Michigan Press, 1967, pp. 58–60.
35 E. R. Bebb, *Nonconformity and Social and Economic Life 1600–1800*, Epworth Press, 1935, p. 48.
36 *Ibid.*, pp. 51, 57.
37 Figures on the growth of Dissent cited in this paragraph are based on a variety of sources: censuses of Dissent carried out in 1715–16 by John Evans and Daniel Neal respectively; John Collett Ryland's survey of Particular Baptist strength in 1751 (analysed by A. S. Langley, *Trans. Bapt. Hist. Soc.*, vii, 1918–20, 138–62); the 'Compton Census', relating to 1676, CSP (D), 1693, King William's Chest 14:89; and 'List of Returns . . . of Certified places of Religious Worship of Protestant Dissenters'; *PP*, 1852–53, lxxviii, 164. The

best secondary sources are Bebb, *op. cit.*, pp. 36–42, Appendices II, III, and V–VIII; *Trans. Cong. Hist. Soc.*, v, 205–7, 378–81, 384–5; and *Trans. Bapt. Hist. Soc.*, ii, 95–109, v, 172–89, and vii, 138–62.

38   Quoted by J. H. Overton, *The English Evangelical Revival in the Eighteenth Century*, London, 1886, p. 153.

39   *Free Thoughts on the most probable Means of Reviving the Dissenting Interest Addressed to the Author of the Enquiry into the Causes of the Decay of the Dissenting Interest*, London, 1730; reprinted in the *Protestant Dissenters Magazine*, vi (1799), 382ff.

40   J. Berington, *State and Relations of English Catholics*, London, 1781; quoted by Watkin, *Roman Catholicism in England*, p. 113.

41   Wesley, *Journal*, London, 1938, ii, 172.

42   Peter L. Berger, *The Social Reality of Religion*, Faber, 1969, p. 137.

43   See Josiah Woodward, *An Earnest Admonition to All, but Especially to Young Persons to turn to God . . . To which is added an account of the rise and progress of the religious societies . . .*, London, 1697.

44   Adam Clark, ed., *Memoirs of the Wesley Family, collected primarily from original documents*, 2nd edn, London, 1836, pp. 155–6.

45   *Ibid.*, pp. 144–5.

46   For an elaboration of this subject see J. S. Simon, *John Wesley and the Religious Societies*, London, 1921.

47   Cf. Woodward, *An . . . Account of the Rise and Progress of the Religious Societies*, pp. 199–200, with Wesley's 'Rules for the Methodist Societies', *Works*, vi, 304–7.

48   *Wes. Conf. Min.*, 1744, i, 14.

49   Wesley, *Letters*, iii, 152.

50   *Wes. Conf. Min.*, 1744, i, 13.

51   [Anon], *Some Papers Giving an Account of the Rise and Progress of Methodism at Wednesbury in Staffordshire, and other Parishes adjacent; as likewise of the late riot in those parts*, London, 1744, pp. 8–10.

52   'Rules for a Helper', enunciated at the 1744 Conference, Wesley, *Works*, vi, 350.

53   *Wes. Conf. Min.*, i, 46.

54   Wesley, *Works*, vi, 388.

55   Wesley, *Sermons*, iii, 202.

56   Wesley, *Letters*, iv, 143.

57   Wesley, *Works*, iv, 189–95. The original letter and the three replies are reproduced in full.

58   *Ibid.*, vi, 383.

59   *Ibid.*

Chapter 2   *Patterns of religious practice, 1740–1914*

1   H. U. Faulkner, *Chartism and the Churches*, London, 1916; K. S. Inglis, *Churches and the Working Classes in Victorian England*, Routledge, 1963; B. Harrison, *Drink and the Victorians: the temperance question in England 1815–1872*, Faber, 1971; E. J. Hobsbawm, 'Methodism and the threat of revolution in Britain', in *Labouring Men: studies in the history of labour*, Weidenfeld & Nicolson, 1964;

and E. P. Thompson, *The Making of the English Working Class*, 2nd edn, Penguin Books, 1968.

2 Charles Y. Glock and Rodney Stark have elaborated their dimensional schema in various publications including *American Piety: the nature of religious commitment*, Univ. of California Press, 1965, pp. 14—16. Cf. G. Lenski, *The Religious Factor: a sociological study of religion's impact on politics, economics, and family life*, Doubleday, 1963.

3 C. Y. Glock and R. Stark, *Religion and Society in Tension*, Rand McNally, 1965, p. 22.

4 Roland Robertson, *The Sociological Interpretation of Religion*, Oxford U.P., 1970, pp. 38—54. The suggestion is made initially in the form of a question (p. 38), but the subsequent analysis represents a firm endorsement.

5 N. J. Demarath, *Social Class in American Protestantism*, Rand McNally, 1965, pp. 7—8.

6 The two most famous statistical surveys initiated at government level were the Compton Census of the late seventeenth century and the Census of Religious Worship, 1851 ('Report on the Census of Religious Worship in England and Wales, 1851', *PP*, 1852—53, LXXXIX).

7 G. S. Bain, *The Growth of White Collar Unionism*, Oxford U.P., 1969, is a study distinguished by its extensive yet critical use of statistical evidence about trade union growth. For discussions of the problems of using these and other forms of social statistics, see the relevant introductory section of B. R. Mitchell and P. Deane, *Abstract of British Historical Statistics*, Cambridge U.P., 1962.

8 For a fuller discussion of the improvement of statistical records relating to English religion see A. D. Gilbert, 'The growth and decline of Nonconformity in England and Wales, with special reference to the period before 1850: an historical interpretation of statistics of religious practice', University of Oxford, D.Phil. thesis 1973, pp. 9—11, 42—3. A much more comprehensive study of the subject will appear in a reference work on religious statistics in Britain and Ireland at present being prepared by R. Currie, A. D. Gilbert, and L. H. Horsley, and due to be published by the Clarendon Press.

9 Here defined so as to include Methodism.

10 Gilbert, *op. cit.*, pp. 100—49.

11 The sample, which includes all parishes for which data are available at each of these time points, comprises the following: Alvescot, Ardley, Britwell Salome, Charlton, Cowley, Deddington, Ducklington, Goring Lower Heyford, Hook Norton, Horspath, Kencot, Mixbury, Northleigh, St Clements (Oxford), St Giles (Oxford), St Mary Magdalene (Oxford), St Thomas (Oxford), Piddington, Great Rollright, Salford, Shilton, Shiplake, Shipton-on-Cherwell, Stoke Talmage, Stonesfield, Swerford, Waterstock, Watlington, and Wroxton parishes. Source: 'Oxford Diocesan Papers', Bodleian Library MSS. This sample, and other related data, will be analysed at greater length in the forthcoming study by Currie, Gilbert, and Horsley (see note 8 above).

12   The early analyses of R. Yates, *The Church in Danger: a statement of the cause, and of the probable means of averting that danger attempted...*, London, 1815, and *The Basis of National Welfare: considered in reference chiefly to the prosperity of Britain, and safety of the Church of England: With an examination of... the population of parishes, and the capacity of churches and chapels*, London, 1817, have not been altered substantively by subsequent research. Cf. Best, *Temporal Pillars*, pp. 11—184; W. L. Mathison, *English Church Reform 1815—1840*, London, 1923, pp. 17—19; and R. A. Soloway, *Prelates and People: ecclesiastical social thought in England 1783—1852*, Routledge, 1969, pp. 279—96.

13   Mitchell and Deane, *Abstract*, pp. 5, 20. The population of Wales, around 500,000 in 1740, has been subtracted from the estimates quoted on p. 5.

14   For more or less pessimistic interpretations see Inglis, *Churches and the Working Classes in Victorian England*; P. T. Marsh, *The Victorian Church in Decline*, Routledge, 1969; and M. A. Crowther, *Church Embattled*, David & Charles, 1970. The most optimistic of the recent histories is D. Bowen, *The Idea of the Victorian Church*, McGill U.P., 1968.

15   B. Heeney, 'On being a mid-Victorian clergyman', *J. Rel. Hist.*, vii, no. 3 (June 1973), 208.

16   For which see A. Mearns, *The Statistics of Attendance at Public Worship, 1881—2*, London, 1882; R. Mudie-Smith, *The Religious Life of London*, London, 1904; R. B. Walker, 'Religious changes in Liverpool in the nineteenth century', *J. Eccles. Hist.*, xix, no. 2 (October 1968), 202.

17   For annual series equivalent to the quinquennial series presented in Table 2.2 see Gilbert, 'The growth and decline of Nonconformity', Appendix I, pp. 458—62. Comparable figures covering the British Isles have been used by several scholars.

18   Extrapolating from 1739, when Wesleyanism made its first converts, to 1767, when it published its first statistics, obviously requires little imagination. The pattern was one of accelerating growth.

19   In the broadest sense the constituency from which English Methodism sought to recruit members was the adolescent and adult population of the country, here defined as the population aged 15 plus and described for the sake of brevity as the 'adult population'.

20   See C. G. Bolam, *et al.*, *The English Presbyterians: from Elizabethan Puritanism to modern Unitarianism*, Allen & Unwin, 1968, pp. 73—218.

21   *An Enquiry into the Causes of the Decay of the Dissenting Interest. In a letter to a Dissenting Minister*, 2nd edn, London, 1730, p. 4.

22   E. Halévy, *England in 1815*, Benn, 1961, p. 404. For Halévy's admirably concise survey of the development of eighteenth-century Dissent see *ibid.*, pp. 401—10, 417—28.

23   Quite apart from the fact that there is no simple relationship between church building and growth, the interpretation of this official material is complicated by the fact that the distinction between 'temporary' places of worship (houses, dwelling houses,

rooms, etc.) and 'permanent' (chapels and meeting houses) was mis-leading. George Graham, Registrar General in 1852, explained that when the status of a place of worship had not been defined un-ambiguously by its occupants, a building not definitely known to be 'permanent' had been classified as 'temporary'. This was an altogether unsatisfactory way of making a distinction which was important: the opening of a permanent chapel was an event signify-ing something quite different from the registration of a building for use as a temporary preaching station. The series on 'permanent' places of worship thus underestimate the progress of Dissent in every decade.

24 Wesley, *Works*, vi, 234—8.

25 For a summary of the principal cases in which the Deputies were involved during the eighteenth and early nineteenth centuries see [Anon], *A Sketch of the History and Proceedings of the Deputies Appointed to Protect the Civil Rights of the Protestant Dissenters*, London, 1814, pp. 155—81.

26 Apprehension about the spread of Dissent and Methodism underlay the various attempts in the 1790s and the first decade of the nine-teenth century to tighten registration procedures. See, e.g., *Hansard*, 1st series, 1809, xv, 663; *Ibid.*, 1810, xvii, 762; and [Anon], *The State of the Established Church: in a series of letters to the Right Hon. Spencer Percival, Chancellor of the Exchequer*, London, 1809, pp. 5—15; cf. W. R. Ward, *Religion and Society in England 1790—1850*, Batsford, 1972, pp. 48—62.

27 John Evans's Census of Dissent, 1716, Dr Williams's Library *MS*, 'Records of Nonconformity', no. 4. Edited and corrected versions of the manuscript include those in *Trans. Bapt. Hist. Soc.*, ii (1910—11), 95—109; *Trans. Cong. Hist. Soc.* v (1911—12), 205—7, 378—81, 384—5; and Bebb, *Nonconformity and Social and Economic Life*, Appendices II, III, and V—VII.

28 'Thompson's List', 1773, Dr Williams's Library MS, 'Records of Nonconformity', no. 5. The above figure is drawn from the corrected version of the manuscript in *Trans. Cong. Hist. Soc.*, v, 380.

29 Bogue and Bennett, *Dissenters*, iv, 327—8.

30 The figures for 1716 and 1808 are from the Evans and Bogue and Bennett surveys cited in the three preceding references; the 1751 figure is based on a survey by John Collett Ryland of Particular Baptist strength in England, published and analysed by A. S. Langley in *Trans. Bapt. Hist. Soc.* vii (1918—20), 138—62; and the figures for 1830 and 1840 are from the *Bapt. Mag.*, 1841, pp. 273—4.

31 *Cong. Ybk*, 1872, p. 82.

32 Bogue and Bennett, *Dissenters*, iv, 329.

33 On which see H. Gow, *The Unitarians*, Methuen, 1928; and H. McLachlan, *The Unitarian Movement in the Religious Life of England: its contribution to thought and learning, 1700—1900*, Allen & Unwin, 1934.

34 For a careful analysis of these growth processes see J. S. Rowntree, *Quakerism Past and Present: being an inquiry into the causes of its decline . . .*, London, 1859, pp. 68—88.

35 For two contemporary accounts of the dichotomy, one sympathetic, the other hostile, see W. Wilson, *The History and Antiquities of Dissenting Churches and Meeting Houses in London, Westminster and Southwark; including the lives of their ministers, from the rise of Nonconformity to the present time*, 4 vols, London, 1808—14, iv, 550—62; and *Meth. Mag.* xxxvii (1814), 376. The latter passage has been quoted at length by Ward, *Religion and Society in England*, p. 70.

36 The meetings of the General Body of London Dissenting Ministers in Salters Hall in February and March of 1719 were concerned with the regulation of doctrinal disputes among Dissenters, and particularly with the problem of Trinitarian orthodoxy. The meetings saw the General Body split into two factions along doctrinal lines: a paradigm for the future of the original dissenting tradition.

37 The Society of Friends, with its historical antipathy towards liturgical and ceremonial forms and its rejection of a professional ministry, provides an obvious exception to some of these generalisations. Ironically, however, by the close of the eighteenth century the Friends had become one of the most insular of all the Old Dissenting movements: a religious culture 'almost entombed in its own traditions', as Horton Davies has put it in *Worship and Theology in England from Watts and Wesley to Maurice 1690—1850*, Princeton U.P., 1961, pp. 119—23.

38 Wilson, *The History and Antiquities of Dissenting Churches and Meeting Houses . . .*, iv, 561.

39 *Ibid.*, pp. 556—7.

40 Bolam *et al.*, *The English Presbyterians*, pp. 222—3; E. E. Hagen, *On the Theory of Social Change*, Homewood, Ill., Dorsey; (London, Tavistock), 1962, pp. 294—309; A. T. Patterson, *Radical Leicester: a history of Leicester 1780—1850*, Leicester U.P., 1954, pp. 214—21. See also R. V. Holt, *The Unitarian Contribution to Social Progress in England*, Allen & Unwin, 1938; and E. Isichei, *Victorian Quakers*, Oxford U.P., 1970.

41 'Report on the Census of Religious Worship', p. clxxxii.

42 *Ibid.*

43 *Cong. Mag.*, 1833, pp. 25—9, quoting the *Unitarian Chronicle* of Sept.—Nov. 1832.

44 'Report on the Census of Religious Worship', p. clxxxii.

45 *Cong. Mag.*, 1833, p. 28.

46 A. H. Drysdale, *History of the Presbyterians in England: Their Rise, Decline, and Revival*, London, 1889, pp. 605—8; *J. Presbyt. Hist. Soc. England*, iii, no. 3 (May 1926), 105—6.

47 These figures have been derived from statistical returns in *The Record*, 26 Sept. 1839; the 'Report on the Census of Religious Worship', *op. cit.*, p. clxxviii; the *Proc. Assembly of the United Presbyterian Church of Scotland*, May 1871, p. 349; and *Whitaker's Almanack*, 1871.

48 In the decades immediately before and after the union of 1876 many individual churches which had moved into the orbit of Congregationalism when the old Presbyterianism had disintegrated in the late

eighteenth and early nineteenth centuries decided to return to Presbyterianism. This was perhaps the most important reason why Congregational growth slowed even more than Baptist growth in the second half of the nineteenth century (cf. Table 2.4).

49   *Minutes of the Synod of the Presbyterian Church of England, 1882*, p. 101.

50   *Ibid.*, 1915.

51   The union produced the United Reformed Church, inaugurated in October 1972.

52   R. Robertson, 'The Salvation Army: the persistence of sectarianism', in B. R. Wilson, ed., *Patterns of Sectarianism*, Heinemann, 1967, pp. 90–102.

53   J. Highet, 'Scottish religious adherence', *Brit. J. Sociol.*, iv, no. 2 (June 1953), 148n.

54   Plymouth Brethren, *Assemblies in Great Britain and Other Parts*, London, 1959, *passim*.

55   P. Embley, 'The early development of the Plymouth Brethren', in Wilson, *op. cit.*, p. 243.

56   Ernest Payne, *The Free Church Tradition in the Life of England*, 3rd edn, S.C.M. Press, 1951, p. 131.

57   David Martin, *A Sociology of English Religion*, Heinemann, 1967, p. 16.

58   Many such movements, too small during the pre-1914 period or confined largely to the twentieth century, have been excluded from the present survey. The *Church of Jesus Christ of Latter-Day Saints* (Mormons) grew from a membership of 600 in 1837 to 32,894 in 1851, was reduced by emigration to fewer than 3,000 members by the 1890s, but grew rapidly after 1945 to reach 72,899 members by 1969. *Seventh-Day Adventists* numbered 1,160 in 1903, a year after their British Union Conference had been organised, and 11,666 in 1968. As late as 1906 there were only five *Christian Science* churches in England, and the number grew thereafter to 349 in 1956 before declining to 324 in 1968. The *Jehovah's Witnesses* had 6,000 'publishers' (distributors of the sect's literature) in 1926 and 55,876 in 1969. The *Assemblies of God* grew from 70 individual assemblies in 1924 to 534 in 1971.

59   In contrast, the rise of Wesleyan offshoots such as the Primitive Methodist and Bible Christian connexions during the period of early organisational consolidation in Wesleyanism before 1840 does *not* appear to have brought diminishing returns to the Methodist movement as a whole. The newer Methodist bodies appear to have capitalised on a diminution of Wesleyan expansion at a time when the demand for Methodist type religiosity persisted more or less undiminished. Cf. R. Currie, 'A micro-theory of Methodist growth', *Proc. Wesley Hist. Soc.*, xxxiv (Oct. 1967), 66ff.

60   Mormons, Christadelphians, Christian Scientists, etc.

61   *The History of Catholic Emancipation and the Progress of the Catholic Church in the British Isles (Chiefly in England) from 1771 to 1820*, London, 1886, i, 279.

62   J. O. Power, 'The Irish in England', *Fortnightly Review*, March 1880,

p. 411; D. R. Gwynn, *One Hundred Years of Catholic Emancipation, 1829–1929*, Longmans, 1929, p. 25; cf. *Catholic Times*, 30 October 1891, p. 4.

63   S. Leslie, ed., *Letters of Herbert Cardinal Vaughan to Lady Herbert of Lea, 1867 to 1903*, Burns Oates and Washbourne, London, 1942, p. ix; *Tablet*, 19 April 1884, p. 602.

64   *The Catholic Directory, 1912*.

Tables

2.1   (i) *PP*; *Convocation of Canterbury Report*, 1876; *C. of E. Year Books*; *Facts and Figures about the Church of England*; J. J. Halcombe, ed., *The Church and Her Curates*, London, 1874.

(ii) 'Churches and Chapels, 1881–1901' are estimates based on data relating to church building.

(iii) Easter Day communicant figures for 1891–1914 are from *Facts and Figures about the Church of England*. Earlier figures are estimates derived from various indices of Anglican growth, including sample studies of trends of Easter Day communion in local areas covered by Episcopal Visitation records, and clergy–communicant ratios computed for years and areas in which both are available.

2.2   (i) Population data on which density has been computed are from *Annual Reports of Registrars-General* and (for the nineteenth century) from *Census Reports*. Where census figures have been used interdecennial data have been extrapolated.

(ii) With the exception of those on Wesleyan Reformers all figures are derived from relevant *Conference Minutes*.

(iii) The figure on Wesleyan Reformers was collected by Dr R. Currie and is cited with his permission.

2.3   *PP*, 1852–53, lxxviii, p. 164.

2.4   (i) Figures on the General Baptist New Connexion are from *General Baptist Handbooks*, 1773–1891.

(ii) Congregational and Particular Baptist figures, 1750–1851 are based on a variety of sources, including A. S. Langley, 'Baptist ministers in England about 1750 A.D.', *Trans. Bapt. Hist. Soc.*, vii (1918–20), 138–62; *Bapt. Ann. Reg.*, iii (1798), 40; Bogue and Bennett, *Dissenters*, iv, 327–8; *The Record*, 26 Sept. 1839; *The Protestant Dissenters' Almanack*, 1849–62; 'Report on the Census of Religious Worship', *PP*, lxxxix, 1852–53; and *Bapt. Hbk*, 1870–78. For more complete notes on sources of eighteenth- and nineteenth-century Nonconformist statistics, see Gilbert, 'The growth and decline of Nonconformity', *loc. cit.*, p. 463.

(iii) All other figures are from the *Baptist Handbook* and the *Congregational Yearbook for England and Wales*.

2.5   *Protestant Dissenters' Almanack*, 1849–57; J. S. Rowntree, *Quakerism Past and Present: being an inquiry into the causes of its decline in Great Britain and Ireland*, London, 1859, pp. 75–6; extracts from the Minutes of the London Yearly Meeting of Friends.

2.6   Figures for 1878–86 are from R. Sandall, *The History of the Salvation Army*, vol. ii, 1878–1886, Nelson, 1950. The figure for officers

for 1896 is from the same history, vol. iii, *1886–1896*, by A. R. Wiggins. All other figures are from the *Salvation Army Yearbook*.
2.7 *Churches of Christ Year Book and Annual Report.*
2.8 *Catholic Directory*; H. Thurston, 'Statistical progress of the Catholic Church', in D. R. Gwynn, *One Hundred Years of Catholic Emancipation, 1829–1929*, Longmans, 1929; *The Month*, lix, February 1887; A. E. C. W. Spencer, 'The demography and sociography of the Roman Catholic community of England and Wales', *Downside Symposium*, 1965; Watkin, *Roman Catholicism in England*; and (note 4), *PP*.

Chapter 3 *The rise of Evangelical Nonconformity*

1 Bogue and Bennett, *Dissenters*, iv, 341.
2 E. A. Payne, *The Baptist Union: a short history*, Carey Kingsgate Press, 1959, pp. 3–4.
3 A. Peel, *These Hundred Years: a history of the Congregational Union of England and Wales, 1831–1931*, London, Independent Press, 1931, p. 41.
4 Cf. K. Slack, *The British Churches Today*, Student Christian Movement Press, 1961, pp. 158–9.
5 W. Wilson, *The History and Antiquities of Dissenting Churches and Meeting Houses*, p. 560.
6 Halévy, *England in 1815*, p. 420. Halévy has noted the emergence of a new emphasis on 'emotional or "experiential" Christianity' in the Congregational and Baptist bodies; see pp. 419–20.
7 *Protestant Dissenters' Magazine*, i (1794), 502ff.
8 Thompson, *The Making of the English Working Class*, p. 402, argues that this label was not applicable to the older bodies, but he has underestimated the extent to which the New Dissent represented a departure from older dissenting traditions.
9 J. G. Rogers, *An Autobiography*, London, 1903, pp. 20–1.
10 N. H. Marshall, 'The Baptist churches', in W. B. Selbie, ed., *Evangelical Christianity*, London, 1914, p. 144.
11 Wesley, *Letters*, iv, 198. For a similar attitude on the part of a leading Calvinist see J. Eyre, *Union and Friendly Intercourse Recommended Among Such of the Various Denominations of Calvinists, and the Members of the late Mr Wesley's Societies, as agree in the Essential Truths of the Gospel*, London, 1798.
12 Wesley, *Sermons*, ii, 226–7.
13 For a contemporary recognition of this irony see *Bapt. Mag.*, 1815, p. 270.
14 B. Greaves, 'An analysis of the spread of Methodism in Yorkshire during the eighteenth and early nineteenth centuries (1740–1831), with special reference to the environment of this movement', University of Leeds M.A. thesis, 1961, p. 21.
15 See, e.g., J. C. C. Probert, *The Sociology of Cornish Methodism*, Cornish Methodist Historical Association Occasional Publication, no. 8 (1964), pp. 19–20.

16   *Bapt. Mag.*, 1831, p. 589.

17   *Ibid.*

18   [Anon], *Temporal Prosperity and Spiritual Decline: Or, Free Thoughts on Some Aspects of Modern Methodism*, London, 1866, p. 12.

19   *Cong. Ybk*, 1855, p. 75.

20   *Wes. Conf. Min.*, 1768, p. 79, provide an example of this warning which Wesley issued repeatedly.

21   Bogue and Bennett, *Dissenters*, iv, 313.

22   *Bapt. Ann. Reg.*, iii, 40ff.

23   *Ibid.*, p. 2ff.

24   *Ibid.* In 1797 George Burder published the first volume of his widely used *Village Sermons*, 7 vols, London, 1797–1816.

25   *Bapt. Ann. Reg.*, iii, 40ff. The clearest indication of the general adoption of itinerancy and village preaching is to be found in the annual reports of regional or county associations, itinerant societies, and interdenominational evangelistic committees. These reports were published irregularly (but with sufficient frequency to permit confident generalisation) in the major denominational and interdenominational periodicals of the period.

26   J. Blackburn, 'Congregational Associations', *Cong. Ybk*, 1846, pp. 81ff; and [Anon], 'Associational life to 1815', *Trans. Bapt. Hist. Soc.*, v (1916–17), 19–34.

27   It has been so described by B. Nightingale, *The Heroic Age of Congregationalism*, London, 1921, p. 50; cf. R. W. Dale, *The Old Evangelicalism and the New*, London, 1889, p. 15.

28   Gilbert, 'The growth and decline of Nonconformity . . .', pp. 451–7.

29   *Cong. Ybk*, 1848, pp. 70–1.

30   J. Petty, *The History of the Primitive Methodist Connexion*, new edn, London, 1864, p. 13; and *Bapt. Mag.*, 1815, pp. 76–7.

31   *The Substance of two Addresses on Laying the Foundation Stone of the Stockport Sunday School*, Stockport, 1805, *passim*.

32   See e.g. *Cong. Ybk*, 1848, p. 88; Probert, *The Sociology of Cornish Methodism*, pp. 30–3; and E. P. Stigant, 'Methodism and the working class, 1760–1821: a study in social and political conflict', University of Keele M.A. thesis, 1968, pp. 11–12.

33   There was no formal or effective denominational leadership in the Independent denominations.

34   Wesley, *Works*, vi, 166.

35   Jabez Bunting to George Marsden, 28 Jan. 1813, Methodist Archives MS.

36   Wilson, *The History and Antiquities of Dissenting Churches and Meeting Houses*, iv, 556–61.

37   *Ibid.*, pp. 556–7; cf. *The Causes and Reasons of the Present Declension of the Congregational Churches in London and the Country*, London, 1766, pp. 1–27.

38   R. W. Dale, *The Old Evangelicalism and the New*, pp. 26–7, and p. 17.

39   *The Substance of two Addresses on . . . the Stockport Sunday School*; J. Toulmin, *The Rise, Progress and Effects of Sunday*

School, Taunton, 1789, pp. 8–10, 15; A. P. Wadsworth, 'The first Manchester Sunday Schools', *Bulletin of the John Rylands Library*, no. 33, 1950–51.

40 *Bapt. Ann. Reg.*, ii, 466.

41 Peel, *These Hundred Years*, pp. 12–13.

42 *Bapt. Ann. Reg.*, iii, 6, 424–5; *Ev. Mag.*, 1795, p. 257; 1797, pp. 383–4, 472–3; 1798, pp. 424–6, 511; 1802, p. 290; 1832, p. 113; S. Greathead, *General Union Recommended to Real Christians. In a Sermon, Preached at Bedford, October 31, 1797. With an introductory account of an Union of Christians of various denominations, which was then instituted to promote the knowledge of the Gospel; including a plan for Universal Union in the genuine Church of Christ*, London, 1798.

43 For elaboration of this hypothesis see Currie, *Methodism Divided*, p. 86; and B. R. Wilson, *Religion in Secular Society*, Watts, 1966, pp. 125–6, 138–42, 176.

44 Currie, *op. cit.*, pp. 314–15.

45 Wesley, 'Advice to the people called Methodists', 1745, *Works*, vi, 410.

46 *Proc. Wes. Hist. Soc.*, iv, 94–6; *ibid.*, xii, 76ff.

47 Wesley, 'Advice to the Methodists'.

48 *Wes. Conf. Min.*, 1746, pp. 32–3.

49 *Ibid.*

50 Quoted by A. C. H. Seymour, *The Life and Times of Selina, Countess of Huntingdon*, London, 1839, i, 8.

51 Wesley, *Sermons*, iii, 325; cf. W. J. Warner, *The Wesleyan Movement in the Industrial Revolution*, Methuen, 1930, especially Chapter 6.

52 W. H. Thompson, *Early Chapters in Hull Methodism*, London, 1895, p. 41.

53 J. G. Hayman, *History of Methodism in North Devon*, London, 1871, p. 51.

54 Quoted in *Wes. Hist. Soc. Proc.*, xv, 220.

55 Warner, *The Wesleyan Movement in the Industrial Revolution*, p. 165.

56 Bogue and Bennett, *Dissenters*, iii, 333.

57 *Ibid.*, iv, 124.

58 *The Causes and Reasons for the Present Declension among the Congregational Churches in London and the Country*, pp. 9–10.

59 Wilson, *The History and Antiquities of Dissenting Churches and Meeting Houses*, iv, 561–2.

60 *Ibid.*, p. 552.

61 For example, the fictional local society in 'Cowfield' in Mark Rutherford, *The Revolution in Tanner's Lane*, London, 1887, and Rogers's descriptions of Prescot in *An Autobiography*, pp. 19–20.

62 *Prim. Meth. Conf. Min.*, 1875, pp. 92–3; *Cong. Ybk*, 1848, pp. 9–11.

63 Thompson, *The Making of the English Working Class*, pp. 259ff., and E. J. Hobsbawm, 'Custom, wages and work-load in nineteenth-century industry', in A. Briggs and J. Saville, eds, *Essays in Labour History*, Macmillan, 1960.

64   *Cong. Ybk*, 1848, p. 84.
65   Rogers, *Autobiography*, pp. 158—9.
66   *Cong. Ybk*, 1848, p. 88.
67   *Ibid.*, p. 83.
68   Thompson, *The Making of the English Working Class*, p. 266.
69   Wells, *op. cit.*, p. 88.
70   *Prim. Meth. Conf. Min.*, 1875, pp. 92—3.
71   C. Booth, *Life and Labour of the People in London*, 3rd series, vii, London, 1903, 132.
72   Patrick Colquhoun, *A Treatise on Indigence*, London, 1806. Colquhoun's data, with certain corrections and adjustments, have been reproduced in Perkin, *The Origins of Modern English Society 1780—1880*, pp. 20—1.
73   R. Guest, *A Compendious History of the Cotton Manufacture*, Manchester, 1823, p. 43, corroborates the evidence of 'Non-Parochial Registers' on the importance of this occupational group.
74   G. D. H. Cole and R. Postgate, *The Common People 1746—1946*, 2nd edn repr. Methuen, 1961, p. 71.
75   A term here used to describe all persons, irrespective of status, gaining a livelihood from land ownership or from employment associated with the agrarian economy.

Table

3.1   'Non-parochial Registers', PRO, R.G.4.

Chapter 4 *The functions of 'Church' and 'Chapel'*

1   Norman Sykes, *Church and State in England in the Eighteenth Century*, Cambridge U.P., 1934, p. 145.
2   S. L. Ollard and P. C. Walker, eds, *Archbishop Herring's Visitation Returns, 1743*, v, 12; published as vol. lxxix of the Yorkshire Archaeological Society Record Series, 1931.
3   J. H. Overton and F. Relton, *A History of the Church of England from the Accession of George III to the end of the Eighteenth Century*, London, 1906, p. 93.
4   S. C. Carpenter, *Eighteenth Century Church and People*, Murray, 1959, p. 191.
5   *Ibid.*
6   A. F. C. Wallace, 'Revitalization movements', *American Anthropologist*, lviii (1956), 26.
7   J. Gilbert, *Memoir of the Rev. Edward Williams*, London, 1825, pp. 351—2.
8   Wesley, *Sermons*, ii, 319—20.
9   *Bapt. Ann. Reg.*, iii (1798), 40.
10   Bogue and Bennett, *Dissenters*, iv, 313.
11   T. F. O'Dea, *The Sociology of Religion*, Prentice-Hall, 1966, pp. 72—3.
12   Wesley, *Works*, i, 341.

13   H. R. Murphy, 'The ethical revolt against Christian orthodoxy in early-Victorian England', *Am. Hist. Rev.*, lx, no. 4 (1955), 816.

14   *Bapt. Mag.*, Oct. 1832, p. 447.

15   *Wes. Meth. Mag.*, 4th series, v, pt 2 (1849), p. 1263.

16   Wesley, *Works*, vi, 340.

17   H. S. Skeats and C. S. Miall, *History of the Free Churches of England, 1688–1891*, London, 1891, p. 424.

18   [Anon], *A Statement of Facts Relative to Mrs H. More's Schools, Occasioned by some late Misrepresentations*, 2nd edn, London, 1801, pp. 15–16.

19   *Ibid., passim.*

20   W. Roberts, *Memoirs of the Life of Mrs Hannah More*, London, 1834, i, 451.

21   Cf. T. Bere, *The Controversy between Mrs Hannah More, and the Curate of Blagdon; relative to the conduct of her teacher of the Sunday School in that parish, with the original letters and explanatory notes*, London, 1801, *passim.*

22   *Ev. Mag.*, Dec. 1793, p. 251.

23   Bogue and Bennett, *Dissenters*, iv, 316, and Wilson, *The History and Antiquities of Dissenting Churches and Meeting Houses in London*, iv, 560, both emphasised that this was a general phenomenon.

24   *Ev. Mag.*, Dec. 1793, p. 251.

25   D. Nicholls, ed., *Church and State in Britain Since 1820*, Routledge, 1967, p. 29.

26   *Ibid.*, p. 31.

27   T. F. O'Dea, *The Sociology of Religion*, Prentice-Hall, 1966, p. 14.

28   E. Durkheim, *The Elementary Forms of the Religious Life*, trans. J. W. Swain, Free Press of Glencoe, 1954, p. 387.

29   Joseph Addison, *Spectator*, 9 July 1711; quoted by Carpenter, *Eighteenth-century Church and People*, p. 171.

30   Best, *Temporal Pillars*, p. 153.

31   'Diocesan returns 1682', Oxford Diocesan Papers, MS *c.* 430, Bodleian Library.

32   Neil Smelser, *Social Change in the Industrial Revolution: an application of theory to the Lancashire cotton industry, 1770–1840*, Routledge, 1959, p. 408.

33   The editor of the official edition of Wesley's *Works* which appeared in 1810 described this 'entirely new' anti-Methodist campaign in an extended editorial note (*Works*, vi, 234–8).

34   *PP*, 1865, i, 128, where the relevant legislation is summarised.

35   Wesley, *Works*, vi, 236.

36   Skeats and Miall, *History of the Free Churches of England*, pp. 412, 443; W. R. Ward, *Religion and Society in England, 1790–1850*, Batsford, 1972, pp. 50–62.

37   On which see J. Bennett, *The History of Dissenters . . . 1808–1839*, London, 1839, pp. 41–8; Ward, *op. cit.*, pp. 56–62; and [Anon] *A Sketch of the History and Proceedings of the Deputies Appointed to Protect the Civil Rights of the Protestant Dissenters. To which is annexed a summary of the laws affecting Protestant Dissenters.*

With an appendix of statutes and precedents of legal instruments, London, 1814, pp. 105–54.

38   For a rough index of this increase see *A Sketch of the History and Proceedings of the Deputies,* pp. 155–81, which provides a summary of cases dealt with by the Deputies between 1740 and 1811.

39   Wesley, *Works,* iii, 216–17.

40   *Ibid.,* iv, 256.

41   *Ibid.,* iv, 289.

42   *Ibid.*

43   *Ibid.,* iv, 346.

44   See Thomas Arnold, *Principles of Church Reform,* London, 1833, p. 27; and Thompson, *The Making of the English Working Class,* pp. 85, 619–20.

45   For example, *A Sketch of the History and Proceedings of the Deputies Appointed to Protect the Civil Rights of the Protestant Dissenters,* 1814, pp. 155–81; Skeats and Miall, *History of the Free Churches of England,* p. 404; *Prim. Meth. Mag.,* 1822, p. 162; *Cong. Mag.,* 1825, pp. 166, 339; *Ibid.,* 1834, p. 374; *Wes. Conf. Min.,* 1843, ix, 557; *Home Missionary Mag.,* 1843, pp. 2–6; *Freeman,* 1860, p. 639; *Nonconformist,* 1875, p. 1223.

46   W. R. Ward, 'The tithe question in England in the early nineteenth century', *J. Eccles. Hist.,* xvi, no. 1 (April 1965), 72, 74.

47   *The Church Reformers' Magazine for England and Ireland,* vol. i, (the only issue) London, 1832, published a table showing the numbers of clerical and lay magistrates in each county of England and Wales. Lay magistrates outnumbered clerical by 4,017 to 1,354, but the editor cited evidence to show that the number of clerical magistrates was 'in many cases underrated' (pp. 63, 249–50).

48   McClatchey, *Oxfordshire Clergy,* p. 190, presents statistical evidence substantiating this popular assumption.

49   William Cobbett, *Rural Rides* (ed. G. Woodcock), Penguin Books, 1967, p. 106.

50   *Ibid.,* p. 180.

51   *Ibid.* On the whole question of the anti-Establishment element in agrarian radicalism there has been a good recent study by E. J. Hobsbawm and G. Rude, *Captain Swing,* Lawrence & Wishart, 1969; see especially pp. 112–13, 219–20, 229–33, 289–91.

52   Thomas Paine, *The Rights of Man,* ed. H. Collins, Penguin Books, 1969, p. 109.

53   Emilio Willems, 'Protestantism and cultural change', in W. V. D'Antonio and B. Pike, eds, *Religion, Revolution and Reform: New Forces of Change in Latin America,* New York; London, Burns & Oates, 1964, pp. 234–8.

54   Wesley, 'Advice to the people called Methodists', *Works,* vi, 412.

55   A. C. H. Seymour, *The Life and Times of Selina, Countess of Huntingdon,* 1839, i, 27.

56   *Bapt. Mag.,* 1815, pp. 446–7.

57   Thompson, *The Making of the English Working Class,* pp. 417, 418, 419.

58 *Ibid.*, p. 412.
59 Wesley, *Sermons*, iii, 327.
60 *Ibid.*, iii, 323. This sermon was preached in Dublin in 1789.
61 See, for example, 'On a single eye', *Ibid.*, iii, 341—2.
62 For example, 'The use of money', *Sermons*, ii, 140—53; 'The danger of riches', *Ibid.*, iii, 1—16; 'On riches', *Ibid.*, pp. 240—9.
63 Hagen, *On the Theory of Social Change*, pp. 185—236.
64 *Ibid.*, pp. 185—6, and T. Burns and S. B. Saul, eds, *Social Theory and Economic Change*, Tavistock, 1967, pp. 2—3.
65 'Advice to the people called Methodists', *Works*, vi, 412.
66 Robert Hall, *Christianity Consistent with a Love of Freedom: being an answer to a sermon, lately published by the Rev. John Clayton*, London, 1791, p. 29.
67 Smelser, *Social Change in the Industrial Revolution*, p. 408.
68 On the contemporary use of this concept see A. Briggs, *The Age of Improvement 1783—1867*, Longmans, 1959, pp. 1—4.
69 Wesley, *Sermons*, ii, 142.
70 Wesley, *Sermons*, ii, 147.
71 Bebb, *Nonconformity and Social and Economic Life*, pp. 101—3.
72 Warner, *The Wesleyan Movement in the Industrial Revolution*, pp. 191—2.
73 For a discussion of the concept of the 'world-taken-for-granted', the shared 'universe of meaning' which for a given social group constitutes the 'natural' way of interpreting reality, see P. Berger and T. Luckmann, 'Sociology of religion and sociology of knowledge', *Sociology and Social Research*, xlvii (1963), 422—3.
74 *A Compendious History of the Cotton Manufacture*, 1823, p. 38.
75 *Ibid.*, p. 43.
76 Thompson, *The Making of the English Working Class*, p. 411.
77 Wesley, *Sermons*, iii, 34.
78 *Bapt. Mag.*, 1815, p. 101.
79 Wesley, *Works*, vi, 304—7.
80 *Methodism Exposed*, London, 1813, pp. 14—15; quoted by E. P. Stigant, 'Methodism and the working class, 1760—1831', p. 85.
81 Wesley, *Works*, vi, 306.
82 Wesley, 'On friendship with the world', *Sermons*, ii, 526—7.
83 *Ibid.*, p. 405.
84 Membership Roll, Hale Leys Chapel, *Non-Parochial Register*, 240, P.R.O., R.G.4.
85 Social disorganisation — the breakdown of established social and cultural systems — in which there is a loss of *solidarity* produced by the collapse of old social structures, and a loss of *consensus* as norms and values previously taken for granted are challenged or overthrown.
86 Wilbert Moore, *Industrialization and Labor* (Ithaca, 1951; repr. Russell 1965), p. 21.
87 See e.g., R. T. Anderson, 'Voluntary associations in history', *American Anthropologist*, 73, no. 1 (1971), 209, 214—15; and B. Hoselitz and W. E. Moore, eds, *Industrialization and Society*, Paris, 1963, pp. 353—424; Moore, *Industrialization and Labor*, p. 21.

88 Donald McGavran, *Understanding Church Growth*, Grand Rapids, Michigan, Eerdmans, 1970, p. 219.

89 'Report from the Select Committee of the House of Lords, appointed to inquire into the deficiency of means of spiritual instruction and places of divine worship in the Metropolis, and in other populous districts in England and Wales, especially in the mining and manufacturing districts; and to consider the fittest means of meeting the difficulties of the case', *PP*, 1857–58, ix, 59, 62.

90 Thompson, *The Making of the English Working Class*, p. 918.

91 G. Whitefield, *The Two First Parts of his Life with his Journals. Revised, corrected and abridged by George Whitefield, A.B.*, London, 1756, p. 143.

92 *Prim. Meth. Mag.*, 1822, p. 208.

93 *Churchman*, April 1836, pp. 87–90; cf. Cobbett, *Rural Rides*, pp. 182, 188–9.

94 *Prim. Meth. Conf. Min.*, 1827, p. 6.

95 A. G. Cumberland, 'Protestant Nonconformity in the Black Country 1662–1851', University of Birmingham M.A. thesis 1951, pp. 156–7.

96 R. M. Cameron, *The Rise of Methodism: a source book*, New York, Philosophical Library, 1954; pp. 308, 355, 381 note 21.

97 *Methodism Exposed, with the History and Tendency of that Sect*, London, 1813, pp. 7–8; quoted by Warner, *The Wesleyan Movement in the Industrial Revolution*, p. 191.

98 J. Taylor to T. Jackson, Birmingham, 5 May 1812, Methodist Archives MS.

99 *Ibid.*; *Wes. Conf. Min.*, 1847, p. 567.

100 Rutherford, *The Revolution in Tanner's Lane*, 1893, p. 86.

101 *Wes. Conf. Min.*, 1847, p. 567.

Chapter 5 *The pattern of Nonconformist encroachment*

1 In the following discussion, which focuses on the context of growth rather than the religious-cultural nature of the collectivities involved, the distinction between 'Evangelical Nonconformity' and 'Nonconformity' generally (i.e., including the Old Dissent), is in most cases unnecessary.

2 Cf. Best, *Temporal Pillars*, pp. 251–2.

3 Roberts, *Memoirs of the Life of Mrs Hannah More*, i, 452.

4 [Anon], *The State of the Established Church; in a Series of Letters to the Right Hon. Spencer Percival, Chancellor of the Exchequer*, London, 1809, p. 24.

5 *Ibid.*, pp. 5, 15, 27, 39 and 64ff. Cf. [Anon], *A Treatise on the Causes which have Contributed, and do contribute to the increase of Methodists and Dissenters . . .*, Macclesfield, 1813, pp. 29–30.

6 Thomas Arnold, *Principles of Church Reform*, London, 1833, pp. 24–5.

7 Quoted by R. A. Soloway, *Prelates and People: Ecclesiastical Social Thought in England 1783–1852*, Routledge, 1969, p. 341.

8   *Cong. Mag.*, 1832, p. 821.

9   The tendency is evident in the constitutions of denominational Itinerant and Home Missionary Societies, which committed their members to evangelize the unchurched (and not to compete with existing religious agencies) and at the same time defined 'neglected populations' as those 'destitute of an evangelical ministry'.

10 Rogers, *Autobiography*, pp. 2—3.

11 'Visitation Returns,· 1831', Oxford Diocesan Papers, MS b.38, Bodleian Library.

12 *PP*, 1812, x, 157—9.

13 Best, *Temporal Pillars*, p. 204.

14 E. W. Bovill, *English Country Life 1780—1830*, Oxford U.P., 1962, p. 233.

15 'Clerical returns prior to the Bishop of Oxford's Visitation, 1854', Oxford Diocesan Papers, MS d.701, Bodleian Library.

16 *Ibid.*

17 Cf. [Anon], *A Letter to a Country Gentleman, on the Subject of Methodism, Confined Chiefly to its Causes, Progress and Consequences in His own Neighbourhood. From the Clergyman of his Parish*, Ipswich, 1805, p. 11; and Best, *Temporal Pillars*, pp. 166—9.

18 J. Thirsk, ed., *The Agrarian History of England*, Vol. iv, *1500—1640*, Cambridge U.P., 1967, pp. 2—14.

19 'A brief sum of all the Parishes, Impropriations, Preachers, Communicants, and Recusants certified for the several dioceses of both the provinces of Canterbury and York', Brit. Mus., Harleian MS. 280, 157—72; analysed in R. G. Usher, *The Reconstruction of the English Church*, i, 279.

20 Cf. The Maps in J. D. Gay, *The Geography of Religion in England*, Duckworth, 1971, p. 271; and W. S. F. Pickering, 'The 1851 Religious Census: useless experiment?', *Brit. J. Sociol.*, xviii (1967), 399.

21 A. Everitt, 'Farm labourers', in Thirsk, *The Agrarian History of England*, iv, 162.

22 J. C. G. Binfield, 'Nonconformity in the Eastern Counties, 1840—1885, with reference to its social background', Cambridge University Ph.D. thesis 1965, pp. 6—13; C. W. Chalklin, *Seventeenth-century Kent*, Longmans, 1965, pp. 228—9; Everitt, 'Nonconformity in county parishes', *Ag. Hist. Rev.*, xviii (Feb. 1970), Supplement, *passim*; W. G. Hoskins, *Devon*, Collins, 1954, pp. 3, 72, 174—5; H. Pelling, *Social Geography of British Elections, 1885—1910*, Macmillan, 1967, pp. 74, 97, 101, 107—8, 122, 127, 226; and Thirsk, *op. cit.* Pelling's study represents an excellent digest of local studies relating religious behaviour and socioeconomic factors, and is relevant to periods much earlier than 1885.

23 In the Diocese of York in 1743, for example, there were only 711 clergymen and 903 parishes. Of the clergymen 335 were pluralists, and of the parishes 393 had non-resident incumbents (Ollard and Walker, *Archbishop Herring's Visitation Returns, 1743*, vol. i, pp. ix—xii).

24 Oxford Diocesan Papers, MS b.38, Bodleian Library; 'Report of the Commission appointed to Inquire into the Practicability and Mode

of Subdividing Parishes, respecting the immediate Want, as reported by them, for Six Hundred New Churches . . .', *PP*, 1852–53, lxxviii, 23–60.

25 'Articles of inquiry addressed to the clergy of the Diocese of Oxford at the Primary Visitation of Dr Thomas Secker, 1738', *Oxfordshire R. S.*, xxxviii (1957), 12–13.

26 Ollard and Walker, *Archbishop Herring's Visitation Returns, 1743*, i, 73.

27 Greaves, 'An analysis of the spread of Methodism in Yorkshire, during the eighteenth and early nineteenth centuries (1740–1831), with special reference to the environment of this movement', University of Leeds M.A. thesis 1961, p. 8.

28 T. Taylor, 'The life of Thomas Taylor, chiefly written by himself', in T. Jackson, ed., *The Lives of Early Methodist Preachers*, London, 1838, iii, 343.

29 C. S. Orwin and C. S. Orwin, *The Open Fields*, 3rd edn, Oxford U.P., 1967, p. 24.

30 G. J. Cuming and D. Baker, eds, *Popular Belief and Practice*, Cambridge U.P., 1972, p. 269.

31 'The grass roots of history', *The Times Literary Supplement*, 28 July 1972, p. 890.

32 W. G. V. Balchin, *Cornwall: the history of the landscape*, Hodder & Stoughton, 1954, pp. 17–18; Hoskins, *Devon*, pp. 4, 72; and W. Page, *The Victoria History of the County of Somerset*, London, 1911, ii, 533.

33 'Report of the Royal Commission on Land in Wales and Monmouthshire', *PP*, 1896, xxxiv, 148.

34 Pelling, *Social Geography of British Elections*, p. 290.

35 Probert, *The Sociology of Cornish Methodism*, pp. 30–6.

36 This generalisation is based on a comparison of disaggregated data from the 1851 Census. The county figures conceal the presence of significant Bible Christian strength in central Dorset.

37 B. Greaves, 'Methodism in Yorkshire 1740–1851', University of Liverpool Ph.D. thesis 1968, pp. 42–4.

38 Pelling, *Social Geography of British Elections*, p. 107.

39 'Dioceses of Oxford Visitation Returns, 1854', Oxford Diocesan Papers, MS d.701, Bodleian Library.

40 *Wes. Meth. Mag.*, 1849, pp. 1011–12.

41 Chalklin, *Seventeenth-century Kent*, p. 229; A. Everitt, 'Nonconformity in country parishes', *Ag. Hist. Rev.*, xviii (Feb. 1970), *passim*; and H. P. R. Finberg, 'A chapter of religious history', in H. P. R. Finberg and W. G. Hoskins, eds, *Devonshire Studies*, Cape, 1952.

42 D. C. Coleman, 'English economic history 1485–1760', in M. W. Thomas, ed., *A Survey of English Economic History*, 2nd edn, Blackie, 1960, pp. 105–6.

43 Thirsk, *The Agrarian History of England and Wales*, iv, 14.

44 For an explication of the administrative and legal status of extra-parochial places see, *PP*, 1812, vol. xi, p. xv.

45 Orwin and Orwin, *The Open Fields*, pp. 19–20.

46 For an elaboration of these demographic and agrarian trends see, *Ibid.*, pp. 15—20.

47 Everitt, 'Nonconformity in country parishes', *loc. cit.*, pp. 188—97.

48 For example, 'Report to the Board of Agriculture from J. Billingsley, Somerset, 1798', quoted in A. E. Bland, P. A. Brown, and R. H. Tawney, eds, *English Economic History Select Documents*, London, 1914, p. 533; similar reports have been quoted by W. E. Tate, *The English Village Community and the Enclosure Movements*, Gollancz, 1967, pp. 164—5.

49 Tate, *op. cit.*, p. 165. 'Commoner' here refers to a squatter on common land.

50 Everitt, 'Nonconformity in country parishes', *loc. cit.*, pp. 194—5.

51 Thompson, *The Making of the English Working Class*, p. 201.

52 E. P. Thompson, 'The moral economy of the English crowd in the eighteenth century', *Past and Present*, 1 (Feb. 1971), 118—19.

53 This is evident in occupational registrations in *Non-Parochial Registers*, PRO MS R.G.4.

54 *Adam Bede* (1859) London, n.d., p. 10.

55 *Ibid.*

56 *Ibid.*, pp. 11, 73—80.

57 'A sketch of the ministerial labours of the Rev. Messers Saffery, of Salisbury, and Steadman, of Broughton, as itinerant ministers in Cornwall, with remarks on village preaching', *Bapt. Ann. Reg.*, ii (1896), 459—64. The assistant was Joseph Webb (1779—1815). For his role in the itinerancy of Cornwall see *Bapt. Mag.*, 1815, p. 223—4.

58 *Ibid.*, p. 461.

59 Cf., e.g., the observations of Congregational itinerants in *The Reports of the Committee of the Congregational Society in London, for Spreading the Gospel in England*, London, 1798, etc.; and, subsequently, in the *Home Missionary Magazine*.

60 'Report of the Select Committee on Parliamentary and Municipal Elections', *PP*, 1868—69, viii, 257—9, qu. 6557—6624.

61 R. A. Ingram, *Causes of the Increase of Methodism*, London, 1807, pp. 84—6.

62 *Quarterly Review*, xxiii (1820), 546.

63 *PP*, 1812, vol. xi, p. xiii.

64 W. Laud, *Works*, ed. W. Scott and J. Bliss, London, 1847—60, v, 327.

65 C. Hill, *Reformation to Industrial Revolution*, Penguin Books, 1969, pp. 195—6.

66 Malcolm Thomis, *Politics and Society in Nottingham 1785—1835*, Blackwell, 1969, pp. 2, 148, etc.

67 P. Deane, *The First Industrial Revolution*, Cambridge U.P., 1969, p. 14.

68 On the 'demographic revolution' see, e.g., H. J. Habakkuk, *Population Growth and Economic Development since 1750*, Leicester U.P., 1971, pp. 25—51.

69 Cf. the surveys of Gregory King (1688) and Patrick Colquhoun (1803), in Perkin, *The Origins of Modern English Society*, pp. 20—1.

70   Mitchell and Deane, *Abstract*, p. 60.
71   Deane, *The First Industrial Revolution*, p. 14; and Perkin, *op. cit.*, p. 117.
72   Cf. Table 2.1 above.
73   Mitchell and Deane, *op. cit.*, pp. 5–6.
74   Wesley, *Works*, v, 346.
75   A. Redford, *Labour Migration in England, 1800–1850*, Manchester U.P., 1926, pp. 11–12.
76   P. Deane and W. A. Cole, *British Economic Growth 1688–1959*, Cambridge U.P., 1967, p. 143.
77   Redford, *Labour Migration*, p. 14.
78   Cf. Everitt, 'The grass roots of history', p. 889.
79   Smelser, *Social Change in the Industrial Revolution*, pp. 136–7.
80   *PP*, 1852–53, vol. lxxxix, pp. cxxviii, cclxxxiii; K. S. Inglis, 'Patterns of religious worship in 1851', *J. Eccles. Hist.*, xi, no. 1 (1960), 82–5; and Pickering, 'The 1851 Religious Census', pp. 402–4.
81   'Report on the Census of Religious Worship', *op. cit.*, p. cxxviii.
82   Cf. C. R. Sumner, *A Charge Delivered to the Clergy of the Diocese of Winchester in October, 1833*, London, 1834, pp. 16–18; R. A. Nisbet, *The Quest for Community*, Oxford U.P. (Toronto), 1953, pp. 50–4, 179–80, 244; E. R. Wickham, *Church and People in an Industrial City*, Lutterworth, 1957, pp. 237, 262.
83   Wickham, *Ibid.*, p. 237.
84   Cf. V. Jones, ed., *The Church in a Mobile Society: A Survey of the Zone of Industrial South West Wales*, Swansea, C. Davies, 1969, pp. 94–9.
85   E. Halévy, *The Birth of Methodism in England*, trans. and ed. by B. Semmel, Univ. of Chicago Press, 1971, p. 72.
86   *Methodist Times*, 30 Sept. 1886, p. 653.
87   Redford, *Labour Migration in England*, p. 18.
88   Even in the middle of the nineteenth century only a minority of the inhabitants of industrial areas had been born in their town of residence. The bulk of the early industrial population was comprised of migrants from surrounding areas, many of whom moved several times. Cf. Redford, *Ibid.*, pp. 14–18; and J. H. Clapham, *An Economic History of Modern Britain. The early railway age 1820–1850*, Cambridge U.P., 1939, pp. 536–7.
89   *Charge Delivered by William Lord Bishop of Chester, to the Clergy of his Diocese; . . . 1799*, Oxford, 1799, p. 12.
90   Cf. *Hansard*, xiv (2 June 1809), 854; xvii (18 June 1810), 765.
91   Quoted by Soloway, *Prelates and People*, p. 310.
92   *Wes. Conf. Min.*, 1847, pp. 564–5.
93   'A micro-theory of Methodist growth', *Wes. Hist. Soc. Proc.*, xxxvi (Oct. 1967), 68.
94   For example, Gay, *The Geography of Religion in England*, chs 4 and 8; Greaves, 'An analysis of the spread of Methodism in Yorkshire. . . . 1740–1831', Leeds M.A. thesis, 1961, ch. 1; and F. Tillyard, 'The distribution of the Free Churches in England', *Sociol. Rev.*, xxvii, no. 1 (January 1935), 1–18.
95   Tillyard, *ibid.*, pp. 10–13.

96 'A micro-theory of Methodist growth', *op. cit.*, p. 68.
97 Cf. Gay, *The Geography of Religion in England*, maps 8–9, 27, 35, and 43–4, pp. 271–310.
98 *Ibid.*, p. 117.
99 *The Report of the Committee of the Congregational Society in London, for Spreading the Gospel in England*, London, 1798, pp. 3, 15–16. The percentage relates to the fifty-eight identifiable localities in which the Society was operating in 1798. Reports were also received from twelve unidentifiable localities.
100 Yates, *The Basis of National Welfare*, 1817, p. 122.
101 *PP*, 1850, xx, 29–34.
102 'Abstract of returns of the names of all parishes in England and Wales, in which (during the last fifteen years) Church Rates have been refused, and since that refusal have ceased altogether to be collected', *PP*, 1856, lxviii, *passim.*
103 *PP*, 1851, ix, 736.
104 *PP*, 1856, lxviii, 10.
105 See Table 5.4, note 2.
106 In a call for Baptist 'Church extension' in the north, the Rev. William Barnes, a leading Particular Baptist, wrote in 1841: 'The progress made in the north is, I admit, considerable, when the former weakness of our body there is taken into account. The northern churches themselves have perhaps done well for the region around about them; but that part of the kingdom — teeming with population, the emporium of commerce and wealth — has not sufficiently attracted the enterprise of the whole denomination' (*Bapt. Mag.*, 1841, p. 274). Similarly, statistical evidence about individual Congregational churches (a few of which maintained statistical records), indicates that where the older denominations were established in the north, they enjoyed the same receptivity as that exploited by Methodist societies. (*Cong. Mag.*, 1840, pp. 607–9.)
107 *Report from the Clergy of a District in the Diocese of Lincoln. Convened for the purpose of considering the State of Religion in the Several Parishes in the said District, as well as the best mode of promoting the Belief and Practice of it . . .*, London, 1800. The statistical returns from seventy-nine parishes were themselves evidence of the holding of services and the presence of a clergyman.
108 The total population of the parishes was 15,042 and the 'average congregations' totalled 4,933 (*ibid.*, p. 6). This index of attendance of 32.7 per cent compared with the top county indices of Anglican attendance in 1851 of 32 in Rutland and 30 in Dorset and Suffolk.
109 *Ibid.*, pp. 7, 9, 12, 15.

Tables
5.1 and Fig. 5.1 'Population Abstract, 1811', *PP*, 1812, vol. xi. The breakdown of counties on a parish basis is on p. xxix.
5.2 and Fig. 5.2 First and Second Report from his Majesty's Commissioners appointed to consider the state of the Established Church, with reference to Ecclesiastical Duties and Revenue, *PP*, 1835, xxii and 1836, xxxvi, 22–3.

5.3   'Report of the Census of Religious Worship, 1851', p. cxxvi.

5.4   'Abstract of Returns of the Names of all Parishes in England and Wales, in which (during the last Fifteen Years) Church Rates have been refused, and since that Refusal have Ceased altogether to be Collected', *PP*, 1856, lxviii.

Chapter 6   *The metamorphosis of the religious Establishment*

1   Arnold, *Principles of Church Reform*, p. 27.

2   Best has called the entire period 1820–35 'The crisis of Church reform' (*Temporal Pillars*, pp. 239–95).

3   *Hansard*, xiii (25 April 1825), 141–2.

4   *British Magazine*, 1833, p. 215; *British Critic*, 1834, p. 487; and O. Chadwick, *The Victorian Church*, 3rd edn, A. & C. Black, 1971, i, 26–47.

5   Chadwick, i, 35.

6   R. P. Flindall, ed., *The Church of England 1815–1948: A Documentary History*, SPCK, 1972, p. 76.

7   Of fifty new churches planned by Queen Anne's Parliament only ten were actually erected, and her provision for the progressive augmentation of poor livings produced no marked improvement in the effectiveness of the eighteenth century Church. See Yates, *The Basis of National Welfare*, pp. 158ff; and Best, *Temporal Pillars*, pp. 11–136.

8   *PP*, 1851, xlii, 93ff.

9   Bowen, *The Idea of the Victorian Church*, p. 9, and 9n.

10   The *British Review*, 1815, no. 12, p. 276, describes a typical case: the failure of an attempt to build a new church in St Pancras, when the parish contained 50,000 people but had church accommodation for only 300. There is a more general discussion of the problems in Sir R. Phillimore, *The Ecclesiastical Law of the Church of England*, London, 1876, ii, 2167ff.

11   Smith to Blomfield, 1840; quoted by Flindall, *The Church of England, 1815–1948*, p. 76.

12   Quoted by Soloway, *Prelates and People*, p. 247.

13   J. Bentham, *Church-of-Englandism and its Catechism Examined*, London, 1818, pp. 198–9.

14   The Bill, which provided for the suppression of some sees and the suspension of some benefices in the minority Anglican Establishment in Ireland, aroused immense hostility in England partly because it seemed to represent a precedent for 'spoliation' which might be applied to the English Church.

15   Bowen, *The Idea of the Victorian Church*, p. 6.

16   *Plan of Church Reform*, 4th edn, London, 1832, p. 16.

17   Debates did not resume in the Convocation of York until 1861.

18   'Report from the Select Committee on the Ecclesiastical Commission', *PP*, 1847–48, vii, p. iii. The name of the new body was the Ecclesiastical Duties and Revenues Commission.

19   *Ibid.*, p. iv. For a fuller discussion of the formation and work of the

Commission there is no better source than Best, *Temporal Pillars*, pp. 239–347.

20   Queen Anne's Bounty was not superseded by the Ecclesiastical Commission, but operated concurrently with it between 1836 and 1948, when the two bodies united to form the Church Commissioners for England.

21   Granted the dimensions of the problems confronting it, this remained true despite the receipt of over £1 million from Parliament between 1809 and 1820.

22   Best, *Temporal Pillars*, p. 131.

23   Cathedrals Act 1840. Chapters were reduced in most cases to a Dean and four resident canons; other offices were abolished or reduced to honorary status. The very considerable savings were redistributed nationally on the basis of need, a decision strongly opposed between 1836 and 1840 by advocates of a so-called 'principle of locality'.

24   'An Act to make better provision for the spiritual care of populous parishes', 6 Vict. 1843, *PP*, 1843, i, 465–77.

25   Yates, *The Basis of National Welfare*, p. 125.

26   So called in recognition of Sir Robert Peel's responsibility for the crucial 1843 Act facilitating parochial subdivision.

27   *PP*, 1837, xli, 217; *ibid.*, 1843, xl, 1; and J. J. Halcombe, ed., *The Church and her Curates*, London, 1874, *passim*.

28   G. A. Selwyn, *The Work of Christ in the World: four sermons preached before the University of Cambridge on the four Sundays preceding Advent in the year of Our Lord 1854*, Cambridge, 1855, p. 7.

29   Bowen, *The Idea of the Victorian Church*, p. 9.

30   Chadwick, *The Victorian Church*, i, 522. The trend is clear, but the proportion of non-graduates fluctuated significantly from year to year; cf. Heeney, 'On being a mid-Victorian clergyman', p. 224.

31   McClatchey, *Oxfordshire Clergy*, pp. 190–1.

32   *Ibid.*

33   Bryan Wilson, *Religion in Secular Society*, p. 137.

34   Heeney, 'On being a mid-Victorian clergyman', p. 217.

35   *Ibid.*

36   Cf. pp. 114–18 above.

37   Cf. Bowen, *The Idea of the Victorian Church*, pp. 285–311, 348–52.

38   Thomas Arnold, *Principles of Church Reform*, p. 47.

39   *Ibid.*, pp. 24–5.

40   His efforts to adduce principles of reform broad enough to comprehend orthodox Dissenters were regarded as particularly impractical.

41   A. P. Stanley, *The Life and Correspondence of Thomas Arnold, D.D.*, London, 1844, i, 274.

42   On which see P. d'A. Jones, *The Christian Socialist Revival 1877–1914*, Princeton, 1968.

43   Chadwick, *The Victorian Church*, i, 450.

44   R. S. Dell, 'Social and economic theories and pastoral concerns of a Victorian Archbishop', *J. Eccles. Hist.*, xvi (Oct. 1965), no. 2, 203, 204.

45 McClatchey, *Oxfordshire Clergy*, p. 92.
46 Chadwick, *The Victorian Church*, i, 454.
47 See p. 31 above.
48 [Anon], *Temporal Prosperity and Spiritual Decline*, pp. 72–3.
49 See pp. 3–17 above for a survey of the growth of the post-Reformation Church of England.
50 William Thomson, Archbishop of York; quoted by Inglis, *Churches and the Working Classes in Victorian England*, p. 22.
51 Inglis, *op. cit.*, pp. 21–61, 250–336.
52 The church-sect typology grew out of the major debate initiated by Max Weber in his famous articles on 'Die protestantische Ethick und der Geist des Kapitalismus' (*Archiv für Sozialwissenschaft und Sozialpolitick*, XX–XXI, 1904–05); and particularly from Ernst Troëltsch's defence of Weber in his massive study, *Die sozialen Lehren der christlichen Kirchen und Gruppen* (first published in 1912, and published in English translation by O. Wyon, *The Social Teaching of the Christian Churches*, Allen and Unwin, 1931).
53 J. Milton Yinger, *Religion, Society and the Individual*, New York, Macmillan, 1957, pp. 147–55.
54 See pp. 74–81 above.
55 See pp. 51–68 above.
56 Ernst Troëltsch, *The Social Teaching of the Christian Churches*, trans. O. Wyon, Allen & Unwin, 1931, ii, 993, 443.
57 Cf. Robertson, *The Sociological Interpretation of Religion*, p. 123.
58 William H. Mackintosh, *Disestablishment and Liberation: The Movement for the Separation of the Anglican Church from State Control*, Epworth Press, 1972, p. xvi and *passim*.
59 K. A. Thompson, *Bureaucracy and Church Reform: The organizational response of the Church of England to Social Change, 1800–1965*, Oxford U.P., 1970, pp. 217–18.
60 H. Richard Niebuhr, *The Social Sources of Denominationalism*, New York, Peter Smith, 1963, pp. 3–25, 264–84.
61 From the Advertisement to the first edition of J. Keble, *Assize Sermon on National Apostacy*, Oxford, 1833; quoted by Bowen, *The Idea of the Victorian Church*, p. 43.
62 Such concessionary ecclesiastical legislation as that opening the ancient universities to Dissenters, removing religious oaths for public offices, or abolishing compulsory church rates, was adopted by a predominantly Anglican Parliament in much the same manner as parliamentary reform and Corn Law repeal passed a Parliament dominated by the landed interest. In each case not enthusiasm for the measures passed, but strategic acquiescence with opposing interests was the motive for legislative change.
63 The first edition of the *Nonconformist* appeared in April 1841.
64 Berger, *The Social Reality of Religion*, pp. 137–8.

Tables

6.1 *Convocation of Canterbury Report*, 1876, pp. 22–7.

6.2 *PP*, 1812, x, 159; 1830, xix, 35; 1837, xli, 217; 1843, xl, 1; 1847—48, xlix, 37; 1852—53, lxxviii, 1.

Chapter 7 *Church and Chapel in denominational relationship*

1 In the case of the cotton industry, the process has been well analysed by Smelser, *Social Change in the Industrial Revolution*, pp. 136—49.
2 Probert, *The Sociology of Cornish Methodism*, p. 33.
3 Thomas Luckmann, *The Invisible Religion*, Macmillan, 1967, p. 30.
4 *Ibid.*
5 Discussed below, pp. 59—68.
6 The relatively depressed state of the agrarian economy in the periods after the Napoleonic Wars and in the twenty years after 1873 were particularly important in this process of elimination.
7 *Bapt. Hbk*, 1894, p. 77.
8 G. Kitson Clark, *The Making of Victorian England*, Methuen, 1965, pp. 159—60.
9 *Cong. Mag.*, 1833, p. 818.
10 Robertson, *The Sociological Interpretation of Religion*, Blackwell, 1969, p. 114.
11 Wesley, *Works*, vi, 350.
12 *Wes. Conf. Min.*, 1848, p. 103; cf. pp. 102—5 *passim*.
13 Wesley, *Works*, vi, 375—6.
14 *Bapt. Mag.*, 1815, pp. 394—5.
15 For example, B. R. Wilson, 'The pentecostal minister: role conflicts and contradictions of status', in Wilson, ed., *Patterns of Sectarianism*, Heinemann, 1968, pp. 138—57.
16 The process of religious-cultural and organisational development has been explored by J. C. Bowmer, 'Church and ministry in Wesleyan Methodism from the death of John Wesley to the death of Jabez Bunting', University of Leeds Ph.D. thesis 1967 *passim*; and J. Kent, *The Age of Disunity*, Epworth Press, 1966, pp. 44—85.
17 O'Dea, *The Sociology of Religion*, p. 91.
18 Ward, *Religion and Society in England, 1790—1850*, p. 102.
19 *Meth. Mag.*, 1815, p. 79. Quoted by Ward, *op. cit.*
20 In the Deed of Settlement of 1784 Wesley had appointed a 'Legal Hundred' in which his authority was to be perpetuated after his death. It soon became customary, however, for these 100 preachers (and the successors who replaced them) to share their power with their fellow itinerants. It was thus the Conference of ministers which assumed in the nineteenth century the immense authority which Wesley had reserved for himself.
21 Wesley, *Works*, iii, 381.
22 *Wes. Conf. Min.*, 1847, pp. 551—2.
23 Cf. Table 2.2 (pp. 31—2 above).
24 This subject is discussed in some detail in Gilbert, 'The growth and decline of Nonconformity', pp. 385—92.
25 W. Wilson, *The History and Antiquities of Dissenting Churches and Meeting Houses*, iv, 550—7 *passim*.

26 *Cong. Mag.*, 1844, pp. 125—7.
27 *Ibid.*, p. 127.
28 E. Halévy, *History of the English People in the Nineteenth Century*, Benn, 1961, iv, 389.
29 Union meetings were reported fully in *Cong. Mag.* before the *Congregational Year Book* was first published in 1846. Peel, *These Hundred Years*, pp. 155—9, has summarised the proceedings of these meetings insofar as they dealt with ministerial affairs.
30 *Bapt. Record*, 1846, pp. 357—9, 391, 491.
31 *Cong. Mag.*, 1842, p. 127.
32 *Ibid.*, pp. 125, 234, 499, etc.
33 Binney, in *Cong. Ybk*, 1848, p. 11.
34 *Cong. Mag.*, 1842, p. 125.
35 Edward Miall, in *Nonconformist*, 1849, p. 923.
36 Binney, *Cong. Ybk*, 1848, p. 13.
37 M. Arnold, *Culture and Anarchy*, London, 1901, pp. xi—31.
38 Wesley, *Sermons*, iii, 325.
39 For example, *Ibid.*, p. 326.
40 McGavran, *Understanding Church Growth*, pp. 262—75.
41 *Ibid.*, p. 271.
42 *PP*, 1852—53, vol. lxxxix, pp. clix—clx.
43 Cited in *Cong. Mag.*, 1840, p. 607.
44 *Ibid.*, p. 609.
45 *Ev. Mag.*, 1849, p. 128.
46 T. F. O'Dea, 'Five dilemmas in the institutionalization of religion', *Journal for the Scientific Study of Religion*, i, no. 1 (1961), 30—9.
47 Cf. A. Hume, *Missions at Home or A Clergyman's Account of a Portion of the Town of Liverpool*, London, 1850, pp. 10ff., and, *The Church of England the Home Missionary to the Poor, especially in our large towns*, London, 1862. For an early expression of the argument that a large, imposing chapel might in some circumstances be the best available instrument of growth, cf. J. Bunting to G. Morley, 25 January, 1815, Methodist Archives, MS.
48 John Betjeman, *First and Last Loves*, Murray, 1952, pp. 105—6.
49 *Cong. Mag.*, 1844, p. 127.
50 *Cong. Ybk*, 1855, p. 76.
51 Algernon Wells, in *Cong. Ybk*, 1849, p. 65.
52 See pp. 115—21 above.
53 *Nonconformist*, 1849, p. 923.
54 John Blackburn, in *Cong. Ybk*, 1847, p. 150.
55 Illustrated and often lengthy sections devoted to architectural aspects of chapels erected in the previous year became staple fare in denominational yearbooks, handbooks, and annual minutes from the 1860s onwards.
56 Blackburn, *Cong. Ybk*, 1847, p. 162.
57 *Ibid.*, p. 82.
58 W. Wilson, *The History and Antiquities of Dissenting Churches and Meeting Houses*, iv, pp. 556—7.
59 Miall, in *Nonconformist*, 1849, p. 921.

60   G. Kitson Clark, in *The Making of Victorian England*, Methuen, 1965, p. 162.
61   J. Vincent, *The Formation of the Liberal Party 1857–1868*, Constable, 1966, p. 5; cf. pp. 1–53 *passim*.
62   A. T. Patterson, *Radical Leicester: a history of Leicester 1780–1850*, Leicester U.P., 1954, pp. 27, 198–213, 147–55; R. Newton, *Victorian Exeter 1837–1914*, Leicester U.P., 1968, pp. 22–3; and M. I. Thomis, *Politics and Society in Nottingham, 1785–1835*, Oxford, Blackwell, 1969, p. 128.
63   R. Cobden, *Speeches on Questions of Public Policy*, ed., J. Bright and J. E. T. Rogers, London, 1870, p. 183.
64   Vincent, *The Formation of the Liberal Party*, pp. 68–9.
65   *Ibid*. The *Protestant Dissenters' Almanack* in the 1850s contained the Annual Reports of the Church Rate Abolition Society, the Liberation Society, the Parliamentary Reform Committee, The Society for the Promotion of Permanent and Universal Peace, and the Ballot Society.
66   The first of these phases pre-dated the Anti-State Church Association and the Liberation Society, but in it Nonconformists were spurned into actions which led to the formation of these permanent nationwide organisations.
67   Perhaps the most detailed survey of Liberation Society organisation is I. G. Jones, 'The Liberation Society and Welsh politics, 1844–68', *Welsh History Review*, i, no. 2 (1961), 193–224.
68   The definitive study of the 'Temperance Question', which deals in depth with all the points raised in this paragraph, is B. Harrison's *Drink and the Victorians*, Faber, 1971.
69   In 1860, for example, of Anti-Church Rate petitions associated with a Church Rate Abolition Bill then before Parliament, specifically 'Wesleyan' petitions were outnumbered by 'Independent' petitions by 668 to 130, and 'Baptist' petitions numbered 756, *Nonconformist*, 1860, p. 261.
70   Cf. p. 82–5 above.
71   *Wes. Conf. Min.*, 1843, p. 149.
72   J. B. Sweet, *A Memoir of the Late Henry Hoare*, London, 1869, p. 61.
73   Cf. p. 11 above.
74   Chadwick, *The Victorian Church*, ii, 359.
75   *Proceedings of the Church Congress*, Cambridge, 1861, p. iv.
76   *Church Congress Report*, 1880, p. 460.
77   Sweet, *A Memoir of the Late Henry Hoare*, pp. 446–51.
78   For an appreciation of the importance of such pressure see the *Nonconformist*, 1875, p. 1073.
79   *Freeman*, 14 Dec. 1859, p. 14.
80   *Protestant Dissenters' Almanack*, 1859, p. 55.
81   J. A. James, quoted by Peel, *These Hundred Years*, p. 149.
82   *Churchman*, viii (1843), 367–8.
83   Chadwick, *The Victorian Church*, i, 441; cf. *Bapt. Mag.*, 1846, pp. 274–85; and *Cong. Mag.*, 1845, p. 321.
84   Cf. Table 6.1, p. 130 above.

85 James, quoted by Peel, *These Hundred Years*, p. 149.
86 *Wesleyan Times*, 21 Jan. 1850, p. 39.
87 *Prim. Meth. Conf. Min.*, 1896, pp. 183—4.
88 *Baptist Union British and Irish Home Mission and General Chronicle*, June, 1884, p. 46.
89 *Ibid.*, July 1884, p. 58.
90 Chadwick, *The Victorian Church*, ii, 168—9.
91 See Chapter 6, note 20.
92 Cf. Table 2.8, p. 46 above. The Catholic historian, Denis Gwynn, has written: 'Any statistical study of the Catholic Church in England and Wales during the past century is . . . largely a study of Irish immigrants and their descendants' (in G. A. Beck, ed., *The English Catholics, 1850—1950*, Burns & Oates, 1950, p. 282).
93 Controversy over a Cabinet decision to increase a parliamentary grant to the Royal College of St Patrick, Maynooth, County Kildare (a grant inherited by Westminster under the Act of Union of 1801), assumed the character of a national political issue in 1845, precipitating the resignation of Gladstone from the Peel Government.
94 Newman was received into the Catholic Church in October 1845.
95 G. Albion, 'The restoration of the hierarchy', in Beck, ed., *The English Catholics*, pp. 86—116.
96 For an analysis of the techniques of William Murphy, probably the most notorious of these itinerants, see H. J. Hanham, *Elections and Party Management: politics in the time of Disraeli and Gladstone*, Longmans, 1959, pp. 304—8; cf. G. F. A. Best, 'Popular Protestantism in Victorian Britain', in R. Robson, ed., *Ideas and institutions of Victorian Britain*, Bell, 1967, pp. 115—142; and E. R. Norman, *Anti-Catholicism in Victorian England*, Allen & Unwin, 1968, pp. 17—18.
97 *The Vatican Decrees in their bearing on Civil Allegiance: a political expostulation*, London, 1874.
98 Leslie, *Letters of Herbert Cardinal Vaughan*, p. ix.
99 *Ibid.*, p. 18.
100 Irish Catholicism was of course involved in what was a major preoccupation of British politics throughout the nineteenth century: the relations of England with Ireland. But this was an issue which, however much it influenced individuals, did not draw the English Catholic Church, as a Church, into the political arena. There was not, in the case of Catholicism, the kind of definite party political alignment which Nonconformity had with the Liberal Party and Anglicanism with the Tories.
101 Cf. Currie and Gilbert, 'Religion', in A. H. Halsey, ed., *Trends in British Society*, Macmillan, 1972, p. 409.

Tables

7.1 Mitchell and Deane, *Abstract*, p. 187. The figures for 1788 and 1801 are from Smelser, *Social Change in the Industrial Revolution*, p. 137.
7.2 *Wes. Conf. Min.*, 1791—1911.

Chapter 8 *The Churches and the world*

1   Perhaps the best examples are Mrs Humphry Ward, *Robert Elsmere*, 2 vols., London, 1888; and William Hale White, *The Autobiography of Mark Rutherford, edited by his friend Reuben Shapcott*, London, 1881, and *Mark Rutherford's Deliverance*, London, 1885.

2   Tennyson, *In Memoriam*, Sect. liv.

3   For example, by A. N. Whitehead, *Science and the Modern World*, Cambridge U.P., 1926; B. Willey, *More Nineteenth Century Studies: a group of honest doubters*, Chatto & Windus, 1949; and H. Davies, *Worship and Theology in England from Newman to Martineau, 1850–1900*, Princeton U.P., 1962. The reference is from Davies, *op. cit.*, p. 176.

4   J. G. Watson, for example, has argued that 'Up to the nineteenth century, discussion of religion had been continued on the same basis for hundreds, if not thousands, of years. A Roman sceptic would have been as much at home discussing the validity or otherwise of Christianity with eighteenth-century sceptics as with his contemporaries. No more materials, essentially, lay to hand.' But, he has added, 'With the nineteenth century not only did biblical criticism destroy the possibility of a literal interpretation of the scriptures, but natural science brought in new and, in their effects devastating problems' ('From secularism to humanism: an aspect of Victorian thought', *Hibbert Journal*, lx (January 1962), 136.)

5   Joseph Butler, quoted by A. S. Wood, *The Inextinguishable Blaze*, Church Hist. Soc., Paternoster Press, 1960, p. 15.

6   Kitson Clark, *The Making of Victorian England*, p. 147.

7   H. G. Wood, *Belief and Unbelief since 1850*, Cambridge U.P., 1955, p. 121.

8   See, for example, G. H. Curteis, 'Strauss, Renan, and "Ecce Homo" ', *Edinburgh Review*, cxxiv (October 1866), 467.

9   *Contemporary Review*, xxix (January 1877), 169. Cf. B. Maitland, 'Belief and unbelief', *Quarterly Review*, cli (January 1881), 128–9.

10   For this information I am indebted to Dr R. Currie of Wadham College, Oxford, who has worked on London City Mission records.

11   On which see, for example, J. M. Robertson, *History of Freethought in the Nineteenth Century*, 2 vols., Watts, 1929; and W. S. Smith, *The London Heretics, 1870–1914*, Constable, 1967.

12   Currie, *Methodism Divided*, pp. 112–40, deals with this aspect of Victorian Methodism as part of a detailed examination of changes in the beliefs and values of the movement under the influence of wider intellectual and social influences.

13   *Methodist Monthly*, August 1892, pp. 254–5; quoted by Currie, *ibid.*, p. 114.

14   C. H. Spurgeon, in *Sword and Trowel*, August 1887, p. 400.

15   The lecture was delivered finally in 1887 after being delayed for seven years.

16   For a detailed analysis of these data see Gilbert, 'The growth and decline of Nonconformity', pp. 126–49.

17   That is, losses resulting from the transfer of membership from one congregation to another.

18   *Contemporary Review*, xxxi (March 1878), 708.

19   A. G. Dickens, *The English Reformation*, Batsford, 1967, p. 436.

20   *Wes. Conf. Min.*, 1847, p. 565.

21   Thomas Allen, recorded in *Wes. Conf. Min.*, 1900, p. 404.

22   W. E. Gladstone, 'The county franchise', *Nineteenth Century*, November 1877, p. 552.

23   Mackintosh, *Disestablishment and Liberation*, pp. 154–5, 163, 173, 230–5; J. Morley, *The Life of W. E. Gladstone*, London, 1903, ii, 134–5; and Rogers, *Autobiography*, p. 216 and chapter xi.

24   *Wes. Conf. Min.*, 1847, p. 565.

25   *Ibid.*, 1890, pp. 354–5.

26   J. H. Rigg, *The Class-Meeting Fellowship of Wesleyan Methodism*, London, 1907, p. 4.

27   'Report of the Committee on Church-Membership, as adopted by the Conference of 1889, having special reference to the class-meeting', *Wes. Conf. Min.*, 1889, p. 408.

28   *Ibid.*, p. 406.

29   *Congregationalist*, 1885, p. 849.

30   C. Booth, *Life and Labour of the People in London*, 3rd series, vol. vii, London, 1903, pp. 112–38; C. T. Bateman, 'Week-evening services', in R. Mudie-Smith, ed., *The Religious Life of London*, London, 1904, pp. 307–13.

31   Currie, *Methodism Divided*, p. 137.

32   Spurgeon, *Sword and Trowel*, August 1887, p. 397.

33   H. P. Hughes, recorded in *Wes. Conf. Min.*, 1898, p. 423.

34   A. W. W. Dale, *The Life of R. W. Dale of Birmingham*, London, 1902, p. 312.

35   Wood, *Belief and Unbelief Since 1850*, p. 30.

36   Cf. Chadwick, *The Victorian Church*, ii, 423–5.

37   D. Bonhoeffer, *Letters and Papers from Prison*, trans. R. H. Fuller, S.C.M. Press, 1953, pp. 106–7; G. Smith, ed., *World Come of Age*, Collins, 1967, p. 14.

38   Horton Davies, *Worship and Theology in England From Newman to Martineau 1850–1900*, p. 193. Cf. H. R. Murphy, 'The ethical revolt against Christian orthodoxy in Early Victorian England', *Am. Hist. Rev.*, lv, no. 4 (1955), 800–17; Smith, *The London Heretics*, pp. 1–2; and Wood, *Belief and Unbelief Since 1850*, pp. 44–6.

39   W. F. Cannon, 'The normative role of science in Early Victorian thought', *Journal of the History of Ideas*, October 1964, pp. 487–502.

40   E. De Laveleye, 'The future of religion', *Contemporary Review*, liv (July 1888), 2.

41   *Quarterly Review*, clxxvii (July 1893), 122–3.

42   Sir James Stephen, in *Nineteenth Century*, lxxxviii (June 1884), 917.

43   Cf., for example, J. M. Keynes, *Essays in Persuasion*, Macmillan, 1931, p. 360.

44   Berger, *The Social Reality of Religion*, p. 132.

45   H. R. Murphy, 'The ethical revolt against Christian orthodoxy in Early Victorian England', *Am. Hist. Rev.*, lx (1955), 816.

46   De Laveleye, in *Contemporary Review*, liv (July 1888), 3.

47   On which see p. 28, Table 2.1.
48   Figure 8.1 deals with the period 1845–85 only. The Methodist series can, of course, be extended backwards to 1767 (in the case of Wesleyanism), but for the pre-1845 period the idiosyncrasies produced by schisms within Methodism create complicated problems of interpretation.
49   Currie and Gilbert, 'Religion', in Halsey, ed., *Trends in British Society since 1900*, pp. 410–12.
50   Cf., for example, Gilbert, 'The growth and decline of Nonconformity. . .', pp. 121–2, and J. E. Orr, *The Second Evangelical Awakening in Britain*, Morgan, Marshall & Scott, 1949, p. 269 and *passim*.
51   The problem of the relationship between political agitation, economic recession, and Methodist growth, raised especially by E. P. Thompson and E. J. Hobsbawm, has been addressed effectively by E. P. Stigant, 'Methodism and the working class, 1760–1821 . . .', University of Keele M.A. thesis 1968, pp. 250–333, and by Ward, *Religion and Society in England*, pp. 84–95. In the present context what is significant about these studies is their demonstration of a negative correlation between early Methodist recruitment and both recession and political agitation.
52   Cf. pp. 82–5 above.
53   T. Cooper, *The Life of Thomas Cooper, Written by Himself*, London, 1872, pp. 85–6.
54   *Freeman*, 4 April 1860, p. 213.
55   *Congregationalist*, 1884, p. 1022.
56   R. W. Dale to Sir E. R. Russell, October 1875; quoted by A. W. W. Dale, *The Life of R. W. Dale of Birmingham*, p. 385.
57   J. S. Lidgett, *My Guided Life*, Methuen, 1936, p. 184; cf. Liberal Publication Department, *Pamphlets and Leaflets*, 5 vols, London, 1902–06.
58   *Liberator*, April 1904, pp. 58–70.
59   K. O. Morgan, *Wales in British Politics 1868–1922*, rev. edn, University of Wales Press, 1970, p. 218.
60   *Liberator*, April 1905, p. 58.
61   N. J. Richards, 'The Education Bill of 1906 and the decline of political Nonconformity', *J. Eccles. Hist.*, xxiii, no. 1 (January 1972), 57.
62   For an examination of the impact of cholera on religion in the United States see C. E. Rosenberg, *The Cholera Years: the United States in 1832, 1849, and 1866*, Chicago U.P., 1962.
63   *Cong. Mag.*, 1932, p. 223.
64   Cf. for example the *Bapt. Mag.*, 1832, pp. 263, 447; *Christian Witness*, 1849, pp. 437–9; *C. of E. Mag.*, 1849, no. 799; *Ev. Mag.*, 1832, pp. 23, 108–9, 399; *Nonconformist*, 1849, pp. 717, 722; and *Wes. Meth. Mag.*, 1849, pp. 1028, 1263.
65   *Nonconformist*, 1875, p. 729.
66   *Wes. Meth. Mag.*, 1860, p. 741.
67   Cf., for example, Dale's comment, *Congregationalist*, 1875, p. 195; and the report in the *Christian*, 23 April 1874, p. 11: 'This work has

been not so much among the profane and godless as among the children of godly parents.'

68 C. of E. Mag., 1860, p. 204.
69 W. Bradfield, Church Membership: Scriptural Ideals and Methodist Rules, Cambridge, 1907, p. 5.
70 Cong. Mag., 1819, pp. 153, 170.
71 Cong. Ybk, 1904; Mudie-Smith, The Religious Life of London, p. 271.
72 Primitive Meth. Conf. Min., 1880 and 1932.
73 Wes. Conf. Min., 1959, p. 82.
74 Best, Temporal Pillars, pp. 444–5.
75 PP, 1888, xxxv, 320.
76 Ibid.
77 Church Times, 13 June 1902, p. 5.
78 See pp. 55–7 above.
79 R. W. Dale, History of English Congregationalism (completed and edited by A. W. W. Dale), London, 1907, p. 600.
80 Wes. Conf. Min., 1819, p. 63; ibid., 1820, pp. 343–4.
81 Ibid., 1826, p. 170.
82 Ibid., 1827, pp. 69, 285.
83 Watchman, 1849, p. 261. Cf. Wes. Conf. Min., 1846, pp. 359–61.
84 Cong. Ybk, 1848, p. 62.
85 J. L. Poore, reported in ibid., p. 70.
86 Cf. e.g., Bapt. Mag., 1841, p. 134; J. C. G. Binfield, 'Nonconformity in the eastern counties, 1840–1885, with reference to its social background', Cambridge Ph.D. thesis, 1965, pp. 79, 155; Cong. Ybk, 1861, pp. 48ff; United Methodist Free Church Magazine, 1875, pp. 599–600.
87 Dale, History of English Congregationalism, p. 600.
88 For the results of a large-scale survey on the subject conducted in 1874–75 by the Congregational Union see Cong. Ybk, 1875, pp. 100–8.
89 Henry Pelling, Popular Politics and Society in Late Victorian Britain, Macmillan, 1968, p. 31.
90 Wes. Conf. Min., 1866–1931.
91 Cong. Ybk, 1907–62.
92 For Baptist data see Bapt. Hbks of the period after 1870.
93 28 March 1918.

Tables

8.1 See notes to Table 2.2 (p. 32).
8.2 Bapt. Hbk, 1870–78.

Conclusion

1 W. B. Selbie, The Life of Andrew Martin Fairbairn, London, 1914, p. 257.
2 A Sociology of English Religion, p. 109.

Index

248

Church growth, viii, 16, 23–48 *passim*,
51, 55, 59, 78, 96, 110, 115, 120–1,
130–1, 138, 145, 147, 149, 155–6,
159, 168–70, 172–4, 179, 187–202
passim
Church Pastoral Aid Society, 136
Church Pluralities Act (1838), 132
Church rates, 118–20, 163, 165, 194–5,
197
Churchman, The, 169
Clark, G. Kitson, 162, 176–7
Class meeting (Methodist), 20, 54, 92,
181–2
Cleaver, Bishop, 114–15
Clergy (Anglican), 4–9, 11, 18–19,
21–2, 27–8, 70, 73–4, 76, 79–81,
94–9, 101–3, 109, 111, 114,
117–19, 121, 125–8, 131–7, 169;
Broad churchmen, 134–6;
Evangelicals, 21–2, 70, 73, 96,
133–7; High churchmen, 10, 11, 70,
128, 133–5; Tractarians, 96, 128,
134, 135, 142, 157, 173
Cobbett, William, 81
Cobden, Richard, 164
Coleridge, Samuel Taylor, 74–5, 136
Colquhoun, Patrick, 66
Community-sense, 75–6, 80–1, 88–91,
93, 113–14
Conferences (Methodist), 21–2, 150–2,
154, 158, 166, 170, 181, 193, 198,
201
Congregationalism, 16, 34–40, 42–4,
48, 51–3, 58, 59, 61–5, 71–2, 78,
83, 86–7, 89, 90–1, 94, 96, 116–17,
120, 145–7, 150, 155–6, 162, 169,
178, 181, 183, 199, 200–2, 206
Congregational Magazine, 41, 96, 156,
161, 197
Congregational Union, 52, 56, 64–5,
156–7, 161, 178, 201
Congregationalist, The, 182
Convocation, 11, 13, 128, 166
Culture and anarchy, 158
Currie, R., 115–16, 178, 182

Dale, R. W., 59, 183, 195, 202
Davies, H., 184
Davies, Howell, 3, 19
Deference, 13, 76–8, 80–1, 84–5, 97,
106–7, 146
Deism, 6, 176
Demerath, N. J., 24
Denominationalisation, 138–43, 149,
154–5, 167, 179

Density, 28–30, 37, 44
Dependency system, the, 13, 79, 84–6,
97–115 *passim*, 139, 146
Dickins, A. G., 180
Disestablishment, 141–2, 163–5, 195,
197, 205
Disraeli, Benjamin, 174
Dissent, vii, 4, 8–10, 12, 14–17, 20–2,
27, 32–6, 46, 60, 71, 73, 76–8, 81,
84–5, 87, 95–6, 101–2, 104, 108,
115, 125, 156, 162, 165–6, 179,
200; *see also* New Dissent, Non-
conformity, Old Dissent
Dissenters' places of worship, 33–6
Dissenting academies, 36
Doddridge, Philip, 16, 61
Domestic industry, 99, 104, 107–9,
112–13, 146
'Downgrade' controversy, 178–9

Ecclesiastical Commission, the, 117,
128–32, 172, 199
Eclectic Review, The, 52
Economic recession, 91–2, 126, 193
Ecumenism, 58–9
Education, 163, 165, 194–6, 200
Eliot, George, 70, 108
Elizabeth I, 4
Enclosure, 77
Essays and Reviews, 175, 178
Established Church, *see* Church of
England
Establishment theory, 3, 8, 12–13, 71,
74–6, 125, 128, 132, 134, 139–40,
142
Evangelical alliance, 169
Evangelicalism, 22, 51–3, 71–2, 82–3,
92, 96, 183–4
Evangelical Nonconformity, viii, 26,
51–69 *passim*, 71–3, 81–3, 85–6,
89–91, 94, 137, 140, 144–52,
154–5, 157, 159–60, 162, 192–3,
196, 200
Evangelical Revival, vii, 40, 45, 51, 61,
71, 74, 82, 120

Fairbairn, A. M., 206
Faulkner, H. U., 23
Field preaching, 3, 17, 55; *see also*
Village preaching
Finney, Charles Grandison, 197
Free Church Council, 196
Freeholders and freehold tenure, 98,
103–5, 112, 148